MAN–ENVIRONMENT PROCESSES

PROCESSES IN PHYSICAL GEOGRAPHY

Editor: Darrell Weyman

1. *Landscape processes* Darrell and Valerie Weyman
2. *Soil processes* Brian Knapp
3. *Atmospheric processes* James D. Hanwell
4. *Tectonic processes* Darrell Weyman
5. *Biogeographical processes* Ian Simmons
6. *Man–environment processes* David Drew

MAN–ENVIRONMENT PROCESSES

David Drew

Department of Geography,
Trinity College,
University of Dublin

London
GEORGE ALLEN & UNWIN
Boston   Sydney

George Allen & Unwin (Publishers) Ltd,
40 Museum Street, London WC1A 1LU, UK

George Allen & Unwin (Publishers) Ltd,
Park Lane, Hemel Hempstead, Herts HP2 4TE, UK

Allen & Unwin Inc.,
9 Winchester Terrace, Winchester, Mass 01890, USA

George Allen & Unwin Australia Pty Ltd,
8 Napier Street, North Sydney, NSW 2060, Australia

First published in 1983

British Library Cataloguing in Publication Data

Drew, David
    Man–environment processes.
1. Anthropo-geography
I. Title
304.2   GF41
ISBN 0–04–551063–6

Library of Congress Cataloging in Publication Data

Drew, David (David Philip)
    Man–environment processes.
(Processes in physical geography; no. 6)
Bibliography: p.
Includes index.
1. Man – Influence on nature.   I. Title.   II. Series.
GF75.D73   1983   574.5'222   82–13736
ISBN 0–04–551063–6 (pbk.)

Set in 10 on 11 point Times by Nene Phototypesetters Ltd
and printed in Great Britain by W. S. Cowell Ltd, Ipswich

Preface

Mad scientists or unpleasant invaders from space were at one time the science-fiction writer's standard characters for transforming our world – usually for the worse. In the late 20th century, such devices have become redundant in fiction and fact as man himself is altering the planet by accident and by design, sometimes on a dramatic scale. Other than the changes in climate that occur on a timescale of thousands of years, man is now the single most powerful agent for altering conditions on Earth.

Until comparatively recently, geographical studies were concerned with the functioning of particular aspects of the human or physical (natural) world or with the extent to which man's actions reflected his environment. Factors in the natural environment were used, in part at least, to 'explain' human patterns, for example 'spring-line' settlements or studies of natural vegetation patterns. Economic, social and technological forces lessened this direct man–environment relationship. Environmental and ecological studies were largely concerned with the 'natural' environment into which man was often seen as an unwelcome intruder, to be ignored if possible. Neither approach can be considered to be wholly realistic today, for although humans are one of the planet's life-forms, they are now far more than passive organisms occupying an ecological niche. Not only can man transform and expand his niche, but he can also affect the workings of the Earth system to a greater or lesser extent, on a larger or smaller scale. At an accelerating rate, man is trying to change the environment to suit himself rather than changing his practices in order better to adapt himself to the environment.

Man is not master of the Earth. It is still true to say that he cannot live in large numbers where he cannot grow food – on more than half of the land surface – but everywhere his dependence on the fickleness of nature is less than total. He can buffer the raw realities of the environment. Because of this, modern geography must expand its horizons to take account of man's impact on nature as being a very important aspect of the world today. This book is intended as an introduction to this aspect of geography.

This book is divided into three parts. Part A summarises man–environment relationships in the past and the present, and gives an overview of how man functions as an agent for environmental change. Part B (Chs 3–8) is concerned with man's impact upon particular aspects of the natural environment (soil, vegetation, land-forms, oceans, fresh water) with especial regard to the modification of natural processes. The high degree of interconnectedness between these 'compartments' of nature means that it is impossible to isolate the effect of man's activities. In Part C, case studies illustrate the overall impact of agriculture and of the growth of industry and towns on the environment, and the final chapter looks at prospects and policies as the potential for environmental change by humans grows ever greater.

DAVID DREW
Dublin, March 1982

Acknowledgements

I would like to thank the following organisations and individuals for permission to reproduce illustrations (numbers in parentheses refer to text figures unless otherwise stated):

W. R. Mead (1.2); Central Office of Information, HMSO (1.5); D. A. Gillmor (1.8, 1.9); Figure 2.3 adapted from *Geoforum*, vol. 10, 1972 (R. Wright), with the permission of Pergamon Press; Figure 2.7 adapted from *Food agriculture and the environment* (J. Tivy), with the permission of Blackie and Son; Figure 2.8 adapted from *The Florida experience* (L. J. Carter), published for Resources for the Future, Inc. by The Johns Hopkins University Press, with the permission of The Johns Hopkins University Press; Figures 2.13–2.16 reproduced with permission from the *Annals of the Association of American Geographers*, vol. 66, 1976, p. 225 Fig. 1, p. 227 Fig. 2, p. 230 Fig. 4 and p. 232 Fig. 5 (P. Gersmehl); British Ecological Society (2.19, 9.11); Figure 2.20 reproduced by the courtesy of NASA and the USGS EROS Data Center; Figure 3.2 adapted from *Modern farming and the soil* (Agricultural Advisory Council) with the permission of HMSO; Figure 3.5 adapted from *Journal of Biogeography*, vol. 2, 1975 (E. Maltby) with the permission of Blackwell Scientific Publications; M. Conry (3.6); C. B. Cox (4.1); Figure 4.2a reproduced from *Evolution of crop plants* (N. Simmonds), with the permission of the Longman Group; US Department of Agriculture (4.2b); W. B. Johnston (4.4); Figure 4.9b adapted from *Science*, vol. 174, p. 16, Fig. 3 (W. I. Aron & S. H. Smith), with the permission of the American Association for the Advancement of Science, © 1971 American Association for the Advancement of Science; T. R. Oke (5.1, 5.3); Figure 6.4a adapted from *Proceedings of the International Forest Hydrology Symposium* (W. E. Sopper & H. W. Lull (eds); A. R. Hibbert), with the permission of Pergamon Press; Forest Service, US Department of Agriculture (6.4b); H. C. Pereira (6.6, 6.20b); F. H. W. C. Green (6.10); Field Drainage Experimental Unit, Cambridge (6.11); Figures 6.14 and 6.17 adapted from *Hydrogeology of the London basin* and *Water resources in England and Wales 1973* (Water Resources Board), with the permission of the Controller of Her Majesty's Stationery Office; Illinois Geological Survey (6.15); C. Kirby (6.19); M. Murphy (6.21, 6.24); American Society of Limnology and Oceanography (6.25, 6.26); H. M. French (7.6); McGraw-Hill (7.7); R. V. Ruhe (7.9); E. C. F. Bird (7.11); Figure 7.13 adapted from *Transactions of the Institute of British Geographers*, no. 21, 1955 (A. Coleman) with the permission of the Institute of British Geographers; J. F. Poland (7.14); Figures 8.4 and 10.8 first appeared in *New Scientist*, London, the weekly review of science and technology; Nature Conservancy Council (9.4, 9.22); Figure 9.5 adapted from *Vegetation and soils – a world picture*, 2nd edn (S. R. Eyre), with permission from Edward Arnold; J. G. Evans (9.7, 9.10); E. Plunkett Dillon (9.14); Editorial Committee, *The East Midland Geographer* (9.16); *Farmer's Weekly* (9.17); G. E. Hollis (10.3); Figure 10.4 adapted from *The climate of London* (T. J. Chandler), with the permission of the Hutchinson Publishing Group; J. L. Goldman (10.5); Figure 10.6 reprinted from the *Geographical Review*, vol. 56, 1966 (P. A. Leighton), with the permission of the American Geographical Society; Figure 10.7 from Acid rain (G. E. Likens *et al.*), copyright © 1979 by Scientific American, Inc., all rights reserved; US Geological Survey (11.2).

Contents

PREFACE   *page* v
ACKNOWLEDGEMENTS   vi

Part A   Introduction to man and the environment

  1   ENVIRONMENT   1
1.1   Culture and the environment   1
1.2   The extent of human control of nature   3
1.3   Gradients of manipulation   9
1.4   Conclusions   10

  2   MAN AND THE WORKINGS OF
      THE NATURAL ENVIRONMENT   12
2.1   The Earth system   12
2.2   Natural systems and human
      intervention   22

Part B   Man's impact on aspects of the
         environment

  3   SOILS   30
3.1   Introduction   30
3.2   Altering soils   31
3.3   Physical change   33
3.4   Chemical change   34
3.5   Creating new soils   36
3.6   Conclusions   38

  4   PLANTS AND ANIMALS   39
4.1   Introduction   39
4.2   Vegetation   39
4.3   Animals   46
4.4   Conclusions   49

  5   THE ATMOSPHERE   50
5.1   Introduction   50
5.2   Leverage points in the atmospheric
      system   50
5.3   Scales of change   51
5.4   Inadvertent climatic change   53
5.5   Deliberate climatic change   54
5.6   Conclusions   57

  6   WATER   58
6.1   Introduction   58
6.2   The hydrological cycle – points of
      intervention   59

6.3   Large-scale modification of
      surface water   *page* 72
6.4   New sources of water   79
6.5   Conclusions   80

  7   LANDFORMS   81
7.1   Introduction   81
7.2   Permafrost regions   83
7.3   Fluvial landforms   85
7.4   Coastal environments   86
7.5   Mass movement   88
7.6   Artificial tectonics – land subsidence   88
7.7   Conclusions   90

  8   THE OCEANS   91
8.1   Introduction   91
8.2   Man and the oceans   91
8.3   Conclusions   94

Part C   The overall human impact

  9   THE RURAL–AGRICULTURAL
      ENVIRONMENT   95
9.1   Introduction to agriculture   95
9.2   Scales of agriculture   95
9.3   Effects of agriculture   96
9.4   The British landscape   99
9.5   Amazonia   114

 10   THE URBAN–INDUSTRIAL
      ENVIRONMENT   118
10.1 Introduction   118
10.2 Urban hydrology   119
10.3 Urban climate   120
10.4 Urban–industrial landscapes   126
10.5 Urban–industrial ecology   128

 11   CONCLUSIONS   129
11.1 Man's impact on the Earth   129
11.2 The future   129
11.3 Investigation of man–environment
      relationships   130

      FURTHER READING   132
      INDEX   133

Part A INTRODUCTION TO MAN AND THE ENVIRONMENT

1 Environment

1.1 Culture and the environment

Man is not a rational creature, though some may pretend otherwise. His attitudes towards the Earth and his response to the environment have varied through time, and still vary between regions and cultures (Fig. 1.1). Early man saw nature as synonymous with God, as do many 'primitive' peoples today, and nature was therefore to be feared, respected and placated. In the developed world nowadays, approaches to environmental change range from 'if it can be done, it should be done' to the 'back to nature' philosophy of the more extreme environmentalists. Cultural tradition has played its part in determining people's attitudes towards their environment. For example, southeastern China and the south-east of the USA have environmental similarities, but are quite dissimilar in terms of human response to those environments.

It has been said that the approach of Western man towards his environment is partly the product of the Christian–Judaic idea that, unlike other creatures, man was created in the image of God, and that therefore man was meant to have dominion over the world.

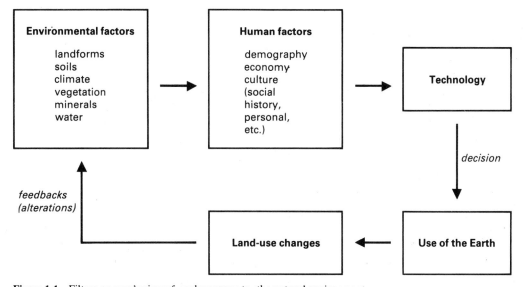

Figure 1.1 Filters on man's view of, and response to, the natural environment.

1

'God blessed them and God said to them: Be fruitful and multiply, and fill the earth and subdue it, and have dominion over the fish of the sea and over the birds of the air and over every living thing that moves upon the earth' (Genesis, Ch. 1, v. 26, Authorised version).

The concept of a world designed for the benefit of man was also articulated by the Ancient Greeks. 'Plants are created for the sake of animals and animals for the sake of man' (Aristotle, *Politics*, 350 BC).

The idea of man as a steward or custodian of the natural world did exist to some extent in pre-Christian thinking, and this lack of total separation of man from nature still persists to a limited extent in Islam and Judaism. Christianity, in its official pronouncements particularly, in part perhaps as a reaction to pagan Earth–fertility cults (for example, the seasonal celebrations such as May Day and Halloween), has continually emphasised the gulf between humans and the remainder of creation. This mental distancing in Western thinking has continued to the present day. Although the Christian ethic is no longer central to the attitude, the idea of nature as an enemy to be fought and subdued has remained as part of our present economic and scientific rationale. Progress is sometimes equated with control over nature and the natural world, which is viewed as consisting of 'factors of production' or means by which man may materially benefit himself. It is interesting to note that the irreligious world of Marxism has also adopted this perception of nature, and perhaps even intensified it. The removal of class exploitation and the proletarian revolution are seen as replacing investment and technology as the prerequisites to dominion over the world.

'Under a planned socialist economy the paths of natural processes progressively diverge from the natural and are transformed directionally' (Marx).

Thus in the eyes of Marx, domination of the natural world was still desirable, and only social conditions prevented its being achieved. Once the workers controlled their lives, domination was certain.

It is debatable whether or not this Western ethic made possible or assisted the development of modern industrial and agricultural technology which has greatly increased man's illusion of mastery over nature, but certainly these innovations were almost entirely the product of Western civilisations. It is this attitude towards life allied with man's ingenuity that has led to the most profound changes in the natural environment.

In other cultures the way of viewing the world has produced very different human responses towards nature. American Indians saw in virgin nature, direct symbols of the spiritual world, and a similar viewpoint characterises areas of high cultural development influenced by the Eastern religions. Unity of man and nature is implicit in south-east Asian Buddhism, Chinese Taoism and Japanese Shinto. In ancient China, aspects of the Earth were seen as manifestations of the cosmic being: the mountains were body, the rocks bone, water was blood, cloud breath. The unity underlying the apparent chaos of nature was emphasised. The Buddhist view of consumption as simply the means to well-being, with the ideal being maximum well-being with minimum consumption, stands in sharp contrast to Western economic thinking which equates inceased consumption with being 'better-off'.

Analytical science, interpreting things in terms of their parts, did not arise in the Eastern world and, until recently, harmony with the environment was a more pervasive attitude than struggle and conquest. In Western thought, man as a part of nature is a relatively recent notion, in part a consequence of Darwinism which showed man to be simply another life-form on the Earth. Adverse changes in the environment resulting from man's activities have lately given impetus to this 'ecological' approach in which man is seen as simply a part of the natural ecosystem.

None of these approaches to nature are necessarily 'right' or 'wrong', but they have powerfully affected the way man has attempted to shape his environment. In the past these differences may have been of only academic interest, but now man's relationship with his environment may be approaching a critical stage whereby the changes he makes may be irreversible or may lead to far-ranging and unforeseen alterations. Man is no longer an aspect of biogeography (simply a unit in an ecosystem), but is setting himself more and more apart from the physical and biological environment in which he lives. When man is able to manufacture or synthesise foodstuffs from inorganic materials – now a not improbable prospect – a basic link, that of man with the living soil, will have been broken.

1.2 The extent of human control of nature

1.2.1 Determinism, possibilism, total control

'The inhabitants of basalt regions are difficult to govern, prone to insurrection and irreligious.' Such were the views of Abbé Giraud Soulavie some 400 years ago. Ellen Semple, early in this century, thought that mountain people were essentially conservative and that, within Germany, climatic difference was the reason for the genial, easy-going nature of Bavarians and the energetic, self-contained nature of the Saxons of northern Germany.

Such opinions are now regarded as belonging to the lunatic fringe of geography but, although the remainder of this book emphasises the importance of man in changing nature, it is worthwhile noting that other views have been expressed. The theory that natural conditions govern man's behaviour and even aspects of his character is called **determinism** or **causation**. It is one of the ideas stemming from the post-Darwinian idea of man as a product of natural selection by inexorable natural processes. The thought that nature has a grand plan to which man should conform, and by conforming prosper, is now highly unfashionable. The alternative view is that of **possibilism**: that man is not passive, but is a geographical agent, able to act on and change his environment within natural limits of space and developmental possibility.

As has already been observed, it is not possible to explain human decisions and activities solely in terms of environmental constraints. If determinism were wholly valid, factory location would be decided by the location of raw materials and power, provided that there was a market. In reality, economic, social and political factors or even the personal whim of the industrialist are at least as important. For example, the location of the world motor-vehicle industry is now almost entirely independent of natural elements, and newer industries (e.g. microelectronic technology) are often located in response to market and personnel factors, natural determinants being confined to finding a pleasant area in which the workers can live. However, it is not true to say that man is independent of his environment. Semple said that: 'Civilisation has lengthened man's leash and padded his collar . . . but the leash is never slipped.' In an obvious sense man is still a prisoner of nature as recent events testify: the Sahelian droughts of the 1970s; the grain-harvest failures in the USSR;

the failure of the Peruvian fisheries when the cold upwelling of the Humbolt current offshore did not occur. Similar disasters are reported by the news media from some part of the world every year. To an extent the degree of human effort required to produce a particular return is related to the degree of compliance with natural conditions – going against the 'natural grain' requires more effort. The applications of ultra-modern technology may have to be very carefully tailored to fit into the environment in order not to cause more harm than good to man.

The examples that follow illustrate the control of nature over man and vice versa to various degrees and over various geographical extents.

1.2.2 Nature in control?

Field boundaries in Yorkshire. The materials used to build field boundaries in a small area of northwestern Yorkshire are shown in Figure 1.2. The underlying geology is also shown and comprises Carboniferous limestone to the north and east, gritstone in the south, and Coal Measures and shales in the west. Until recently, field boundaries would have been built from the most easily obtainable materials that were suitable. In the bare limestone area virtually all of the boundaries are walls of limestone blocks; on the heavier soils with scattered woodland to the south, hedge boundaries account for a third of the total. The Coal Measures and shales are unsuitable for use as wall blocks, and hence there are none made of these materials. Even the results of glaciation are perceptible in the distribution of field-boundary types. Ice movement was generally from north to south over the area, depositing limestone erratics on the younger Coal Measures and grits. Thus there are walls built of limestone boulders on the Coal Measures and walls constructed using both grit and limestone on the gritstone, but there are no walls built of imported rocks on the limestone.

This close relationship between an aspect of the natural environment and an aspect of human activity is now changing, as may be seen from the use of wire or wooden fences. Almost all modern enclosures are made of these materials as are repairs to earlier boundaries. This partly reflects the relative cheapness of erecting fences, but it also demonstrates how, on a small scale, men may distance themselves from the limitations imposed by immediate surroundings and resources.

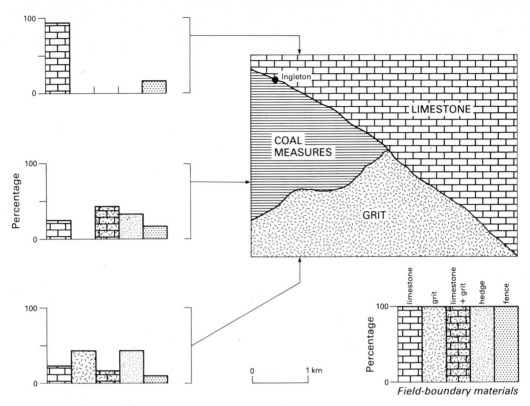

Figure 1.2 Materials used to construct field boundaries, and underlying geology, Ingleton area, Yorkshire. The block diagrams represent the number of boundaries on a particular rock type that are constructed of a certain material. (Based on data from Mead 1966.)

The Mullet of Mayo. The extreme north-west of County Mayo in western Ireland is a narrow peninsula running north–south and called the Mullet of Mayo. Low-lying, remote, and exposed to the full force of the westerly Atlantic gales, it illustrates a degree of subordination or compromise with nature very different from the agricultural areas of lowland Britain. The superficial deposits of the peninsula are shown in Figure 1.3a. The western strip is blanketed with glacially derived sands forming dunes that are relatively stabilised by grasses. In contrast, the eastern shore is underlain by heavy, ill drained clays also of glacial origin. Farming in the Mullet concentrates on raising beef cattle together with limited areas of fodder crops, oats and potatoes. Grazing on the scanty vegetation of the dune area quickly bares the ground and encourages rapid wind erosion of the sand. Equally, cattle cannot be kept on the flat, boggy clay lands at sea level which support only a coarse grass vegetation. However, in a narrow central strip on the peninsula, the blown sand from the west has been mixed with the heavy clays to form a good, well drained loamy soil.

Man's response to these abrupt variations in land quality may be seen in Figure 1.3b. The extreme eastern and western sides of the Mullet are negative areas in human terms, but the central loamy area contains virtually all of the settlements and is intensively farmed. The main roads roughly parallel the soil boundaries enclosing the many tiny fields on the loam. Administrative boundaries, in this instance townlands, are also influenced by the physical environment and form long, thin strips oriented east to west, so enclosing segments of each of the main soil types. Farm holdings also reflect this pattern. In this area man has taken the easiest option available, bowing to the logic of the environment rather than attempting to alter conditions to suit his wishes.

Arid areas. The hot deserts of the world are still virtually uninhabited. The presence of man is determined absolutely by the availability of a

4

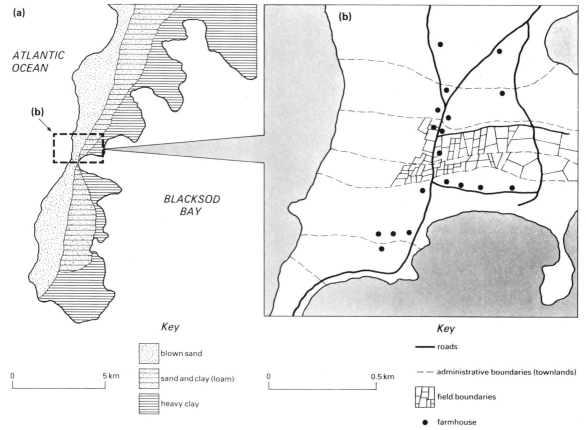

Figure 1.3 The Mullet of Mayo, western Ireland: (a) superficial deposits; (b) cultural features of the landscape.

permanent water supply, and the size of the population is related directly to the quantity of water available. The deserts require the highest inputs of skill and technology in order to transform them, and hence they largely remain bastions of 'primitive' human societies. For example, the traditional Bushmen of the South African Kalahari desert are hunters and gatherers making no provision for the future, using the minimum of artefacts and having no agriculture. They deflect nature only slightly and have a minimum of impact on their environment. However, this society and others of its kind in the world are now subject to pressure from external 'technological cultures', and are unlikely to persist for much longer. The Bushmen are beginning to practise agriculture and to become disturbed by the political currents of southern Africa.

On the margins of the African deserts, pastoral nomadism is still widespread. The search for pasture for their animals means that the nomads have no permanent settlements. They follow the new growth of vegetation induced by the annual rains over routes of several hundred kilometres every year. This degree of dependence on nature is becoming rare in the world, but the semi-arid environment remains a problem area for man, as is shown in Chapter 2.

1.2.3 Man in control

Phoenix, Arizona. An extreme contrast with the adaptation to a semi-arid environment practised by nomadic pastoralists may be found in the similar near-desert region of the southwestern USA. Phoenix in Arizona is a sprawling urban area of 1.2 million people in the Gila desert, the northern extension of the great Sonoran desert. Annual precipitation is highly variable but normally less than 200 mm, temperatures are hot and the natural vegetation is a partial cover of sagebrush and succulents. Yet, as Figure 1.4 shows, the Phoenix area is an oasis some 400 km² in extent in what was formerly near-desert. High-quality cotton is grown around the city, as are lucerne, citrus fruits, dates

5

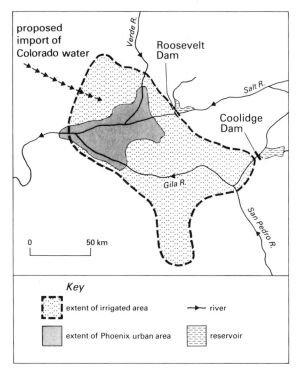

Figure 1.4   The Phoenix oasis.

and figs; spring lambs are reared. This environmental transformation has been achieved by large-scale manipulation of water resources, enabling large areas of the weakly developed soils to be irrigated. Energy imports in the form of oil and as fertilisers further enhance the capabilities of the area. The two seasonal rivers of the area, the Gila and the Salt, were dammed upstream of Phoenix earlier this century to provide stored water for use in the rainless season – this has left the two river courses dry below the reservoirs. The area now consumes 6.5 thousand million m³ of water annually, almost twice the annual input from rainfall. The deficit is made up by extraction of ground water from storage, a process that cannot continue at its present rate for more than a few years as water-table levels fall. It is now intended to import water into Phoenix via canals and pipelines from the Parker Dam on the Colorado river near the Californian border, some 250 km distant. Thus one of the world's most affluent cities has been developed in spite of local environmental constraints.

Individual houses, great urban areas, permanent settlements in Antarctica, battery chicken farms – all are examples on different scales of a high degree of human control over the environment, though always sustained by diversion of resources including energy from elsewhere. Such diversion of resources in order to circumvent local constraints on development is the essence of the developed world. It leads to a greater degree of interdependence between communities and states, and so to the complicated legal, social and economic frameworks that exist in the modern world. In turn, the existence of such a social–economic–political structure allows further environmental control to be undertaken, depending on the technological and economic level of development. Thus, in the example of Phoenix given above, the alteration of the environment to one attractive to people has encouraged more people to live in the area, which has increased demand for goods and services, which has led to further alteration of the environment.

1.2.4   Living with nature?
Regional patterns of agriculture in England. The imprint of man's agricultural activities on the landscape is described in Chapter 9, but a brief examination of regional differences in agricultural practices in England is given here to exemplify a balance between man and environment. England's landscape is typical of the developed world in that little of the surface remains unaltered by man, but the degree of imposed change varies greatly over short distances. The key to Figure 1.5 has been arranged as a vertical progression of increasing control of environment, culminating in large urban areas.

Agricultural patterns might be expected to be strongly influenced by local climate, soil, topographic and perhaps geological conditions, and in broad terms such influences are apparent in Figure 1.5, the distinction between highland and lowland England being evident. However, the effects of historical, social, economic and technological factors have greatly distorted any straightforward, deterministic relationship between man and environment. Three examples illustrate this.

THE LAKE DISTRICT.   The hard Palaeozoic rocks of the Lake District core have developed only a skeletal, stony soil. Only in the valleys are soils deep and fertile. Farms are small (20–40 ha) and usually include sections of valley and upland. Although fodder and root crops are grown in the valleys, agriculture is overwhelmingly oriented towards rearing livestock, particularly sheep. The

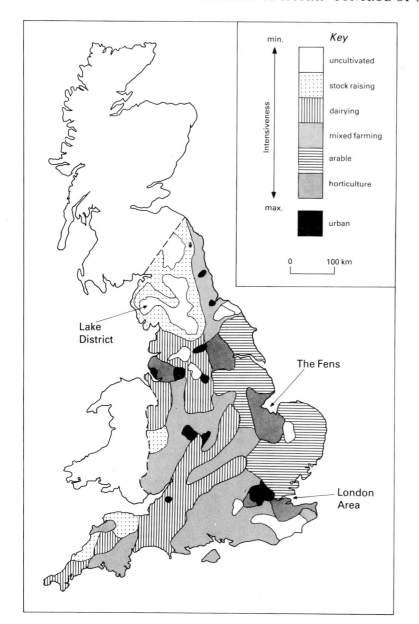

min.

Key

□ uncultivated

⠿ stock raising

▥ dairying

▨ mixed farming

▤ arable

▨ horticulture

max.

■ urban

Intensiveness

0   100 km

Lake District

The Fens

London Area

Figure 1.5 Distribution of agricultural types in England (highly generalised). Agricultural types are ranked according to the degree of intensiveness (value of produce per unit of land). (After Central Office of Information 1971.)

Lake District is representative of much of upland Britain with its apparent conformity with the restraints of climate, topography and soils. Yet, even here, man diverges from nature. Land improvement is widespread, selective breeding of sheep has taken place, dairying is increasing although costs are high and feedstuffs must be imported due to the long winter and lack of spring grass. 'Marginal land' in this sense is really an economic and not an environmental term. In times of high demand and prices, such areas are arti- ficially elevated to a higher level of agriculture, in 'average' times there is reversion to low-intensity livestock rearing and in slump conditions the land may be abandoned altogether. Regional agricultural policies, particularly those of the EEC, also help to sustain such areas of econ- omically marginal land.

THE FENS. This is the area of Britain's most fertile soils extending over some 280 000 ha of uniformly flat land. Much of the true (peat) fen

7

is artificial as it was reclaimed by drainage – the long, narrow fields are bounded by ditches. Arable farming is all important, 85 per cent of the land being used for this purpose; permanent grassland is confined to small patches of heavy boulder clay. The fenland could be used for almost any type of agriculture, but it is sufficiently close to the great population clusters of southern Britain for arable farming to be the economic choice. Again, the relationship between man and environment is blurred. Drainage, addition of trace elements (copper and manganese) to the soil and protection against soil erosion are all necessary to sustain the present pattern of agricultural activity.

THE LONDON AREA. A glance at Figure 1.5 will show the contrast between agricultural activity in the two areas thus far considered, and that in the London area. Diversity is the theme, and it is due more to the proximity of the vast London market than to the variety of natural conditions. Soils and drainage are still of local significance – for example, there are more livestock on the heavy Wealden soils – but overall there is a gradient of increasing control over the environment into the city. Horticulture is widespread especially in north Kent and the Thames valley, and in the Lea valley imposed land-use change is at a maximum with the greatest concentration of commercial greenhouses in Britain. In the area as a whole the relationship between agriculture and soils is weak, as any in-adequacies in the soil can be rectified economically via fertilisers, drainage or whatever is required. The high degree of control is reflected in costs – the investment involved in, say, 1 ha of greenhouses is perhaps 100 times greater than that needed for 1 ha of mixed farming and as much as 1000 times greater than that for 1 ha of a marginal livestock farm. The high land costs also mean that the profit obtained per unit of land from agriculture must be sufficiently great to justify that land use in economic terms. However, the greater the degree of change brought about by man, the smaller the area over which it applies, due to limitations of resources, labour and finance, all of which involve use of energy.

Ontario, Canada. A large-scale example of balance, although an uneasy balance, between man and nature is given in Figure 1.6. Canada is a highly but very unevenly developed country in economic terms. Steep environmental and de-velopmental gradients are characteristic, both

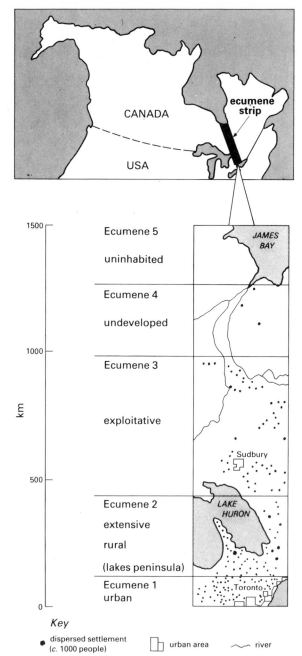

Figure 1.6 Population density and ecumenes in part of Ontario, Canada.

running south to north. The changes in climate (temperate to arctic) and soils (thick and fertile to bare rock) are reflected in the rapid fall-off in population density northwards. Figure 1.6 shows a north–south strip 200 km wide and 1500 km long in Ontario in eastern Canada, giving population density and the major physical features. The contrast between north and south is striking, from the uniform urban area of Toronto through the more scattered but still uniform rural settlement of the agricultural Lakes Peninsula, to the 'pioneer' communities of central and northern Ontario. The strip has been divided into **ecumenes** or degrees of colonisation of the land by man. The types of ecumene shown are:

(1) Intensive – urban, suburban and intensive agriculture, the highest degree of environmental control.
(2) Extensive – wholly agricultural, a high degree of human influence on vegetation and soil.
(3) Exploitative – small and isolated centres of intensive environmental change: in this instance a response to natural resources (timber, hydroelectric power (HEP), copper, nickel, iron, uranium, cobalt). Extensive untouched areas remain between these centres. The use of technology allows man to survive in an otherwise inhospitable taiga (coniferous forest) environment when the economic motivation is sufficient.
(4) Undeveloped – no permanent settlements, an uncomplicated relationship between man and the environment involving trapping and hunting.
(5) Uninhabited apart from military bases and mineral exploration outposts (non-ecumene) – the sub-Arctic zone.

This portion of Canada thus illustrates successive degrees of human impact on the environment and conversely environmental impact on man. A similar strip north to south in the USSR with near-identical physical conditions would show much wider ecumene bands of types 2 and 3.

1.3 Gradients of manipulation

The examples of man–environment interaction given in Section 1.2 show varying degrees of control of nature by man or vice versa. In fact, the case studies lie at different points along a gradient of environmental manipulation that extends from the almost total control of environment achieved in a heated, air-conditioned, gadget-ridden house to the minimal impact on nature exerted by, say, Australian Aborigines. There are two aspects to degrees of control: the intensity of imposed change and the areal extent of change. As was noted in

Section 1.2, as intensity increases, so areal extent diminishes. So, for example, the use of the pesticide DDT by man mainly in temperate and tropical zones has caused this artificial chemical to become diffused throughout the biosphere: penguins in the Antarctic and seals in the Arctic have some DDT in their bodies. This is a low intensity, areally extensive modification of the environment. In an area of open-cast mining the environment is utterly changed, but only over a relatively limited area.

Man's impact on the environment is unevenly distributed over the Earth's surface. Figure 1.7 is a highly generalised classification of the Earth into levels of human dominance over nature that correspond to the ecumene concept discussed in the previous section. Three categories are distinguished: uncontrolled, partially controlled and areas with a high degree of human dominance. Of necessity this distribution largely reflects agriculture or forestry activities as they are responsible for areal changes extensive enough to be mapped on a global scale. The areas of the ice caps and sub-Arctic, deserts, mountains and some areas of rain forest are the conspicuously blank areas on the map and, as Figure 1.8 shows, these correspond to areas of low or zero population density. The physical absence of man from an area does not necessarily mean that his influence is not felt. Changes in climatic or oceanic processes could affect the entire planet.

Another aspect of man's relationship to the environment – that of time – is illustrated in Figure 1.9. To a great extent population numbers, technological innovations and environmental impacts go hand in hand. An improved technology, irrigation for example, allows an increased population to survive, which in turn may lead to further areas of land being 'colonised' or to more intensive use of areas already occupied. In either case human impact on the environment will increase. The rate of increase of human population was very slight until recent times, and in prehistoric times man's numbers were probably kept in check by the same factors that regulate animal populations in the wild. A consequence of man's increasing ability to create his own environment has been the ability to support an ever-increasing population, a phenomenon that distinguishes man from the rest of the living world. However, it has been the advances in industrial, agricultural and medical techniques over the past 200 years that have produced the most dramatic increases in population. Since 1950 alone, the number of people in the

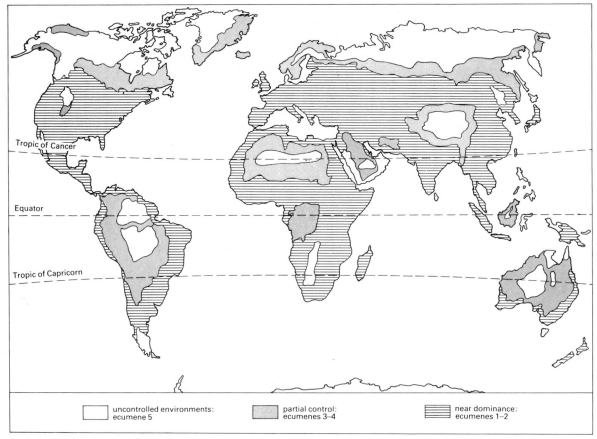

Tropic of Cancer

Equator

Tropic of Capricorn

| | uncontrolled environments: ecumene 5 | | partial control: ecumenes 3–4 | | near dominance: ecumenes 1–2 |

Figure 1.7 Degrees of human control of the Earth's surface.

world has doubled (to *c.* 4.5 thousand million), and estimates for global population in the year 2000 AD range from 6 to 8 thousand million. Environmental change by man is increasing at a similar rate. The increase in lead levels in Greenland ice is shown in Figure 1.9 to exemplify the environmental side-effects of man's impact on his surroundings.

1.4 Conclusions

This chapter has provided a summary of how man views his environment, and has illustrated some ways in which he responds to his surroundings. The degree and scale of environmental manipulation in time and in space has created the varied cultural landscapes of the Earth.

However, the nature of the changes that man imposes on the land is governed by a variety of factors which operate in concert. For example, the overall approach to the natural world is culturally

determined and with cultural change will come a new approach. Within this framework man's ability to change nature is limited by his level of technology and his available economic resources. Finally, there is the degree of motivation for change. The motives are various, but increased material well-being, security or profit are perhaps the most important. Economic forces such as proximity to market (agriculture in the London area) or value of goods produced (oil production in remote regions) can ensure the diversion of resources necessary to intensively 'develop' a particular area. Similarly, security considerations may be considered such a priority as to override both economic and environmental considerations (military bases in the Canadian Arctic) in modifying an area. Increasingly, as man's technological and political–economic sophistication advances, so his behaviour with respect to the environment becomes less predictable in terms of 'natural' factors.

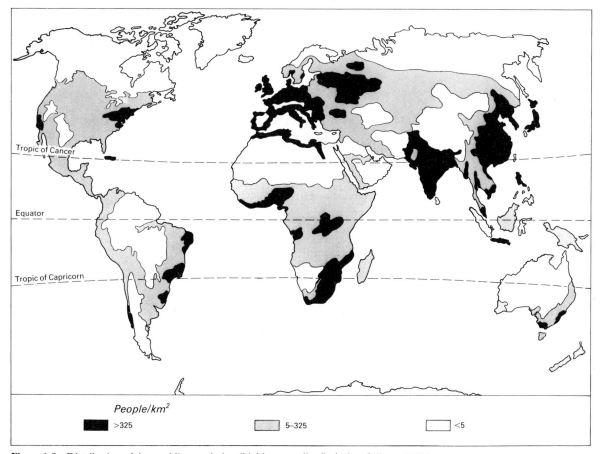

Figure 1.8 Distribution of the world's population (highly generalised). (After Gillmor 1974.)

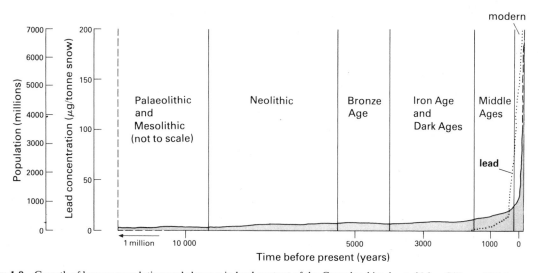

Figure 1.9 Growth of human population and changes in lead content of the Greenland icesheet. (After Gillmor 1974.)

2 Man and the workings of the natural environment

2.1 The Earth system

2.1.1 Introduction

Man has to classify, categorise and compartmentalise in order to make any sense of the world in which he lives. Thus the Ancient Greeks ordered the world into the domains of Fire, Water, Earth and Air, and modern man classifies living things, minerals and soil types. The subject matter of geography is grouped as the titles of the other books in this series suggest. Such an approach is necessary if humans are to begin to understand the immense complexity of the workings of the Earth as a whole.

However, this method of study has its disadvantages. One feature of the Earth is the interdependence of the innumerable parts that make up the whole. Everything is connected to everything else directly or tenuously, and it is impossible to 'understand' any one aspect in isolation without reference to its function as a part of the world as a whole. This is particularly true where the subject matter of this book is concerned. When man makes an alteration to his environment, it is usually to achieve an immediate and obvious end. For example, the construction of a house obviously changes the environment by replacing an area of grass or forest with an assemblage of concrete, timber and glass. Yet that is not the totality of change. The building will fractionally alter the climate around itself, the changed climate will alter the character of the soil and vegetation in the immediate area, and the changed soil and vegetation will further change the local climate. A roof will process rainfall in a different manner from the pre-existing vegetation and so forth. In this example the changes made to the environment have been largely unintentional, and apparently so

small as to be insignificant. However, only the tiny scale of the intervention makes the building of the house of purely academic interest in terms of environmental change. At the other end of the scale, if man were to wage nuclear war, presumably with the sole intention of annihilating his enemies, almost every aspect of our planet would be altered, some beyond all recognition, and chain reactions of change, particularly biological, might be set off leading to an utterly different environment in the distant future.

How then can the complexity and interconnectedness of the workings of the Earth be seen as a comprehensible whole? One method is to view the Earth as a vast, integrated machine, powered by energy, doing work and subdivided into countless smaller machines operating within the overall controls and framework of the Earth machine as a whole.

The energy that powers the Earth machine comes from gravity, from the Earth's interior and from the motion of the Earth itself, but far more importantly from the Sun as solar radiation. It is energy from the Sun that creates landforms, climate and life. Without solar radiation the Earth would be dead, dark and almost unchanging. Solar energy reaches the Earth via the atmosphere, is variously and unequally distributed over the planet, does work and is then returned to space. Over a period of time, incomings are equal to outgoings. Between input and output, energy flows by many different routes (transfers), and is stored for long periods of time (coal, oil) or short periods of time (soil, animals) as is shown in Figure 2.1. Human beings are stores of an infinitesimal fraction of this energy flow.

At a very general level man's intervention in the workings of the Earth deflects the direction of

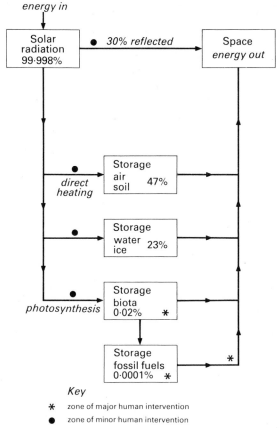

Figure 2.1 Simplified representation of the energy flows through the Earth system.

assemblage of components linked by energy flows and functioning as a unit. Thus the central heating in a house is a system, as is a pond, as is the atmosphere. If the system receives energy from outside and yields back energy, it is termed an **open system**. If energy and, therefore, mass is retained within the system (self contained), it is termed a **closed system**.

Although the Earth may be viewed as one enormous system, it may be divided into innumerable subsystems. There are three obvious such subsystems: the atmospheric system, the Earth (lithospheric) system and the water (hydrospheric) system. It is in the zone of interaction among these three units (Fig. 2.2) that the zone of life (biosphere) occurs. Figure 2.2 is an extreme simplification of the interaction of the three environments, and Figure 2.3 is a more realistic illustration of the degree of complexity of interactions that occur, in this instance within a drainage basin, itself a highly complicated system.

Thus the Earth operates as a hierarchy of systems, each partially independent but firmly linked to other systems. Human intervention cannot significantly affect the workings of the global scale systems such as the atmospheric system, but lower order systems, particularly those involving organisms (**ecosystems**), may be vulnerable to man-imposed changes. The following examples are of global scale subsystems in which some

energy flows (by harvesting crops instead of allowing the plants to decay and return their stored energy to the soil, for example), changes the magnitude of energy flows (abstracting river water) or subtracts from or adds to natural energy stores (coal mining, addition of artificial fertiliser to soil). Looked at in this way, it becomes apparent that man's actions cannot be confined, and that these actions will have consequences in many parts of the environment other than at the actual point of intervention. Whether his intervention has 'good' or 'bad' effects on a large or a small scale will depend on the nature of the imposed change and on the point in the natural world at which the change is applied. Examples of various types of intervention in differing environments are considered in the later sections of this chapter.

2.1.2 Natural systems

We have described the workings of the Earth as those of a gigantic **system**. A system is an

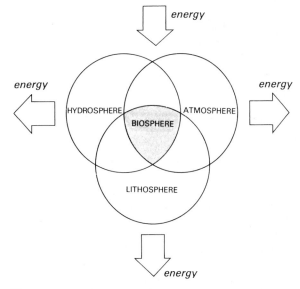

Figure 2.2 Interaction and interconnectedness of the major aspects of the natural environment.

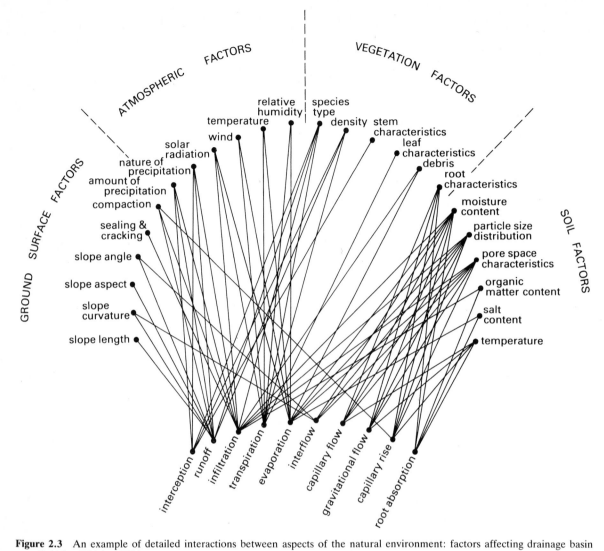

Figure 2.3 An example of detailed interactions between aspects of the natural environment: factors affecting drainage basin runoff. (After Wright 1972.)

degree of human intervention, and hence of modification of the workings of the system, occurs.

The nitrogen cycle. The terrestrial nitrogen cycle (as with the carbon cycle) is a relatively open system with large inputs from the atmosphere and large losses due to denitrification and leaching (Fig. 2.4). Within this flow through the system there is natural cycling between biomass and soil as ammonia–nitrate–nitrate–protein with an overall balance prevailing at least over short time periods. Human intervention in the nitrogen cycle is now considerable. The invention of the Haber process for the synthesis of ammonia from atmospheric nitrogen earlier this century freed man from dependence on natural sources, and has introduced large quantities of 'artificial' nitrogenous compounds into the natural cycle. The amount of industrially fixed nitrogen is now more than a quarter of that fixed biologically, and by 1990 the two sources will probably be equal. Nitrates are used mainly for explosives and for artificial fertilisers, and thankfully it is the second application that has had the greater effect on the cycle.

The general simplification of ecosystems (Ch. 9) resulting from agriculture, together with the practice of harvesting (animals and plants), has lessened biological stores of nitrogen. On the out-

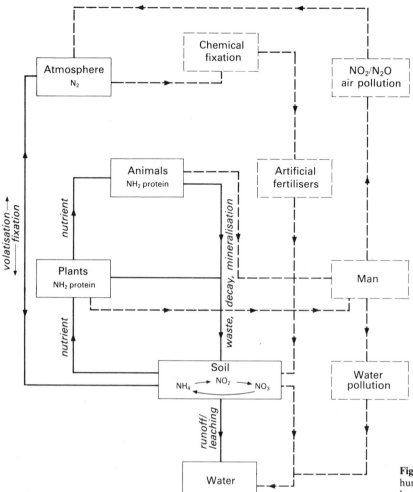

Figure 2.4 The nitrogen cycle: areas of human intervention in the cycle are shown by broken lines.

put side, deforestation and land drainage have encouraged leaching from the soil, thus widening the bore of the outlet pipe to the system (soil store – water store in Fig. 2.4). Thus human intervention has meant a much higher throughput of nitrogen across the biological part of the cycle (a doubling in areas of intensive agriculture), less internal cycling and a short circuiting of parts of the cycle (harvesting). The excess nitrate that is lost to the cycle ultimately reaches rivers and lakes, but in quantities that now sometimes exceed the capability of the natural ecosystem to process it. Hence there is a surplus of nutrients and subsequent changes in freshwater ecology. Excessive algal growth is one symptom of this process.

The phosphorus cycle. In nature the phosphate subcycle, involving the transfer of phosphates among soil, biomass and soil, is a relatively closed system (Fig. 2.5). It forms a part of the larger cycle involving deposition in the oceans, incorporation in phosphatic rocks, uplift, weathering and incorporation in the soil, but the biological cycle has a low level of inputs and outputs. Or rather it *had*: man's actions have greatly compressed the time-scale on which the phosphorus cycle operates. Inputs of phosphatic compounds have been increased by mining natural phosphate-rich substances and mineral phosphate for use as fertilisers and in detergent manufacture. Detergent wastes end up directly in fresh water, and excess soluble

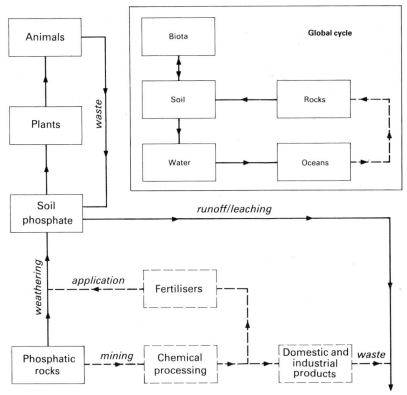

Figure 2.5 The phosphorus cycle. Inset shows the long-term closed cycle. The main diagram shows the biotic subcycle with broken lines indicating areas of human intervention.

fertiliser phosphate follows the same course as nitrate. The pollution of the Baltic sea described in Chapter 8 is largely a consequence of excess phosphates resulting from man's activities. Localised high-intensity phosphate inputs to fresh water from sewage outfalls have further increased phosphate concentrations locally. Again, a natural cycle has been radically altered and a formerly almost closed system been rendered partly open.

The mercury cycle.   Mercury is an example of a substance that is present in only very small quantities in natural systems, a heavy metal, not easily transported but which now has a much amplified flow-through volume because of human extraction, concentration and ultimately disposal, for industrial purposes (Fig. 2.6). Global inputs from mining are now 230 per cent of those from natural weathering processes. Unlike the two previous examples the natural mercury cycle does not have a significant biological component, as mercury does not form a major part of living organisms. However, biological build-up (concentration)

does occur, particularly in marine organisms, because of the accumulation of mercury in body tissues that takes place when the substance is present in the water in higher than natural concentrations. Already this biological amplification has led back to man, from eating contaminated fish (cf. DDT amplification, Ch. 9).

This increase in flow-through or mobilisation rate of natural substances is a characteristic of human intervention in natural systems. For example, the mobilisation rate of iron has been increased by 1300 per cent, of manganese 400 per cent and of lead 1200 per cent. Similarly, sediment loads in rivers affected by human activities show great increases. As natural systems and cycles are speeded up in this manner, so they adjust to the new conditions, often achieving new equilibria.

2.1.3   The stability of natural environments
Although most human activities designed to alter the environment are intended to have beneficial results from man's point of view, the degree of interconnectedness of natural phenomena men-

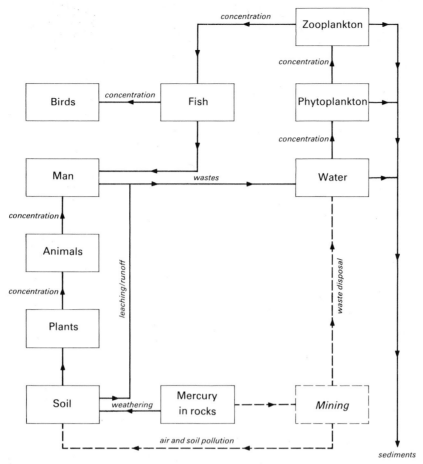

Figure 2.6 The mercury cycle with special reference to biological concentration in the aquatic environment. Areas of human intervention are shown by broken lines.

tioned earlier in this chapter means that un-expected changes or even chain reactions of changes may result from what was intended to be an isolated, 'improvement'. The extent to which such inadvertent changes take place depends first on the stress applied to the system by man and secondly on the degree of susceptibility to change (sensitivity) of the system itself.

Natural systems do change through time, but over long time periods (climatic change, valley incision, vegetational colonisation, for example). On a human timescale most natural systems appear to be static, but even this is true only in a statistical sense, and in reality the systems oscillate around a mean condition – a state known as **dynamic equilibrium**. For example, although the flora of a meadow may fluctuate in species, type and abundance over a period of years in response

to fluctuations in, say, weather conditions and grazing, overall the character of the flora will remain constant unless one or more of the controlling variables (climate, soil, man) imposes a long-term, major environmental change. However, if sufficient external stress (impetus to change) is applied to a system, then the whole system may develop a new dynamic equilibrium at a different level of operation. In the example of the meadow given above, extensive land drainage might sufficiently alter the character and moisture conditions of the soil to cause a shift to a more xeric (drought-resistant) form of dominant vegetation.

All natural systems have a weak link in their chain of cause and effect: a point at which the minimum amount of stress (impetus to change) need be applied in order to bring about changes in the whole system. For example, in the atmospheric system quite small changes in the composition of the atmosphere can trigger changes in climate on a global scale, changes in dust or carbon dioxide levels being probably the most effective. Changes of a few percentage points in carbon dioxide concentrations either way are sufficient to set off the changes (destabilise the system), and the ability to bring about such changes *may* be within man's powers (Ch. 5). Effective intervention at other points in the workings of the atmosphere – changing albedo (reflectivity) levels over a wide area or altering evaporation on a global scale, for example – would require a far greater effort (stress) to achieve the same degree of change in the system. Logically, deliberate human intervention takes place at such vulnerable or **leverage** points in the natural environment where a minimum of effort produces a maximum of result. In water resources, engineering intervention is concentrated at the river-flow stage of the hydrological cycle, rather than at the precipitation stage. Alteration of the biosphere is most easily accomplished by vegetational changes such as deforestation rather than by altering the other interdependent factors of soil character or climate.

The method used to spark off an environmental change is called the **trigger**, and such factors are various: fire; the introduction of an alien plant or animal species; the removal of a limiting factor (by supplying a particular plant nutrient, perhaps) on a plant or animal population; the introduction of a new component to the environment (radioactive fallout, for example).

Although all natural systems are chains with links of varying strengths, it is also the case that some natural systems are more easily disrupted than others, with wholesale and irreversible change in the system being readily provoked. For example, biological systems (ecosystems) respond more quickly to stress and offer less resistance than do inorganic systems. This is reflected in the degree of impact man has made upon aspects of the natural environment ranging from comparatively minor, in the case of landforms, to profound, in the case of life-form assemblages. Soils, being part biotic, part abiotic (inorganic), have consequently suffered an intermediate degree of change.

Even within a particular sphere of the natural environment, there are wide degrees of susceptibility to imposed change. For example, there are climatic, and hence vegetational and soil, environments balanced between two distinct states, in which a slight pressure exerted in a particular direction would tip the balance and cause drastic change. Such a condition is shown in Figure 2.7. These are areas of the world in which a slight deterioration in vegetational status, which could be brought about by natural climatic change or by man's activities in deforestation, would lead to soil erosion on a large scale and hence to altered geomorphology, hydrology, soil characteristics and possibly local climate. Thus the result would be a change in the whole condition of the environment. An example of man's intervention in such a sensitive environment is given in the last section of this chapter, and in another such environment, the tundra, in Chapter 7.

Figure 2.8 shows an attempt to express environmental resistance to change (degree of stability) for a particular area – Florida in the USA. Compare the map of land use with that of environmental resiliance – the degree to which the environment can tolerate imposed change without wholesale system change resulting. In reality, such a map is an oversimplification, as the response to stress will be different for different aspects of the environment – beaches, aquifers (water-bearing rocks), soils and so forth. Each aspect of a natural system has a **threshold** level beyond which imposed change becomes irreversible and a new system equilibrium must be established. Above the threshold level, recovery to the original system state can occur if the stress is removed. Different systems possess different threshold levels, but it is always possible that the magnitude of disturbance exceeds the ability to recover as in the case of glaciation or vulcanicity altering vegetation, soils and geomorphic processes. Figure 2.9 summarises the idea of system thresholds.

A simple illustration of the threshold concept would be the vegetation cover on a footpath over grassland. Continued trampling compacts the soil, lessens infiltration rates and encourages horizontal, ground-hugging plants to predominate. When compaction reaches a certain level and there are sufficient bare patches of soil, rainfall will begin to erode the soil. Prior to this stage a relaxation of trampling pressure would allow the original vegetation to reassert itself over a period of time, but beyond that stage erosion removes topsoil and plant nutrients so that still fewer plants can survive, allowing further erosion (Fig. 2.10). The recovery threshold has been passed, and even if the footpath is no longer used, recovery to the original state of the system is very slow. If the footpath remains in use, it might even become an

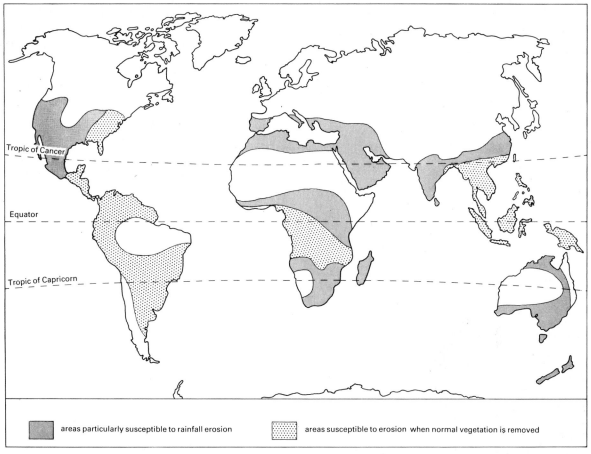

Figure 2.7 Areas of the world liable to extensive rainfall erosion. Areas susceptible under present conditions and those that would be at risk if the vegetation cover were to be removed are shown. (After Tivy 1975.)

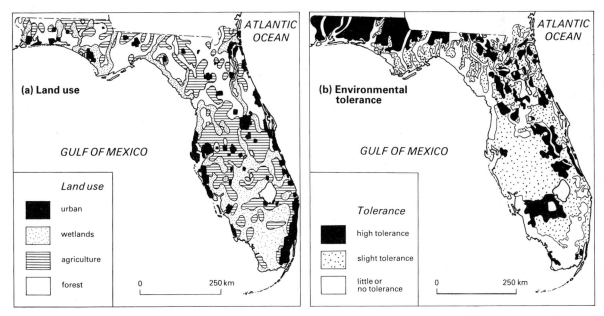

Figure 2.8 (a) Land use and (b) degrees of environmental tolerance to imposed stress, Florida, USA (After Carter 1974.)

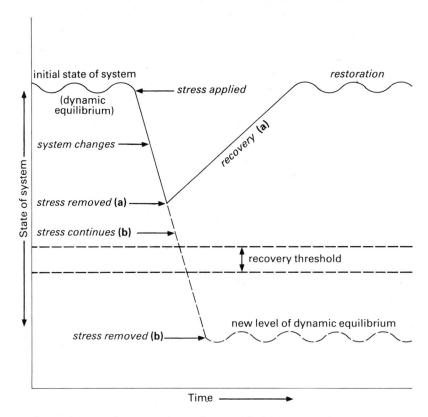

Figure 2.9 Response of an environmental system to imposed stress: (a) with cessation of stress prior to the threshold level and therefore with subsequent recovery; (b) with continuation of stress until the system is beyond the threshold level and cannot return to its original state. A stabilisation will occur at a new equilibrium when the stress is removed.

ephemeral stream course, deepening after every rainstorm, until bedrock is reached (Fig. 2.11). Even with this example the threshold level would vary with climate, slope and soil type. From the examples in later chapters it is apparent that human action is often responsible for pushing natural systems beyond their threshold levels.

The instance of the footpath used to illustrate system destabilisation also exemplifies another aspect of systems functioning – the existence of mechanisms that tend to reinforce or to lessen the tendency of a system to change. These are called **feedback** mechanisms. Although the discussion of systems operation has thus far been seen in terms of unidirectional chains of cause and effect (mass and energy transfers), in real systems things are rarely so simple. Loops exist in systems so that changes in the 'effect' (poorer vegetation in the footpath example) can alter the way the causation mechanism (compaction of the ground) operates, and therefore alter the 'effect' in a different

manner. In a central heating system the thermostat somewhere in the house forms a feedback loop as, by responding to changes in temperature, it can modify the workings of the boiler. Feedback mechanisms serve either to resist or accelerate the effects of imposed change. Positive feedbacks reinforce the direction of the original change. In the footpath example, positive feedback occurs as increased erosion diminishes vegetation cover, which in turn increases susceptibility to erosion. A further example of positive feedback has helped to alter the vegetation and soils of upland Britain (Ch. 9). In upland areas of Britain the high rainfall and low temperatures encourage excessive leaching (downwashing) in soils, removing lime and causing the soil to become more acidic and therefore less fertile with time. Deep-rooted vegetation such as trees can ameliorate the leaching process by drawing up dissolved lime through the roots, incorporating it into plant tissue and then returning it to the ground. If the deep-rooted vegetation

Figure 2.10 Erosion of grassland by trampling pressure: footpaths on a steep slope at Malham Cove, Yorkshire.

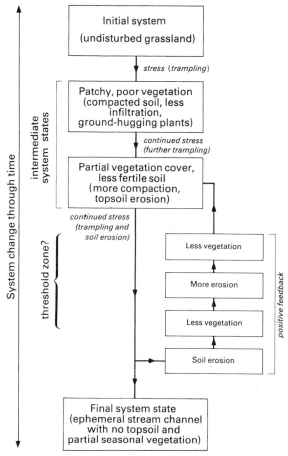

Figure 2.11 Diagrammatic illustration of system state alteration due to continued stress – the example of grassland erosion due to footpath trampling. The system can stabilise at any of the intermediate states shown or may be able to reverse direction if stress is removed before the threshold is passed. A positive feedback loop accentuating the erosion process is shown.

is lost (by human or natural causes), then the succeeding shallow-rooted plants will be unable to bring up lime from depth. The soil will then rapidly acidify until only acid-tolerant vegetation (**calcifuge**) can grow. The litter from these plants will be acid, further acidifying the soil, so allowing only even more acid-tolerant species to grow. This self-intensifying aspect of the acidification of the soil is a positive feedback effect (Fig. 2.12).

Negative feedback is illustrated by the normally stable relationship between valley slopes and the river at their base which transports weathered material derived from the slopes. If the river commences downcutting for whatever reason, the slopes of the valley will be steepened, more weathered material will be brought down to the river, thus giving it extra load to carry until it ceases incision and the dynamic equilibrium between river and slopes is restored. In the chapters that follow are many examples of such

feedback mechanisms: if positive they will accelerate any change initiated by man; if negative they will lessen its effect.

The systems approach described in this chapter is only a means of understanding the natural world, and for it to be of any use we still need detailed information on how particular systems actually work. However, in the context of human interference with the environment, the systems approach may be useful as a way of predicting changes, of assessing the sensitivity of natural systems and of determining the leverage points and thresholds of systems that are to be altered.

In the following section, three detailed studies illustrate some of the concepts discussed in this

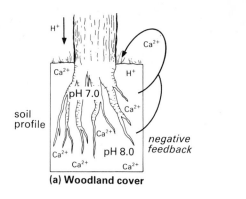

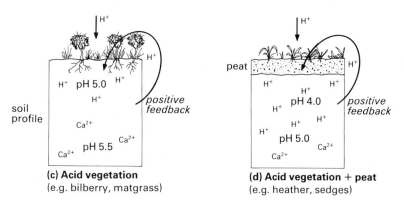

Figure 2.12 Accelerated acidification of a brown-earth soil in a British upland environment following deforestation. (a) Lime (Ca²⁺) recycling from depth (negative feedback) under forest conditions. (b) Loss of forest causes cessation of lime cycling: lime is leached downwards and replaced by H⁺ ions from rain water (acidification). (c) Acid-tolerant vegetation produces acidic litter and therefore accelerates the rate of acidification (positive feedback). (d) Fewer plant species can survive the acid soil. Very acid litter results with consequent inhibition of decay of organic material, formation of peat layer and increased acidification (positive feedback).

chapter, the first examining the workings of a natural system and the effects of human intervention on its operation.

2.2 Natural systems and human intervention

2.2.1 The mineral nutrient cycle

Ultimately, man's food supply depends on the working of the nutrient mineral cycle. This includes the nitrogen, phosphorus, calcium, potassium and integral water cycles together with numerous elements in trace quantities and has been knowingly or unknowingly a focus for human intervention for thousands of years.

A very simplified model of the mineral cycle is shown in Figure 2.13. Minerals are taken up from the soil by plants, incorporated into plant tissue, returned to the surface as litter and reintroduced to the soil via decomposition and leaching. This is shown as a closed system with no gains or losses to

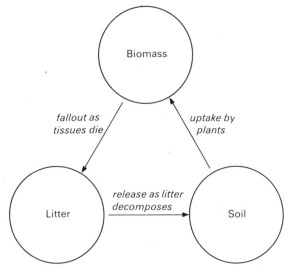

Figure 2.13 The mineral nutrient cycle modelled as a closed system. (After Gersmehl 1976.)

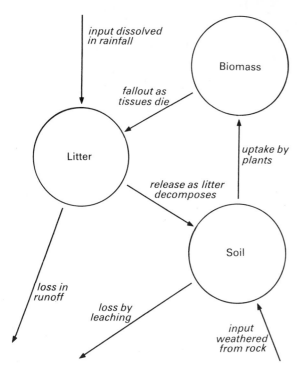

Figure 2.14 The mineral nutrient cycle modelled as an open system. (After Gersmehl 1976.)

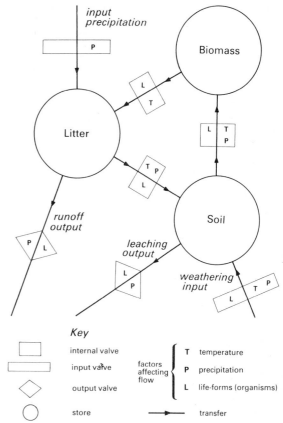

Figure 2.15 Control valves on transfer mechanisms in the mineral nutrient cycle. (After Gersmehl 1976.)

the larger environment, and a more realistic model using the same stores and transfers but showing external inputs and outputs (open system) is given in Figure 2.14. Weathering, precipitation, soil transportation and artificial fertilisers are external inputs; leaching, runoff and harvesting are outputs from the system. There are variations from place to place in the total amount of mineral nutrients within the cycle, and this total amount, the potential fertility, is largely determined by the absolute values of the inputs and outputs. The proportional distribution of nutrients among the three stores also varies. Examples of these variations for selected natural ecosystems (litter and biomass stores) and annual transfer rates (soils to plants, plants to litter) are given below.

Ecosystem	Storage (kg/ha) Biomass	Litter	Total	Transfers (kg/ha/year) Soil–plant	Plant–litter
tundra	160	280	440	40	38
oak forest	6000	800	6800	380	250
prairie	1200	800	2000	700	700
desert	150	0	150	85	85
tropical rainforest	11 000	180	11 180	2000	1500

The great differences in absolute quantities of stored nutrients between ecosystems is apparent, as is the varied distribution of nutrients between the two stores.

The rate of transfer of nutrients internally and externally is dependent on moisture and temperature conditions and on the number and type of organisms present. These factors function as control valves on exchanges between the storages in the system (Fig. 2.15). The relative capacity and degree of utilisation of the stores, together with the magnitude of the various transfer types, are shown in Figure 2.16 for the world's major soil–vegetation–climate types.

Under stable environmental conditions the working of these mineral cycles becomes balanced, inputs closely matching outputs, thus giving a high degree of internal conservation of mass and energy. A change in the environment will destabilise the system to an extent that depends upon the degree of imposed change and the sensitivity of

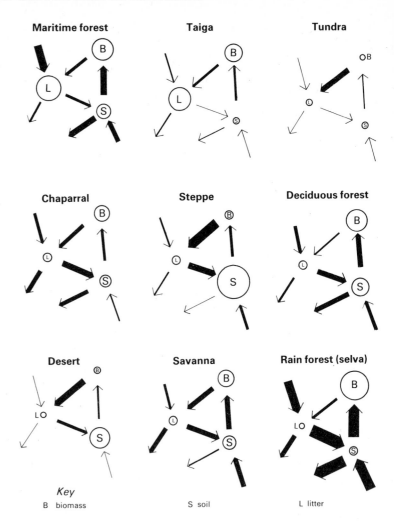

Figure 2.16 The operation of the mineral nutrient cycle in the main world climatic–vegetational–soil regions. The size of the nutrient stores is proportional to the absolute and relative quantities of nutrients stored. The thickness of the transfer arrows is proportional to the amount of nutrients transferred. (After Gersmehl 1976.)

Key
B biomass   S soil   L litter

all or part of the system. If a forest cover is removed from an area, the transfer of mineral nutrients from soil to biomass is sharply reduced as is the amount of biomass storage. Water no longer required for transpiration will remove more nutrients from the soil system via leaching and runoff, while rainfall inputs to the soil increase with the loss of tree-canopy interception. Thus overall storage within the system declines until a new equilibrium is attained at a lower level. If this change in vegetation were due to natural changes (e.g. climate), the system change might be permanent, but the rate of change would be slow and catastrophic responses unlikely. If the change were due to deforestation by man, the system might recover and original vegetation and nutrient levels be restored, provided the threshold point for the nutrient cycle had not been passed. The effects on

the mineral cycle of the cutting down of oak forest is shown in Figure 2.17. Crop harvesting has the same effect, but artificial fertiliser is then applied to compensate the soil store for the litter loss.

Ecosystems with rapid, efficient nutrient transfer systems recover from destabilisation more easily than those with sluggish transfer mechanisms. However, if a high proportion of the nutrients are contained within one of the stores (biomass rather than the soil in tropical rainforest), then stress applied to that store will cause most damage to the system – it is a leverage point. Therefore, Figure 2.16 may be seen as a representation of the degree of stability of the various ecosystems, for the mineral nutrient cycle affects not just soil and vegetation status, but through them local climate, the operation of a part of the hydrological cycle and dissolved and sediment

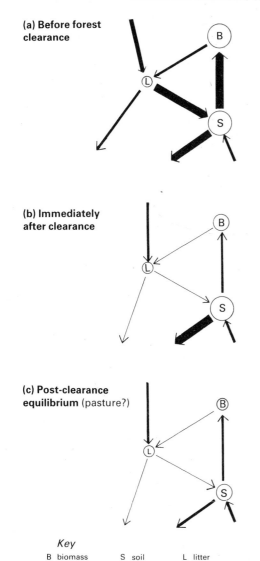

(a) Before forest clearance

(b) Immediately after clearance

(c) Post-clearance equilibrium (pasture?)

Key

B biomass   S soil   L litter

Figure 2.17 Changes in the mineral nutrient cycle in a deciduous woodland before and after tree felling.

loads in streams. Ecosystems with low absolute storages and transfer systems with limited capacities (taiga, tundra, desert) are those upon which man can inflict permanent change most easily (Sec. 2.2.3; Ch. 9). Ecosystems with a dominating store or transfer (soil in the steppe, biomass in the selva (rainforest), litter to soil transfer in chaparral) can most readily be deflected by tampering with that particular aspect. Ecosystems with an approximately equal distribution of nutrients between stores and with transfer mechanisms of comparable efficiency (maritime

forest, deciduous forest) offer the greatest resistance to stress, whether natural or man induced.

The methods used to try and 'improve' the workings of ecosystems are designed to strengthen the weakest link, and therefore differ between environments. In a desert there is a high concentration of nutrients in the soil zone, but weak transfers inhibit their cycling through the other stores. Thus the control valve (water) affecting transfer rates needs to be opened wider by irrigation. Tundra ecosystems are vulnerable to degradational environmental change, to a poorer vegetational cover and less fertile soils, but are difficult to improve. Not only are absolute nutrient amounts within the system small, but transfers are limited by the lack of heat energy, and this is not easily rectified on a large scale (Ch. 7).

2.2.2 Rabbits in Britain

The introduction of alien life-forms into an area by man has often led to a chain reaction of changes quite unforeseen at the beginning. The bringing of the rabbit to Britain by the Normans for food and fur is an example. Originally, rabbits were kept in warrens and though some escaped, the wild population remained tiny until the 19th century – probably well under one million. Although the rabbit had no serious competitors for food and breeding grounds except for the hare, natural predators and a lack of food for part of the year kept numbers in check. Then, a series of unconnected environmental changes obliquely allowed the population to explode – to 30 million in 1939 and to 60–100 million by 1950, with rabbit densities of up to 50 animals per ha over large areas. The enclosure movement provided rabbits with ideal burrow sites in hedges, the growing of fodder crops and the establishment of water meadows allowed more rabbits to survive the 'hungry-gap' in early spring, and the practice of landlords of shooting hares and eliminating the predators on game birds (which were also the predators on rabbits) removed further restraints on population growth. Hedgerow removal in postwar years (Ch. 9) tended to cause rabbits to concentrate in the remaining favourable environments. The effects were remarkable. By the early 1950s the direct effects on agriculture were losses of crops to the value of *c.* £200 million annually at 1980 prices. The rabbits also initiated other changes in the environment.

Landforms were modified as burrowing undermined slopes and caused minor local slope retreat.

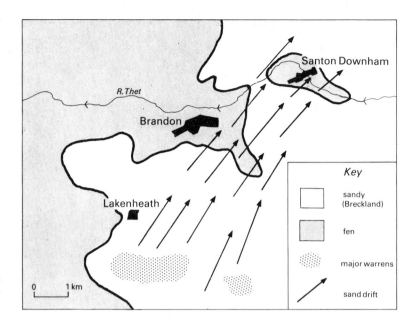

Figure 2.18 Wind erosion due to sand blowouts on rabbit warrens near Lakenheath, Breckland in the 19th century.

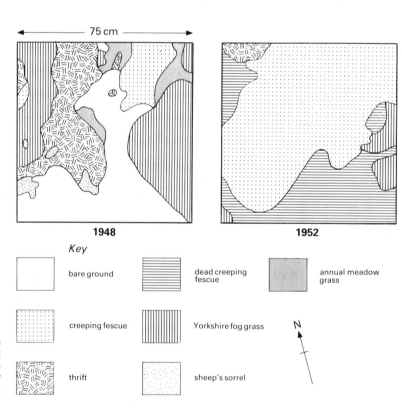

Figure 2.19 Vegetational changes on land within a 75 cm × 75 cm quadrat on Skockholm Island due to the exclusion of rabbits for a 4-year period. (After Gillham 1955.)

River banks and sea defences in Lincolnshire were weakened, causing increased bank bursts and floods. In areas of light soil, destruction of stabilising vegetation and exposure of bare soil led to wind erosion. Figure 2.18 shows the extent of wind erosion that occurred in the 19th century from an extensive area of warrens on the edge of Breckland near Lakenheath. The blown sand drifted northeastwards for over 10 km over a period of years, eventually rendering good fenland near Downham sterile, and almost blocking the navigable channel of the River Thet.

The greatest effect of the rabbit in large numbers has been in modifying vegetation. Rabbits are selective grazers, preferring young plants and avoiding woody or unpalatable species. A low vegetation cover with many species characterises heavily grazed areas, but locally they may induce quite different ecosystems. In the base of the dry valleys of the English chalklands, the disturbed, manured ground used for burrows encouraged nettles and elder to prosper, and in turn this attracted a new fauna including pigeons, crows and voles. Figure 2.19 shows the effect of excluding rabbits from a patch of previously heavily grazed land over a 4-year period. The site was on the rabbit-infested island of Skokholm in Pembroke. After the 4 years of exclusion the vegetation had become dominated by creeping fescue grass, a vegetational pattern identical to that prevailing on the neighbouring, but rabbit-free, island of Grassholm.

2.2.3 Desertification

The semi-arid lands of the world are prime examples of delicately poised environments, liable to rapid degradation when subjected to slight pressure. In human terms the margin for error in the exploitation of these regions is small, and the consequences of mismanagement are continental in extent. Desertification is a broad term including a number of climatic, ecological and geomorphological changes that diminish the biological productivity of an area and ultimately render it useless for agriculture. Almost all of the arid lands are at risk and the United Nations (UN) Food and Agriculture Organisation estimates that the present desert area (8 million km²) could triple. The Third World countries of the Americas, Asia and Africa are the most affected, but the processes of desertification occur even in the rich countries – 10 per cent of the USA has been affected and a further 20 per cent is threatened.

Desertification takes place on the desert margins, in patches rather than over uniform areas. Precipitation is low, but more importantly highly variable: several rainless years (as in the Sahel between 1968 and 1973) may be followed by a wet period. Rainfall is commonly of high intensity. Under natural conditions vegetation cover fluctuates with these precipitation changes, and following drought, wind erosion occurs. However, it is now thought that human actions can intensify these natural processes and perhaps destabilise the environment to a point beyond its recovery threshold. The human trigger factor leading to desertification is overpopulation due to people settling in one place as opposed to having a nomadic way of life. Internationally financed water-resource development schemes have been the unintentional cause of this trigger factor, as by establishing permanent water supply sources the schemes encourage higher stocking rates and the establishment of settled communities around the water. It is these concentrated zones that are most liable to desertification.

Overstocking causes soil compaction and so a lower infiltration capacity; heavy grazing, particularly by goats, destroys even woody vegetation and wood gathering accentuates this trend. Grain growing bares the soil for part of the year. All of these factors combine to alter climates close to the ground (**microclimates**), soil and vegetation status. During a drought period, stock numbers initially increase in an attempt to maintain food yields but, as vegetation becomes even more sparse, large numbers of stock may die, and economic collapse and often famine follow. Wind erosion can proceed more vigorously, acting upon the extensive areas of bare ground. When rains return, the surface is vulnerable to sheet and gully erosion, thus further degrading the land and allowing only a poorer vegetation cover to recolonise. This is an extreme extension of the footpath erosion example given in Section 2.1.3.

It is thought that a further positive feedback may occur accelerating the process of desertification. Albedo values (reflectivity) for the affected land surfaces increase by 5–15 per cent as ground is bared, and therefore there is less heating of the ground and the air above it. In turn, this shortens and lessens the daily convective rise of air, and prolongs and strengthens the natural subsidence of air in the subtropical high-pressure systems that prevail over the semi-deserts. This lessens the chances of precipitation, intensifies the drought,

Table 2.1 Desertification: factors and effects.

Factor affected	Direction of change	Immediate effects	Subsequent effects; feedback effects
Slightly affected			
solar radiation	decreased (dustiness)	surface cooling	atmospheric cooling, less convection, less rain, less vegetation, higher albedo – cooling (+ feedback)
Moderately affected			
albedo	increased	surface cooling	as above (+ feedback)
throughflow	decreased	less flow to water sources	depopulation – less stress (– feedback)
groundwater percolation	decreased	water-table fall, wells dry	decreased population/stock, less grazing, more vegetation, soil improvement, more infiltration (– feedback)
Severely affected			
vegetation	decreased	erosion, depopulation	as above (– feedback) and/or cooling – intensification of drought (+ feedback)
evaporation	increased	vegetation decline	as above
infiltration	decreased	as above	as above
surface runoff	increased	erosion	less ground water, landform changes, less vegetation, etc.

Figure 2.20 Landsat satellite photograph of the Negev desert showing the contrast between the light, desertified (Egyptian) side and the darker, vegetated zone in Israel on the other side of the fence. (Photograph courtesy of NASA and USGS EROS Data Center.)

further weakens the vegetation system and so completes the self-amplifying cycle. Table 2.1 summarises the effect on various aspects of the environment of the desertification processes. Desertification is difficult to demonstrate conclusively, but one example from the Middle East seems unambiguous. In 1969 a fence was erected along the 1948 ceasefire line between Egypt and Israel in the Negev–Sinai desert. On the Israeli side only a few herds of animals were grazed and the natural scrub vegetation remained largely undisturbed. The albedo of this surface was estimated at 25 per cent. On the Egyptian side of the barrier extensive grazing continued by goats, camels and sheep. Bedouin cultivated small plots of land and gathered the leaves of the common shrub *Artemisia* for use as roofing. Within 3 years there was a pronounced difference between the two areas. Viewed from satellites (Fig. 2.20), the Egyptian side appeared much lighter and reflective with an albedo of 37 per cent. The temperature regimes of the two areas began to diverge with summer daily maxima of *c.* 45°C on the darker Israeli side but 40°C on the lighter Egyptian side, and winter daily maxima of 33°C on the Israeli side but 30°C on the Egyptian side. Rainfall differences were not demonstrable, but the darker, warmer area had a greater convective cloud cover. The onset of desertification due to human intervention seemed to be beginning on the Egyptian side of the fence.

Part B MAN'S IMPACT ON ASPECTS OF THE ENVIRONMENT

3 Soils

3.1 Introduction

This section of the book is concerned with the effect of man on particular aspects of the natural environment, although it will become apparent that it is unrealistic to compartmentalise the natural world in this manner. Nowhere is this more true than with the subject of this chapter, soils. The soils of an area represent in many ways a summary, a distillation, of all the factors of the environment, human and otherwise, in the locality. The importance of soils to man as the basis of agriculture is obvious, but their pivotal point in the environment as a whole will become apparent from the many references to soils in the succeeding chapters. (For a fuller account of soil processes and terminology, see *Soil processes*, B. J. Knapp, George Allen & Unwin, 1979.)

Because of their great degree of generalisation, Figure 3.1 and Table 3.1 are a reasonable guide to the broad global variations in soil types. The soil types shown are **zonal** soils, distinguished according to a global classification in which soil, vegetation and climate are presumed to be linked one to another with climate the primary cause, soils and vegetation the effect. Man has not yet altered whole zonal soil groups out of all recognition as he has with vegetation (Ch. 4). However, disturbance of vegetation for agriculture or forestry with a consequent change in microclimate, inevitably leads to modification of soil properties as the three aspects are so closely linked causally. Tillage modifies soil considerably, particularly its chemistry and biology but to a lesser extent its

Table 3.1 Major soil types, climatic regions and vegetation zones.

Climatic zone	Zonal soils Vegetational zone	Zonal soil
tundra	tundra	arctic brown soil
boreal	coniferous forest (taiga)	podsol
temperate oceanic	mixed forest	brown earth
mediterranean	mediterranean forest	red–brown earth
mid-latitude cont.	steppe; prairie	chernozem
semi-arid	semi-arid	sierozem
arid	desert	no true soil
tropical/equatorial	rainforest	latosols

Intrazonal soils	
Modifying factor (to prevent zonal soil developing)	*Examples of resulting intrazonal soils*
parent material	rendzina (limestone)
excess water	gley
excess salt	solonchak/solonetz

Azonal soils	
Cause of immaturity	*Examples of specific soils*
high altitudes (low temperatures)	lithosol
inhibited decay of organic matter	peat (histosol)

texture and structure. More drastic changes are usually attempts, successful or otherwise, to improve soil productivity (fertility), for example by use of fertilisers, by irrigation or by drainage. The extreme instance of human influence on soil is the

30

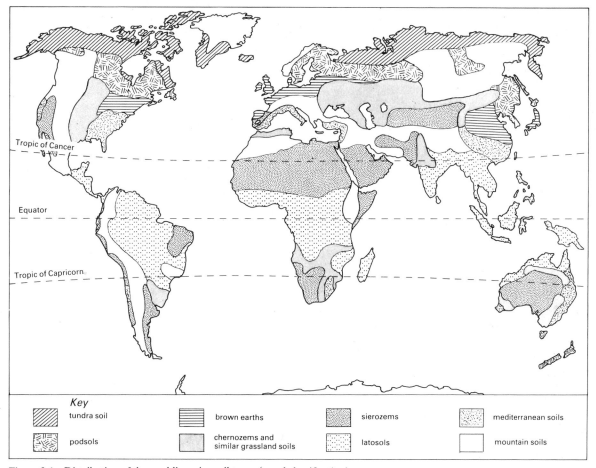

Figure 3.1 Distribution of the world's major soil types (zonal classification).

creation of completely new soils – on the bare, rocky Aran islands off western Ireland, soil was painstakingly created by carrying sand and seaweed from the beaches.

3.2 Altering soils

Soils are in dynamic equilibrium with the factors that determine their characteristics: climate, parent material, topography, biota and time. Changes in any one of these variables will affect the soil, but the response to a given environmental change will vary from soil to soil according to their sensitivity to a particular type of stress. So, for example, the soils of parts of eastern England have an inherent structural weakness. They are liable to compaction and formation of a plough pan (Sec. 3.3.1), if ploughed when too wet. Tropical latosol soils (Fig. 3.1) undergo rapid and degenerative change in terms of fertility when the natural vegetation of rainforest is removed (Ch. 9). Under the newly created extreme microclimate, oxidation and leaching of nutrients render the soil barren.

Human actions should be added to the list of factors determining soil character, as they are, at least locally, of more significance than all of the natural factors combined · (Table 3.2). Some aspects of the soil are readily modifiable, others are less tractable. Soil texture is difficult to change except by adding vast quantities of coarse grained sand or fibrous organic matter, whereas soil chemistry and biology can be varied much more easily with consequential effects on structure and drainage. In a sense the use of artificial fertilisers is an example of man accelerating a natural process – in this case the release of plant nutrients

31

Table 3.2 Some of man's effects on soil characteristics.

Soil factor	'Beneficial' change	Neutral change	'Adverse' change
soil chemistry	mineral fertilisers (increased fertility)	altering exchangeable ion balance	chemical imbalance
	adding trace elements	altering pH (lime)	toxic herbicides and herbicides
	desalinise (irrigation)	alter via vegetation changes	salinise
	increase oxidation (aeration)		over-removal of nutrients
soil physics	induce crumb structure (lime and grass)	alter structure (ploughing, harrowing)	compaction/plough pan (poor structure)
	maintain texture (organic manure or conditioner)	alter soil microclimate (mulches, shelter belts, heating, albedo change)	adverse structure due to chemical changes (salts)
	deep ploughing, alter soil moisture (irrigation or drainage)		remove perennial vegetation
soil organisms	organic manure	alter vegetation and soil microclimate	remove vegetation and plough (less worms and micro-organisms.
	increase pH		
	drain/moisten		pathogens (e.g. slurry)
	aerate		toxic chemicals
time (rate of change)	rejuvenate (deep ploughing, adding new soil, reclaiming land)		accelerated erosion
			overuse of nutrients
			urbanising land

Table 3.3 Changes in soil-profile characteristics in a British lowland soil due to intensive agriculture.

Soil characteristic	Natural state	Under intensive agriculture
organic content	A horizon high (7%)	uniform (3–5%) in plough horizon
	B horizon 0%	
carbonate	A horizon low/zero	uniform distribution if tilled and limed
	B/C horizon max.	
nitrogen	medium/low	seasonally high (nitrate)
exchangeable cation balance	Ca 80%	Ca 70%
	Mg 5%	Mg 4%
	K 5%	K 10%
	P 3%	P 12%
	H 7%	H 4%
structure	A horizon crumb	A/B unstructured/blocky
	B/C horizons blocky	A/B plough pan
pH	increase down profile $c. 5.5–7$	uniform $c. 6.5$
biological activity	high	medium

from bedrock by chemical weathering. Although climate cannot be changed, some of its effects on soil can be, especially those relating to soil moisture. Thus irrigation simulates a wetter climate; the addition of lime restores the removal by leaching of carbonate that occurs in humid region soils.

Although human activity has changed soils over vast areas, by converting forest to pasture for example, man's main effect has been in the creation of artificial **intrazonal** soils – local soils that are deviations to a greater or lesser degree from the climatically determined zonal soil. Although the zonal soils for Britain are brown earths (lowlands) and podsols (uplands) (Ch. 9), the actual soils form a mosaic of variants on these basic types, in part as a result of differing degrees of human activity. Table 3.3 indicates the nature of the changes within the soil profile of a lowland brown earth that have resulted from centuries of use for arable farming. The most altered part of the soil is the upper ploughed horizon called an **agric** horizon, in which constant overturning and mixing has prevented the establishment of normal chemical and physical horizons. Typically, cultivated soils are richer in the basic plant nutrients, especially phosphates, than their uncultivated counterparts, but poorer in organic material.

The remainder of this chapter examines particular ways in which soils have been modified, purposefully or otherwise, by man.

3.3 Physical change

3.3.1 Structural deterioration due to ploughing

The increasing mechanisation of arable farming has allowed land to be ploughed and harrowed at a time of year when the soil would have been too wet and heavy to work in the past. Farmers are under some economic pressure to sow earlier in the season. The net result has been the deterioration in structure of silty clay soils over some arable areas in England. The change in structure (Fig. 3.2) has been from a free-draining, open soil framework to one with a compact, massive-structured horizon that impedes both drainage and root development. The soil in Figure 3.2b has a 'plough-pan' horizon with a horizontal platy structure at a depth of 25–30 cm. The pan is formed when the soil is ploughed while still in a plastic state, easy to mould and smear. The base of the furrow has a layer of fine particles spread over it by the plough and the tractor wheels, and as the soil settles the layer remains as a horizon of low permeability to water infiltration.

3.3.2 Soil erosion

Man's most negative impact on soil is, of course, to create conditions that allow partial or total erosion to occur. Strictly speaking, this is not an alteration of soil character so much as a geomorphic event, and hence case studies of total erosion are given elsewhere in this book.

Catastrophic soil erosion is most common in delicately balanced environments (semi-arid or mountain, in particular) and where the soil is easily erodible (Fig. 3.3). However, physical and chemical soil degradation is much more widespread, and even carefully managed arable agri-

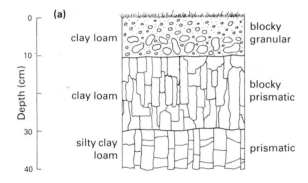

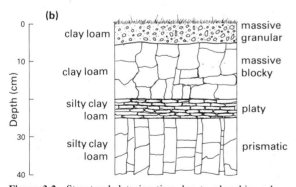

Figure 3.2 Structural deterioration due to ploughing when wet of a brown-earth soil derived from boulder clay in Britain. (a) Original soil profile; (b) after ploughing. (After Agricultural Advisory Council 1970.)

Figure 3.3 Intense soil erosion and gullying associated with the misuse of agricultural land, Oaxaca, Mexico.

culture will increase soil losses five- to 50-fold compared with losses under a natural vegetation cover. In promoting erosion, man is effectively compressing geomorphic time and greatly accelerating a natural process (see Chs 7 & 9). In the great corn-growing belt of the USA the fertile soils were 2 m or more in depth, yet in the 100 years or so for which they have been farmed, one-third of this depth has been removed over wide areas.

Man-initiated erosion need not necessarily be detrimental. In the Mediterranean basin old, deep soils on the slopes had lost almost all nutrients from the A horizon and had a very limited agricultural potential. Forest clearance 1000–5000 years ago led to water erosion of the fragile A (topsoil) horizon leaving the more compact, clayey B (subsoil) horizon at the surface. Since then a new, 'rejuvenated' soil has developed, based on the former subsoil.

3.4 Chemical change

3.4.1 Artificial fertilisers

Attempts to maintain or to improve soil fertility by the use of chemical fertilisers are relatively new practices, although manuring and marling (addition of lime-rich clay) have been undertaken for centuries. With the invention of artificial chemical fertilisers in the 19th century and the recognition of the nature of plant nutrients, it became possible to alter some aspects of soil chemistry at will, and the use of synthetic fertilisers is now universal within the developed countries. The basic artificial fertilisers are combinations of the primary nutrients: nitrogen, potassium and phosphorus. These, together with the use of calcium as a conditioner–nutrient, are a highly simplified version of the cocktail of plant nutrients stored in a natural soil and acquired from rock weathering and the decay of organic matter. Calcium, potassium and phosphorus are stored in soils for long periods in ionic form at the surface of plate-like clay particles, as well as being 'fixed' (turned into an insoluble form) in the case of calcium and phosphorus. If fertilisers are applied over a long period of time, the chemistry of the soil becomes greatly simplified, its store of nutrients being heavily biased towards calcium, phosphorus and potassium (Fig. 3.4). Other cationic elements are displaced from storage and leached out of the soil by rain water. In turn, this can help to create changes in soil structure. Potassium-rich soils may

develop a columnar or prismatic structure that is hard and intractable when dry, slushy when wet. Continued use of ammonium sulphate fertiliser acidifies the soil and so may 'fix' other nutrients, making them unavailable to plants (zinc is one such trace nutrient). Soils that have been manured or grazed for long periods are often rich in phosphate, and it may accumulate in a distinct phosphatic horizon with concentrations of 1000 p.p.m. or more.

Scientific application of fertilisers can be used to control soil chemistry very exactly, varying the balance of nutrients according to the crop being grown and, similarly, the degree of soil acidity (pH) can be kept within the optimum range of slight acidity (pH 5–7) by liming in humid regions. The recognition that plants require certain elements in trace quantities has allowed soils deficient in one or more such elements to be made much more fertile by their addition. Adding molybdate at rates of 100 g/ha to New Zealand hill pasture soils together with phosphatic fertiliser allowed nitrate-fixing bacteria to thrive, which in turn encouraged the growth of clover for fodder in the absence of available nitrate. The use of worked out areas of cut peat for agriculture usually requires the addition of a whole spectrum of major and minor plant nutrients that are absent from the organic soil. Trace elements such as copper, boron, zinc and iron are often lacking in organic soils.

3.4.2 Salinisation and desalinisation

Soils with a high salt content (salts of potassium, sodium, magnesium and calcium) or high alkalinity are characteristic of arid and semi-arid regions. They are intrazonal soils developed at low points in the landscape either due to the concentration and subsequent evaporation of runoff which has dissolved salts from the surrounding area, or to the existence of a water table sufficiently close to the surface to allow upward (capillary) movement of water which evaporates and deposits its dissolved salts. Soils in such areas may be potentially fertile, irrigation being the key to their exploitation. However, irrigation can be used or misused: it can be used to desalinate soils, but it may also cause salinisation of previously fertile soils.

Saline (**solonetz**) soils are reclaimed by prolonged washing, usually by spray irrigation, with high quality water. A system of drainage ditches at the appropriate depth is necessary to carry off the saline water from the leached soil. When the harmful salts, sodium in particular, have been removed, it may be necessary to add calcium to restore soil structure and chemical balance utilising the ion-exchange processes illustrated in Figure 3.4. If the salinisation is due to a high water table, the drainage ditches must be sufficiently below the zone of capillary rise of ground water to prevent the salinisation process from recurring. Saline soils developed by inflow of runoff from surrounding areas may be deep ploughed and treated with gypsum to improve vertical drainage and restore the ionic balance (calcium) to that suited to plant growth. Such methods have been used to reclaim large areas of land, particularly in the USSR steppe and the estuarine areas of Romania. The Russians have used a dilute solution of sulphuric acid to remove salts: the excess runoff water (leachate) then contains sodium and calcium sulphates in solution. The effect of these de-salination techniques is to convert the intrazonal solonetz into a well watered version of the zonal

soil for the area – a chernozem in the case of the steppes – within a few years.

Seen from the air, many croplands that have been irrigated over a period of many years show grey, mould-like patches amongst the green. This is due to salinisation stunting plant growth and is the beginning of a process that will turn the area into near-desert in which only the most salt-tolerant vegetation can survive. Between 20 and 40 per cent of the world's irrigated lands are affected by salinisation to some extent, and it is estimated that each year as much land is lost to cultivation by salinisation as is brought into culti-vation by new irrigation schemes. In India alone 4 million ha are affected.

In arid areas both ground and surface waters are naturally more saline than in humid zones. In addition, the water used for irrigation is the runoff from a much larger area rather than simply the rain that falls on the particular irrigated area. At least 30 ha of catchment is needed to irrigate 1 ha of land

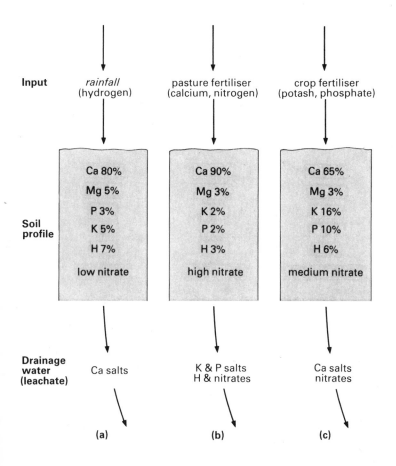

Figure 3.4 Altering soil chemistry by the addition of chemical fertilisers (ion ex-change). (a) 'Natural' chemistry of a brown-earth soil. (b) Chemistry of the same soil following prolonged application of pasture fertiliser (nitrates are not stored in the soil). (c) Chemistry of the same soil following prolonged application of crop fertiliser.

in the semi-arid areas, and therefore the dissolved salts from the 30 ha are concentrated onto 1 ha. Prolonged irrigation raises the soil water table, until, when it is 1–1.5 m below the surface, capillary rise will allow salt deposition to take place in the soil nearer the surface during the dry season. Unless rainfall and irrigation are sufficient subsequently to wash the salt back down the soil profile, it will gradually accumulate until the soil is rendered useless. In the Bhakra area of the Punjab, irrigation raised the water table some 9 m in the first 10 years of irrigation over an area of 2.7 million ha. In the Murray river basin of south-eastern Australia, irrigation schemes during the 1950s were equally short lived, and salt concentrations in the runoff water rose 10-fold within as many years. The effects of this process on the soil depend in part on the predominant salts. If calcium is abundant, then land drainage will restore the soil to its original state but, if sodium salts form more than 12 per cent of the total salt content, the clay-sized soil particles become dispersed, structure is lost and the soil is a true solonetz.

Although careful management allows soils to be irrigated for hundreds of years, in the past salinisation has been an almost inevitable long-term consequence. The gradual increase in salt content of the soils of the Fertile Crescent in Mesopotamia, the cradle of agriculture, can be inferred from the progressively higher salt content of the bricks used for house building in the area over the centuries. The destruction of their farmland by salinisation may have been one of the reasons for the collapse of this and other ancient civilisations of the semi-arid world.

3.5 Creating new soils

3.5.1 Reclamation of Exmoor soils
The very opposite environment to that described above is that of upland Britain. The soils of Exmoor in north Devon and west Somerset at 300–500 m above sea level are peaty gleys, ill drained, acidic and supporting a coarse vegetation dominated by *Molinia* (purple moor grass). Reclamation of these soils has continued intermittently over the past 200 years. Modern techniques consist of deep ploughing, the addition of

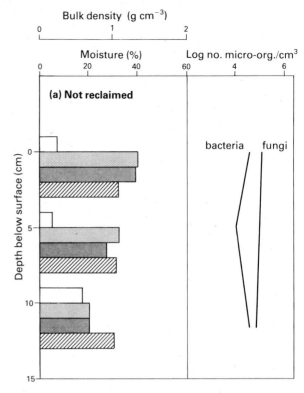

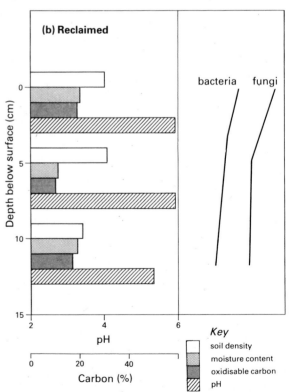

Figure 3.5 Alterations in the characteristics of an Exmoor soil due to reclamation. (After Maltby 1975.)

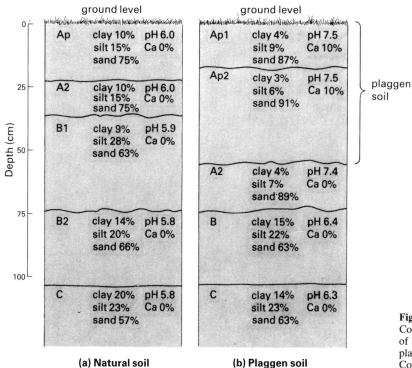

Figure 3.6 Soil profiles near the coast of County Kerry, Ireland: (a) the natural soil of the area; (b) a nearby soil with thick plaggen horizons created by man. (After Conry 1971.)

lime and nitrogenous fertiliser and re-seeding with *Festuca* (sheep's fescue) and *Agrostis* (bent grass) species of grass. The resulting changes in soil character are considerable, as is shown in Figure 3.5. Chemical, physical and biological properties are shown for the natural and reclaimed soil at 5-cm intervals down the profile. The lower soil moisture levels and higher pH of the reclaimed soil increase soil life (bacterial and fungal levels are shown), while oxidation reduces the carbon content. Earthworm numbers increased 100-fold in the reclaimed soil.

Establishing such a soil on the heights of Exmoor is in direct opposition to natural processes, and maintenance of the status of the reclaimed soil requires constant attention. In areas where this has been neglected, the soils have begun to revert to their original character in response to the strong natural controls of upland climate, topography and parent material.

3.5.2 Irish plaggen soils

In areas of naturally infertile soils throughout Europe, man has created small areas of artificial soils, commonly by building up a thick layer of organic-rich material over the original soil. Such soils are termed **plaggen**, meaning 'sod' soils. Figure 3.6 shows the profile of a plaggen soil on the Kerry coast in southwestern Ireland, together with the profile of the natural soil of the area. Intensive agricultural use led to the loss of calcium and plant nutrients from these sandy soils, and the plaggen horizons formed of lime-rich sand, seaweed and manure were added to compensate for these losses. Applications of 10 000 tonnes/ha are needed to account for the 65 cm-deep plaggen layer. The plaggen horizons differ from the original soil in several ways. The pH has been raised from 6 to 7.5, calcium carbonate content from zero to 10 per cent, organic content from zero to 5 per cent and sand content from 75 to 90 per cent. The increased organic content and higher pH allow the plaggen soils to respond well to fertiliser application, as it can be stored in soil in an available form. The overall effect has been to increase the fertility of the soils, and in County Kerry they are used for carrot and onion growing, though in some instances the addition in trace quantities of cobalt, boron and manganese has been necessary to allow the full potential of the soil to be realised.

3.6 Conclusions

The examples of changes in soils brought about by man given in this chapter are but a sample of a vast and important subject which is referred to many times in this book, directly or (as in Ch. 6, dealing with soil water) indirectly.

In recent times increasing awareness of our environment has focused attention on man's relationship with the soil. The results have been various, including the 'organic farming' viewpoint that eschews artificial fertiliser and the 'no-plough' techniques of cropping. Admirable though the motives may be in such movements, man must modify the soil and what grows in it in order to eat. The problem, as yet unresolved, is to what extent and how, the soils of an area may be manipulated to the advantage of agriculture, but without inflicting 'unacceptable' damage on the natural world.

4 Plants and animals

4.1 Introduction

As food is a basic necessity for man, the direct sources of that food, plants and animals, have been subject to a greater degree of control over a longer period of time than any other aspect of the natural environment. The crucial change in the relationship between man and the rest of the living world occurred with the transition from a mesolithic (hunting and gathering) society to a neolithic (agriculture, domestication) economy. This marked the evolution of human beings from being simply another life-form with an appropriate ecological niche to becoming a controlling force on other organisms to the extent where they may be the primary evolutionary controlling factor. To an extent human selection has replaced natural selection.

Man's involvement in the biological world may be viewed as a modification of natural ecosystems (Ch. 2) in which flows of energy and materials between and within the living and physical worlds are deflected, enhanced or diminished either by accident or with the intention of furthering human well-being (see *Biogeographical processes*, I. Simmons, George Allen & Unwin, 1982).

Alterations to patterns of vegetation and animals have been made for a variety of reasons. The safeguarding of human interests has led to the virtual elimination of animal predators and to the partial winning of the fight against diseases borne by organisms. Competitors for food supply, whether carnivores, herbivores, plant pests or rivals for plant nutrients (weeds, natural vegetation), have been suppressed wherever possible. More positively man has operated his version of Darwinism by domestication and selective breeding of plants and animals – the characteristics selected being those of most use to man. The end-products are as various as battery chickens and exotic garden flowers.

Figure 4.1 shows the derivation of some of the domesticated plants and animals now distributed throughout the world. The diffusion of life-forms beyond their natural area of occurrence is a further significant aspect of interference. Many introductions of alien species are made because they are a useful source of food, but other introductions have been made to control existing pests or simply from curiosity to see how the newcomer will cope with its new environment. Equally, many introductions have been accidental rather than deliberate – animals or insects transported on boats, and seeds carried on clothing, for example. Figure 4.2a shows the process of diffusion of the grape vine from its original area of domestication in southwestern Asia 6000 years ago. A much more rapid and less intended diffusion of a species was that of the European starling following its introduction in Central Park, New York in 1891 (Fig. 4.2b). Human impact on the biosphere has not been uniform: for example, it has been animals higher up the food chain and plants close to their limits of environmental tolerance that have suffered most change. However, on a global scale the concept of biogeography as the relationship between organisms and the natural environment is no longer valid. It was mentioned in Chapter 2 that the biosphere is particularly vulnerable to change and, more obviously than in other aspects of the environment, 'everything is connected to everything else.' The result of the intimate linkages that characterise ecosystems has been that human intervention has commonly led to unexpected chain reactions of change.

4.2 Vegetation

4.2.1 Modifying vegetational patterns

A conventional map of the broad types of vegetation is given in Figure 4.3. At this scale and

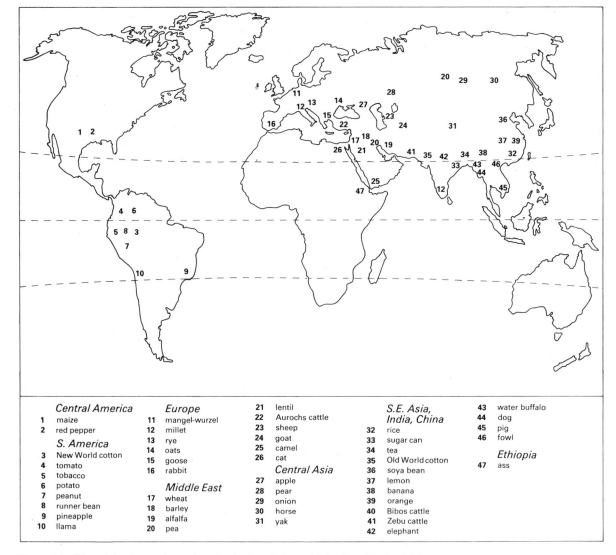

Figure 4.1 The origin of some domesticated animals and plants. (After·Cox, Healey & Moore 1973.)

	Central America		*Europe*	**21**	lentil			**43**	water buffalo
1	maize	**11**	mangel-wurzel	**22**	Aurochs cattle		*S.E. Asia,*	**44**	dog
2	red pepper	**12**	millet	**23**	sheep		*India, China*	**45**	pig
		13	rye	**24**	goat	**32**	rice	**46**	fowl
	S. America	**14**	oats	**25**	camel	**33**	sugar can		
3	New World cotton	**15**	goose	**26**	cat	**34**	tea		*Ethiopia*
4	tomato	**16**	rabbit			**35**	Old World cotton	**47**	ass
5	tobacco				*Central Asia*	**36**	soya bean		
6	potato		*Middle East*	**27**	apple	**37**	lemon		
7	peanut	**17**	wheat	**28**	pear	**38**	banana		
8	runner bean	**18**	barley	**29**	onion	**39**	orange		
9	pineapple	**19**	alfalfa	**30**	horse	**40**	Bibos cattle		
10	llama	**20**	pea	**31**	yak	**41**	Zebu cattle		
						42	elephant		

according to this method of mapping, Britain is blanketed by deciduous forest. In fact, such a map is a historical document indicating idealised relationships among soils, vegetation and climate expressed as climax vegetation types (the optimum vegetation for a particular environment). It bears much less resemblance to reality than does the map of world soils given in the previous chapter. Thus, the European deciduous forest shown on the map has largely been converted to pasture or arable land, most of the mediterranean forest is now agricultural land or scrub and most of the tropical rainforest (selva) is secondary forest or thorn scrub.

Even in regions where agriculture is limited, vegetation is often not wholly native, as in areas used for forestry. In semi-arid regions, such as, for example, the areas of desertification described in Chapter 2, man has commonly upset the natural ecological balance by increasing the number of herbivores (stock), and the net result has been a lowering of the vegetational status, encouraging the spread of plants with more modest environmental requirements – xerophytes (drought-resistant plants), fire-resistant plants and unpalatable plants. This is an example of forced evolution in which defence against the side-effects

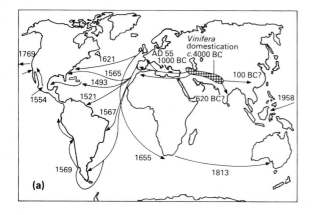

Figure 4.2 The diffusion of animal and plant introductions. (a) The transference of the domestic grape vine from its area of origin (shaded). (After Simmonds 1976.) (b) The spread of the European starling in North America between 1891 and 1928 following its introduction in New York. (After Elton 1958.)

There are gradations of manipulation of natural vegetation. A forested zone may be slightly modified by selective tree felling or may be converted wholly to grassland, arable agriculture or intensive agriculture. Existing grassland may be modified by selective grazing by introduced herbivores or may undergo profound species change via the use of fertilisers and re-seeding as with the Great Plains of North America. The overall tendency has been to degrade vegetational status imposing lower species diversity, less biomass and shifting vegetation towards the arid end of the humid–meso–xeric (wet to dry) moisture gradient.

Irreversible changes in vegetation types can only occur when soil status is also altered. Thus great areas of the world are artificially maintained as grasslands (**plagioclimax vegetation**), but unless the soil has altered radically in response to the new vegetation, climate or erosion, any relaxation of man's imposed pressure will allow vegetation gradually to revert to its natural equilibrium. There are exceptions in sensitive zones, where a threshold has been passed and the original vegetation would not return. The tropical rainforest (Fig. 4.5) and semi-arid regions are probable examples.

Deliberate changes in vegetation (agriculture) are considered in Chapter 9, and the examples of both vegetation and animal distribution modifications given in the remainder of this chapter are of largely accidental changes, particularly those on a small scale.

4.2.2 Small-scale vegetational changes

Primroses. Primroses, once common woodland flowers, and cowslips, open meadow plants, occupied very different ecological habitats. In Britain the loss of woodland and the modification of pastureland has forced both species to occupy a common, compromise niche in man-made hedgerows and managed copses. This proximity has allowed interbreeding and has produced an intermediate plant-form with the long cowslip stalk surmounted by the flowers of the primrose. A second human influence has been the picking or uprooting of both species by flower lovers. The cowslip is now a relative rarity, and the distribution of the primrose has been modified on a gross scale so that now it is virtually absent from the areas around urban centres.

Railway flora. Transportation has always had an influence on the British flora. Whether trackway,

of man's activities is the primary requisite for survival.

Modification of the vegetation of Europe was a long, slow process (Ch. 9), but in recent times elsewhere in the world the pace has accelerated. Figure 4.4 demonstrates the drastic vegetational changes imposed upon an area of deciduous forest in South Island, New Zealand over a 90-year period. The actual vegetation is now pastureland, scrub and isolated stands of the original forest. Such rapid vegetational changes can be demonstrated to have occurred throughout the world.

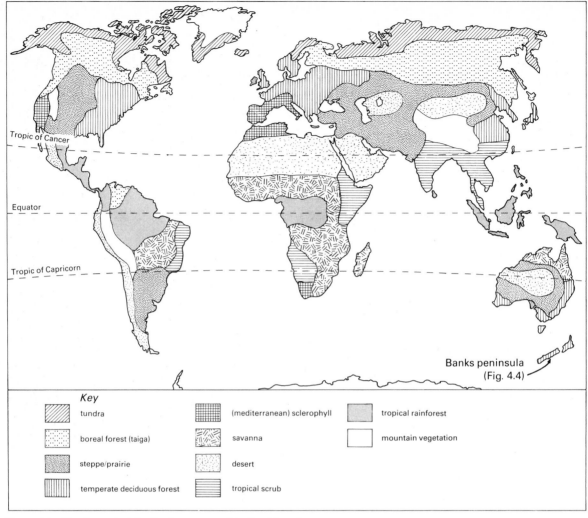

Figure 4.3 The theoretical distribution pattern of the Earth's major vegetational types. (After Drew 1977.)

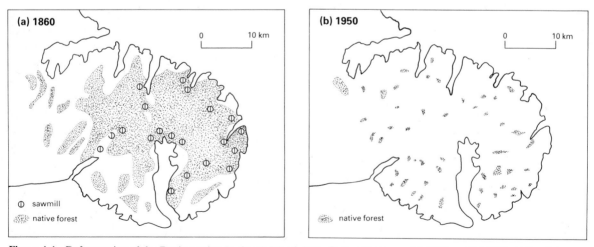

Figure 4.4 Deforestation of the Banks peninsula, South Island, New Zealand between (a) 1860 and (b) 1950. (After Johnston 1968.)

(a)

(b)

Figure 4.5 (a) Undisturbed tropical rainforest in Jamaica. (b) Secondary scrub in the same area following clearance and later abandonment of the land.

motorway, railway or canal, the result has been to provide continuous, relatively uniform, open habitats criss-crossing the country. Thus suitable species are presented with ideal conditions in which to propagate together with the artificial dispersal mechanism of the mode of transport itself. Diffusion of these species has been rapid and linear rather than the more usual slow progression of a broad front of advance. The best known example of railway flora is that of the alien (mediterranean) plant, Oxford ragwort (*Senecio squalidus*) which escaped from the Oxford Botanical Gardens in 1790. Ninety years later it reached the Great Western Railway track in Oxford and thereafter spread rapidly throughout the railway routes of southern England, thriving on the disturbed ground and having its plumed seeds carried along in the currents of air generated by passing trains. Native plants such as sticky groundsel (*Senecio viscosus*) have spread on the arid environment of the track ballast, and the creation of opposite, cool, humid environments at tunnel entrances and shaded platforms has allowed the migration of some fern species. The rusty-back and brittle bladder ferns have spread from their original distribution in north and west Britain to reach much of the remainder of the country. In recent years railway habitats have become much more limited as the network has become truncated. Although modern high-speed trains are powerful agents of dispersal via air currents, the use of herbicide sprays to control embankment vegetation has severely curbed species variety allowing resistant species such as strap-wort (*Corrigiola litoralis*) to prosper accordingly.

4.2.3   Medium-scale vegetational changes
Vietnam. During the war in Vietnam (1954–1973) severe control on vegetation – tropical rainforest – was exerted by man, for purely military purposes. One-fifth of the total forest area (22 000 km^2) was defoliated by the American forces using powerful herbicides at 13 times the concentrations required for agricultural weed killing. The effects are expected to persist for 100 years and the ecological side-effects are largely unknown. Even more impact was created by bombing, which converted 2000 km^2 of jungle into bare earth in 1971 alone.

Prickly pear. The prickly pear cactus was introduced to Australia from South America for use as a highly effective stock fence. In Australia it found a spacious niche and spread uncontrollably, eventually ruining some 250 000 km^2 of agricultural land – an impact comparable to that of the rabbit. Chemical control was found to have no effect and eventually a form of 'natural' ecological control was adopted. Another alien was imported from South America, the moth *Cactoblastis cactorum*, whose larvae burrow into the prickly pear and destroy the plant from the inside. Within 3 years the prickly pear population had declined by 80 per cent, and after 20 years a natural balance had been established between cactus and predator, with prickly pear populations remaining at an acceptable level.

4.2.4   Large-scale vegetational changes – the mediterranean flora
Areas with a mediterranean climate occupy only 3 per cent of the Earth's land surface, but their importance in human terms has been out of all proportion to their extent, particularly in the case of the European mediterranean area, but also in regions such as southern California. Instability and vulnerability are characteristic of the mediterranean vegetation, especially the forests. This is a reflection of the transitional nature of the climate, part temperate, part tropical, and also the rugged, mountainous nature of many mediterranean areas. Drought and downpour typify the precipitation regime, encouraging soil erosion, and the diverse nature of the forest flora (four times the number of species of temperate forests) leave individual species more liable to extinction.

Such a delicately poised environment is very sensitive to human influence and such influence has disrupted the mediterranean ecosystems on a large scale. From man's point of view the mediterranean regions are balanced between fruitfulness and frugality, the way the balance tips depending upon the approach to the land. An ideal model of land use would involve maintaining forests on the hills and practising agriculture on the lowlands, but such a system has rarely been used either in the Mediterranean basin itself or elsewhere in the world. In the European area, in particular, the conflict between pastoralism and agriculture has been decisive in determining the fate of the natural vegetation.

It has been estimated that vegetation types created by man occupy more than three-quarters of uplands in the European mediterranean region. More recently settled areas of mediterranean climate have suffered comparable change. For example, in Chile and California even the grasses and herbs of the pasturelands in areas of cleared forest are dominantly those imported from Europe by settlers, as they tolerate animal trampling better than the natural ground flora.

However, it is in Europe that the changes imposed upon the mediterranean vegetation are best documented. The forests of oak or pine that are the natural vegetation for some 80 per cent of the upland zone have been exploited by man for at least 10 000 years. Much of the timber was used in construction or for charcoal, but large areas were wholly or partially deforested for the creation of pasture. Forest clearance has occurred in bursts of activity at different periods throughout the region, though it is in the past three centuries that maximum loss of forest has taken place. Removal of evergreen forest and the prevention of regeneration by browsing has created more extreme microclimates, allowed extensive soil erosion and, even when the land was abandoned, allowed only a lesser vegetation to recolonise. Figure 4.6 illustrates the sequence of vegetational degradation associated with forest clearance for either arable or pastoral purposes. The rate at which the regression proceeds in any particular instance depends upon local factors of soil, topography and climate together with the degree and duration of stress imposed by man.

Loss of forest encourages plant species that are light and drought tolerant to become dominant, and grazing similarly promotes the spread of unpalatable plants and those that can propagate from shoots. Overall, the change is from a mesophytic to a xerophytic vegetation. The scrub (maquis, chaparral) characteristic of so much of the mediterranean is a relatively rich flora, and if left undisturbed may allow forest to regenerate. However, overgrazed areas or lands exhausted by arable farming may become virtual deserts in which only the most tenacious of plants, asphodel in particular, can survive (Fig. 4.7). Areas such as these have been pushed beyond a threshold and cannot recover their original condition.

Napoleon, who was born in Corsica, claimed that he would recognise his homeland even if blindfolded, just from the scent of the aromatic vegetation. These plants, however, are those of the maquis (high scrub) and petit maquis or garrigue (low scrub) that now cover a large proportion of Corsica and have replaced the original forests of pine and oak. Corsica's vegetation has been degraded by human action to a greater extent

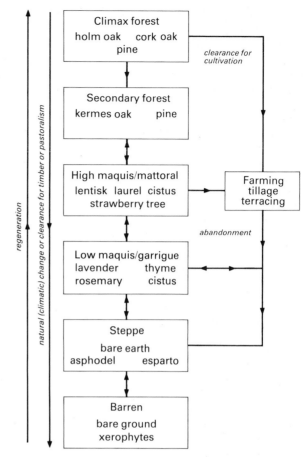

Figure 4.6 The degradation and regeneration sequence for mediterranean vegetation under human or natural influences.

than that of any other comparable mediterranean region (Fig. 4.8a). Over 75 per cent of the potentially important agricultural zone between the high mountains and the coastal plain is now scrubland. Figure 4.8b shows the pattern of vegetation in such a zone around the capital city of Ajaccio. Natural forest is restricted to isolated clumps in a sea of maquis, and the association of even more degraded vegetation (garrigue) with settlements is apparent. These are largely areas of abandoned arable land.

The original forests of evergreen oak on the higher hills were cut for charcoal and tannin extensively in the 15th and 16th centuries, but the oak forest had begun to disappear at a much earlier period. Even by 500 AD beech forest was replacing oak, as the numerous pigs kept in the mountains selectively ate oak saplings and acorns, inhibiting regeneration. Even today Corsica has a

Figure 4.7 Natural and degraded forms of mediterranean vegetation: (a) natural oak forest; (b) low maquis grazed by goats; (c) barren, eroded asphodel steppe.

pig population of 30 000 compared with an estimated optimum population of 4000. The pastoral tradition in Corsica led to clearance of vast areas of beech and pine forest, exposing the soil to severe erosion even on comparatively gentle slopes. Browsing by pigs, goats and sheep has prevented regrowth, and abandonment of land with economic decline has allowed the thorny maquis to form an impenetrable thicket. The vegetation of Corsica is now in large part a product of human intervention; Figure 4.8c shows the potential and actual altitudinal zonation of vegetation on the island.

4.3 Animals

4.3.1 Relation between man and animals

To a greater extent than with vegetation, human interference with animal populations has produced far-reaching and unpredicted effects, for example with the rabbit (Ch. 2). The higher up the food chain are the animals, the greater is the degree of control exerted by man. Despite insecticides, most insect populations are relatively immune to human control and, indeed, often proliferate in otherwise 'controlled' environments. Larger animals are less numerous and easier to manipulate. Eradication of species and selective breeding of others has increased the number of grazing animals (herbivores) at the expense of carnivores (hunted to eliminate predatory species or for man's amusement). Species have also been sharply reduced in numbers or eliminated altogether by habitat destruction, often an unintended consequence of land-use alteration. Extinction and introduction of animal species are opposite aspects of human manipulation, though they may go hand in hand. When goats were brought to the Galapagos Islands in the eastern Pacific, the indigenous populations of giant tortoises and iguanas declined rapidly as all were competing for the same foodstuffs, the goats most successfully. At least 200 species of mammals and birds have become extinct as a result of man's activities over the past 300 years. The rate has been one species per year in this century, and a further 250 species are on the

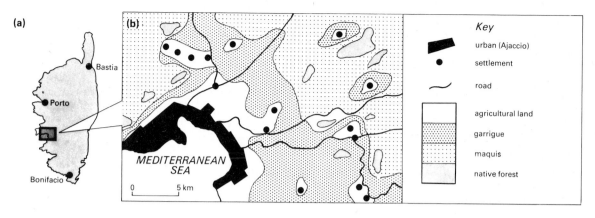

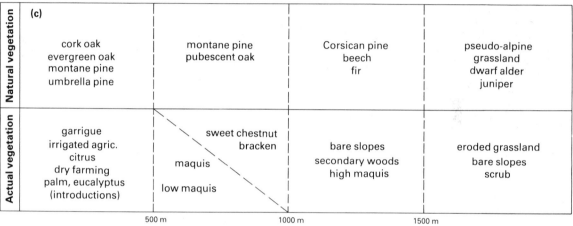

Figure 4.8 Man-induced changes in the mediterranean vegetation of Corsica: (a) location of the area; (b) modified vegetation in the Ajaccio area; (c) actual and probable natural altitudinal vegetational sequences in Corsica.

verge of disappearing. The largest of these, the blue whale, has declined rapidly in numbers in recent years. Catches in Antarctic waters were over 5000 in 1950, 1700 in 1960 and zero in 1970. The effect on the marine ecosystems of the extinction of a species such as this is largely a matter for speculation.

The introduction of animal species into new habitats has been a haphazard affair; part deliberate, scientific or otherwise; part inadvertent. The success of a species in a new habitat depends upon the existence of a vacant niche for it to occupy. Some introduced animals, now naturalised in Britain in greater or lesser numbers, include:

prehistoric	fallow deer, house mouse
mediaeval	rabbit, pheasant, black rat, carp
18th–19th centuries	brown rat, sika deer, grey squirrel

1900	mink, wallaby
1930	coypu
1950	yellow bellied toad
1960	guppy
1970	gerbil, crested porcupine

Populations of many of these immigrants are too small to be significant, but others, the grey squirrel for example, have prospered mightily. The grey squirrel has now largely ousted the native red squirrel from all but western areas, it has few natural enemies and is thought to have a considerable effect on bird populations by destroying eggs. By comparison the wallabies of Derbyshire live a cloistered existence with no natural enemies but man.

European colonies have experienced animal introductions on a greater scale over a much shorter time period. New Zealand is a prime example where, within the past 100 years, the rabbit, hedgehog, rat, hare, stoat, weasel, ferret, fox, goat, cat, dog, deer, opossum, blackbird, rook, mallard, chaffinch, goldfinch and skylark have been added to the native fauna.

Three examples of modifications of animal ecosystems are given below: extinction, proliferation and large-scale changes in an aquatic ecosystem.

4.3.2 Modifying animal ecosystems

The large blue butterfly. Fauna with a small natural population and a very restricted habitat (lack of adaptability) are particularly liable to extinction as a result of man's activities. This may accelerate a natural process or reverse a natural (colonising) trend. Butterflies often fall into this category, as caterpillars of some species are highly selective in their feeding. The large copper butterfly had disappeared from Britain by 1865 due to the draining of the Fens, and its introduced successor, the Dutch large copper, survives only under close management in Woodwalton fen.

It is thought that by 1980 the large blue butterfly (*Maculinea arcon*), a rare native of the downs of southern England, had also become extinct in the United Kingdom. The butterfly's life cycle is highly specialised. The caterpillars feed on the flowers and seeds of thyme for a period of 3 weeks before becoming pupae. These then drop to the ground and are carried underground by a particular species of ant that obtains a sweet secretion from the pupae, but also provides them with a protected environment in the ant's nest until May when the butterflies emerge. The increasing loss of downland to arable agriculture fragmented the large blue population into 'islands', and the decline in rabbit numbers allowed remaining areas of turf to develop a taller form of vegetation, excluding the close grazed turf favoured by the ants. Population levels of the large blue probably dropped below the minimum required for continuation of the species, and thus its extinction is an example of inadvertent loss of a species due to habitat destruction by man.

Cocoa tree parasites, Malaysia. Accidental extinction of an insect species is more than counterbalanced by population explosions due to human removal of some natural check to population growth within the ecosystem. In the Sabah area of Malaysia, jungle was cleared for cocoa tree plantations during the 1950s. The plantations were surrounded by a ring of secondary (degraded) forest with untouched primary (natural) forest farther away. The secondary forest provided a base for numerous pests of the cocoa tree including ring bark borers and bagworms (caterpillars). These pests are sedentary, rarely moving from a single, sheltered site on a tree. Extensive spraying using DDT was undertaken to exterminate the pests, but the results were exactly the opposite. The natural predators of the pests are insects that roam over the trees looking for food and it was therefore they which were exposed the most to the insecticide and severely reduced in numbers. Freed of predators, the cocoa tree pest population exploded.

The Great Lakes fisheries. Although the Great Lakes of North America form one hydrological unit draining to the Atlantic ocean via the St Lawrence river, the lowest lake, Ontario, was originally biologically segregated from the remainder by the existence of the Niagara Falls on the river linking it to Lake Erie. The Falls also formed a barrier to navigation until they were bypassed by the construction of canals in the 19th century. The Erie canal (Fig. 4.9a) linked the Hudson river in New York state with Lake Ontario via the Oswego river (1819) and was then extended to Lake Erie in 1825. The Welland canal (1829) provides a direct route between Lakes Ontario and Erie.

The canals are also biological conduits, but it was many years before the effects, in terms of changes in abundance, composition and distribution of fish species became apparent. Two invasive species were responsible for many of these changes, the alewife and the blood-sucking, parasitic large sea lamprey. Alewife were found in Lake Cayuga and Lake Seneca on the Oswego river in the 1860s, having migrated from the Hudson river. Shortly afterwards the fish reached Lake Ontario and within a few years the lake fisheries had collapsed as the population of whitefish, chubb, pike and lake herring fell drastically from competition by the alewife. Twenty years later the sea lamprey reached Lake Ontario.

The migration continued through the Great Lakes system (Fig. 4.9a), but it was 120 years after the opening of the canals before alewife and lamprey were recorded from the most distant lakes, Michigan and Superior. These deep lakes provided an ideal environment for the lamprey in particular, as it prefers to live in the permanently

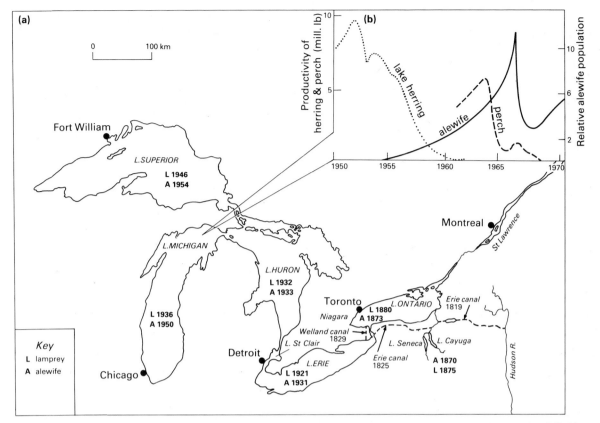

Figure 4.9 Changes in the Great Lakes fisheries. (a) Spread of the lamprey and alewife fish through the Great Lakes following construction of the Erie and Welland canals. (b) Changes in fish populations in Lake Michigan 1950–70. (After Aron & Smith 1971.)

cold waters of the depths. Figure 4.9b shows the changes in fish population in Lake Michigan in recent years since the arrival of the alewife and lamprey. The alewife population explosion did not occur until the mid-1960s, probably because by then the numbers of its main predator, the lake trout, had been greatly reduced by the lamprey. The decline in the numbers of commercial fish was rapid, and in the late 1960s chemical spraying was undertaken to try to kill the lamprey larvae in the spawning streams. Pacific salmon (up to 10 million annually) were introduced into the lake to prey on the alewife, and to try to restore something resembling a pre-canal ecosystem.

4.4 Conclusions

Because undisturbed vegetation represents the biological response to the totality of environmental factors (soil, climate, landforms), so its

linkages to these other global subsystems are very sensitive. Elsewhere in this book the side-effects of man-imposed vegetational changes are noted: on soils (Chs 3 & 9); on climate (Chs 2 & 5); on hydrology (Ch. 6). The consequences of modifications of animal distributions are commonly equally far reaching, but more subtle and less easily detected, as the case studies in this chapter have indicated.

Man's initial interest in the biological world stemmed from his need to eat and to compete with predators – aims now being furthered by genetic control of plants and animals and by attempted control of disease-carrying insects or microorganisms themselves.

However, alongside this 'rational' and empirical approach to the natural world has been a capriciousness in regard to other life-forms, which is only now beginning to change with the acceptance by man of his integration with the natural world.

5 The atmosphere

5.1 Introduction

Man first altered the local workings of the atmosphere and hence the climate some 7000–9000 years ago, when he changed the face of the land by clearing forest, planting crops and irrigating land. However, the climatic changes that resulted were almost imperceptible, as were those resulting from recent deliberate attempts to modify the weather. Man has tended to bend with the wind, literally and metaphorically, where climate is concerned, adapting to existing conditions rather than attempting to control: houses are sited in sheltered positions, frost-sensitive crops are planted on valley sides where temperature fluctuations are least (thermal belt) rather than valley floors, irrigation is employed to compensate for inadequate rain and so forth. Even today, man's control over atmospheric forces is almost entirely defensive, seeking to avert the worst consequences of a drought, a hurricane or a spell of excessively cold weather. Positive climatic control is severely limited in area and intensity, though large-scale schemes to deflect atmospheric processes have been put forward. For example, it has been suggested that the Congo river in Central Africa should be dammed to create a lake 3 million km^2 in area (10 per cent of Africa's area). This water body with its high evaporative loss of water would then inject moisture into the monsoonal airflow which in turn would increase precipitation in the drought-prone Sahel area of North Africa. On a similar scale are the ideas for deflecting major ocean currents such as the Gulf Stream or Kuro Shivo current or for preventing water exchange between the Pacific and Arctic oceans by damming the Bering Strait. All these schemes are probably viable in a technological sense, but our ignorance of the detailed workings of the atmosphere means that the full cause and effect chain that might result from such large-scale interventions is far from

clear. It is certain that no deliberate change on such a scale could be beneficial to people everywhere.

Nevertheless, it is probable that during this century man has inadvertently begun to increase the rate of change of global climate, particularly in the northern hemisphere. It is very difficult to assess the magnitude of these changes or to be sure whether they are natural or man made, but it is thought that the natural cooling trend in global climate since 1950 has now been halted and that a perceptible warming will have taken place by the year 2000. By 2050 we may have the warmest climate for 1000 years. Changes in the polar regions are expected to be two or three times greater than the global average, and any significant ice-cap melting would provoke further major and possibly irreversible distortions of atmospheric circulation and heat-budget patterns. These changes are considered to be a likely direct consequence of altering atmospheric composition, especially of dust and carbon dioxide. Unlike any of the other aspects of the natural environment examined in this book, the atmosphere is a continuous and so a single system and changes can be transmitted throughout its extent. Therefore, alterations in, say, the atmospheric segment of the carbon cycle or in the albedo of large areas of land surface will initiate climatic change possibly on a global rather than a local scale. (The workings of the atmospheric system are explained in detail in *Atmospheric processes*, J. D. Hanwell, George Allen & Unwin, 1980.)

5.2 Leverage points in the atmospheric system

The ultimate determinant of climate is the input of solar radiation which powers the workings of the atmosphere. All the elements of climate: temperature and pressure patterns, wind and precipitation are secondary effects of the differential heating of the atmosphere and the Earth's surface. Therefore, alterations made to the heat budget will cause the maximum climatic change and the greatest sequence of subsequent changes. Alterations made to the functioning of the secondary processes such as precipitation or wind systems are likely to have more restricted effects. All deliberate attempts at climatic modification have been concerned with this secondary level (fog dispersal or rain making, for example).

Fortunately perhaps, the vast scale of the atmospheric system and the enormous energy flows that occur mean that there are relatively few leverage points within the system at which a modest application of stress can produce a very significant change. Some idea of the magnitude of atmospheric energy flows may be obtained if the energy obtained from the burning of 1000 tonnes of coal is represented by 1 energy unit. Then the following·events involving energy may be compared:

	Energy involved (units)
thunderstorm	10
large nuclear bomb	10 000
daily world energy consumption	100 000
a mid-latitude depression	1 000 000
the monsoon circulation	10 000 000
daily global receipt of solar radiation	1 000 000 000

On this basis, man's ability to deflect, if not alter, such flows significantly, let alone to push the system beyond thresholds, seems rather limited, with the exception of finely balanced climatic zones such as the semi-arid regions liable to desertification described in Chapter 2. However, there are weak points within the atmosphere, two of which are now being acted upon by man. Changes in surface reflectivity (albedo) alter the heating of the lower atmosphere and such changes are related to land-use alteration. Secondly, and potentially much more important, is the composition of the atmosphere, particularly the quantity of carbon dioxide gas present. It is the increase in the concentration of this gas due primarily to combustion of fossil fuels and as a secondary effect through deforestation (Sect. 5.4.2) that is thought to be responsible for the warming trend in global climate. Because carbon dioxide is an important

agent for the absorption of long wave radiation, it occupies a key position in the thermal budget and small changes in its concentration can produce large fluctuations in global temperatures.

The case studies of climatic change given in this chapter are arranged first according to scale (micro to macro: house to hemisphere), and secondly according to whether the changes are inadvertent or deliberate. All large-scale changes are accidental, as indeed is the most intense change at meso scale – the distinctive urban climate considered in Chapter 10.

5.3 Scales of change

5.3.1 Microclimatic change

The primary reason for the construction of buildings is to provide shelter, to create a wholly controlled and artificial climate within a very small area. However, any building also creates its own distinctive microclimate in the immediate vicinity, and this microclimate may be desirable or otherwise. It should be one of the duties of modern architects to consider these climatic aspects when designing buildings. Urban climates (Ch. 10) are a formidably complex assemblage of thousands of overlapping local climates created by the structures.

(a) Long section showing flow zones

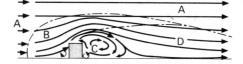

(b) Long section showing wind velocity profiles

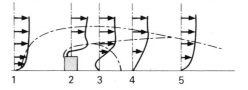

(c) Plan view of air-flow pattern   *Key*

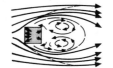

A undisturbed flow
B displaced flow
C turbulence
D downflow (wake)

Figure 5.1 Modification of wind-flow patterns in the vicinity of a building. (After Oke 1978.)

A single building modifies many of the climatic parameters, but only on a minute scale. Figure 5.1 shows the alteration of wind flow in the area surrounding a building. The smooth, laminar flow of air is disrupted, creating a high pressure on the upwind side and a low pressure with eddying on the lee side. A miniature current of concentrated high-speed air flow (jet-stream) is formed above the zone of turbulent flow. The building will convert incoming solar radiation into heat in a different manner from its surroundings depending on the colour, texture and density of the building materials. Most buildings act as miniature heat islands due both to increased absorption and subsequent irradiation of solar energy and to heat produced by combustion. Thus the building will possess its own weak convective cell with ascending warm air. Humidity is lower close to the structure, as surface water is rapidly removed by man-made drains in built-up areas.

5.3.2 Mesoclimatic change

In rural areas climate is altered over wide areas (perhaps hundreds or thousands of square kilometres) by land-use changes. The effects are greatest close to the ground, but atmospheric conditions are altered within a dome 30–100 m in height extending over the area. Such effects are discussed in the context of the tropical forest environment in Chapter 9, but equally striking effects result from clearance of forest in cold, dry climatic regions.

In the North-west Territories of Canada, an area of spruce–lichen forest (taiga) underlain by podsol soils was cleared by burning. Measurements of the microclimate of the burned area, now covered by low shrubs and herbs, some 24 years after firing, showed that its climate remained distinctly different from that prevailing in the surrounding forested area. Albedo levels in the burned area were lower than those in the forest (16 per cent as opposed to 19 per cent). Consequently, the greater absorption of radiation by the ground in the burned area led to higher temperatures both at the surface (10°C higher in the summer) and in the soil (4°C higher). The lack of a 'buffer' zone of ground vegetation led to the higher soil temperatures, but also to a much greater range of day-night variation of temperature (37°C instead of 28°C). Thermal gradients in the lowest 10 cm of the atmosphere increased from 5 to 7°C/cm.

The lack of trees allowed wind speeds to increase close to the ground, lessening snow cover by 20 per cent, decreasing soil moisture, but allowing more rain to reach the ground because of the lack of interception of water on leaf surfaces. In the longer term this will alter soil processes (increased leaching), hence vegetation and so microclimate again.

Although the climatic changes recorded in this example appear to be great, they are largely concentrated in the very lowest layers of the atmosphere, the effects diminishing rapidly with height. Proven examples of medium-scale climatic change due to human activity, other than in urban areas and perhaps newly afforested regions, are rare.

5.3.3 Macroclimatic change

Even more difficult to demonstrate are climatic changes imposed on a macro-scale, for it is always possible to argue that any change is due to natural rather than artificial causes. However, the case of the Rajputana desert on the border between Pakistan and north-west India suggests that man may have triggered climatic change in a marginal area of some $30\,000\,\text{km}^2$. It is an extreme example of the desertification process (Ch. 2), in this instance largely due to overgrazing of the vegetation by goats, leading to cumulative modification of atmospheric processes.

The Rajputana desert was a part of the Indus valley civilisation until *c.* 700 AD – now many of the cities of this period lie overwhelmed by drifting sand. The desert is still relatively densely populated and in climatological terms it is a curious desert. Water-vapour concentrations are much higher than normal for a desert, as is the dewpoint temperature, and the area would seem to be a desert despite, rather than because of, the climatic base: semi-aridity appears to be its natural condition. Dust in the atmosphere may be the reason for the aridity – it is the world's dustiest desert. Concentrations of dust particles of $300–800\,\text{mg/m}^3$ occur in the lowest 5–10 km of the atmosphere – two or three times higher concentrations than are normal in the 1–2 km layer above major industrial cities elsewhere in the world. The suspended dust particles decrease the amount of solar radiation reaching the ground by reflection, causing upper air cooling and lower ground temperatures. In turn this reduces the amount of convective rise of air, a possible source of precipitation, and reinforces subsidence of air as the primary mechanism. Less rain leads to surface desiccation and so more dustiness. At night the dusty atmosphere acts as a blanket, preventing surface temperatures from falling as low as would normally be the case under clear desert skies. Thus there is less chance of temperature falling to below the dewpoint and allowing condensation of water on to ground surfaces as dew.

There can be no proof that the increased aridity over the past 1300 years is a direct consequence of overgrazing and baring of the soil, but more recent experience of desertification in Africa and elsewhere suggests that man can destabilise semi-arid climates. Areas of the Rajputana desert near Jaipur that have been fenced off from grazing animals have developed a cover of high grasses within a few years.

5.4 Inadvertent climatic change

5.4.1 Change induced from the ground
Urban areas cause the most profound changes in land use due to human action, but they occupy only a tiny fraction of the Earth's surface compared with the 20 per cent of the land surface significantly altered by agricultural or forestry activities. Conversion of forest into pasture raises albedo from approximately 12 per cent with evergreen trees to 20 per cent with grass cover. Surface cooling due to this effect has become apparent in Amazonia (Ch. 9). Extensive zones of irrigation generate a zone of higher humidity above and down wind of the area, and this effect may become a significant agent of climatic change in the steppes of the USSR where great areas of land are to be irrigated in the near future (Ch. 6).

5.4.2 Atmospheric composition
Both agricultural and industrial activity are gradually altering the composition of the atmosphere by increasing the quantities of naturally occurring substances in the air and by introducing new compounds. With the exception of carbon and sulphur compounds and some aerosol particles (fluorocarbons), measurable quantities of the man-made substances are present mainly in the vicinity of the source area. Some 90 per cent of the additions to the atmosphere are of gases, the remaining 10 per cent consisting of tiny particles (aerosols) less than 100 μm in diameter which stay aloft for periods of days or weeks in the troposphere or months to years if they reach the stratosphere. Aerosol particles are generated naturally from volcanic and desert dust and sea-salt particles, but man-derived aerosols are produced in large quantities by industrial emissions, motor-vehicle exhausts, crop-residue burning and erosion of ploughland by wind. Dust concentrations in the atmosphere are 10 times greater in the northern hemisphere than in the southern, a reflection of the much greater land area in the northern hemisphere, but also of the much greater degree of human activity. As was noted in the case of the Rajputana desert, aerosols can reflect and scatter incoming solar radiation, thereby stabilising the lower atmosphere and lessening the convective rise of air. On the other hand, in theory a significant increase in aerosols could lead to increased precipitation in some areas of the world, as some of them can function as nuclei of condensation around which cloud droplets form. This effect is known to occur within the limited zone around cities.

Gaseous emissions to the atmosphere are potentially more likely than dust to trigger climatic change, as they can remain aloft indefinitely. Atmospheric carbon dioxide is a part of the global carbon cycle, though a relatively short-term storage zone compared with the oceanic and vegetational stores. Atmospheric carbon dioxide acts as a radiation filter (Sec. 5.2), letting through incoming short-wave radiation but absorbing outgoing radiation in several infra-red bands, thereby heating the lower atmosphere and cooling the stratosphere. Burning of fossil fuels and deforestation have increased atmospheric carbon dioxide concentration from c. 0.027 per cent 100 years ago to c. 0.033 per cent today. Predicted levels for the years 2000 and 2050 AD are 0.044 and 0.06 per cent respectively, if present rates of increase of fossil-fuel use are maintained. Man now accounts for one-fifth of all carbon dioxide production, and he has significantly shifted the global storages of carbon – the same quantity is now stored in the atmosphere as in biomass, though this is due largely to the reduction in biomass caused by deforestation. If carbon dioxide emissions continue to increase at the present rate, a global rise in temperature of c. 0.3°C per decade may take place, though the warming is likely to be uneven with a maximum occurring polewards of latitude 50°S and 50°N.

More important in quantitative terms are emissions of sulphur dioxide gas. Although the gas remains in the atmosphere for a short time only, its effects can be drastic (Ch. 10).

An alien group of substances released into the atmosphere from refrigerants and aerosol propellants are the chlorofluoromethanes (FG-11 and FC-12 being the principal industrial emissions). Such **freons** as they are termed are very stable, non-toxic substances which, if they reach the stratosphere, may persist for up to 70 years – the only large natural sink being a slow breakdown by ultraviolet radiation in the stratosphere. The tropospheric concentration of freons is now approximately 0.0002 p.p.m., but is expected to reach a maximum of almost 0.0003 p.p.m. early in the next century with some 65 per cent consisting of FC-12. From this time onwards natural decay rates will approximate to production rates. It is thought that freons have a direct effect on the Earth's heat budget, as they behave in a manner akin to that of carbon dioxide, absorbing outgoing radiation in the 8–15 μm infra-red range. A concentration of freons of 0.0025 p.p.m. would decrease outgoing infra-red radiation by 0.3 per cent, which in turn would raise surface temperatures by up to 0.5°C.

One group of atmospheric pollutants is largely due to motor-vehicle exhausts including carbon monoxide and nitrogen dioxide. In areas with strong insolation (sunshine) some such substances and hydrocarbons are liable to be chemically altered into new compounds by the action of sunlight (photochemical change) in the atmosphere. Figure 5.2 illustrates the alteration of nitrogen dioxide into the complex compound peroxyacetyl nitrate (PAN), which damages vegetation, perishes rubber and irritates the eyes. Such photochemical alteration of emission products is a wholly urban phenomenon at present (Ch. 10).

The variety of other substances introduced into the air by man is enormous. Many of them are obscure, but the quantities involved are too small to suggest that they can modify the workings of the atmosphere. One such substance that may have an effect, however, is the radioactive gas emitted from nuclear power stations, krypton 85. Although the gas does not form chemical combinations in the atmosphere, its radioactive decay produces electrons that locally ionise the air. The effect is to improve the conductivity of the lower atmosphere, lessening the electrical field between the negatively charged Earth and the positively charged upper atmosphere. In theory this could lead to a lessening of atmospheric electricity (thunderstorms). Total ionisation of the lower layers of the atmosphere has increased by some 10–15 per cent over the past 30 years. However, it has not been shown that the frequency of thunderstorms has been altered as a result.

Although the constituents of the atmosphere are undoubtedly being changed by human activity, the effects of these changes are not yet obvious, nor, as is apparent from the foregoing account, is there any certainty as to what manner or magnitude of changes are to be expected.

5.5 Deliberate climatic change

5.5.1 Frost protection

Deliberate and controlled alteration of heat budgets, other than within buildings, is practicable only on a small scale and over limited areas, if only for economic reasons. So, for example, the richer football clubs can afford electrical soil-heating systems to make pitches playable in frosty weather. Soil temperatures and air temperatures in the lowest few centimetres of the atmosphere can be raised by the use of mulches that lower albedo and delay the re-radiation of energy (Fig. 5.3). With crops that are particularly frost sensitive – citrus fruits are a good example – it may be worthwhile to take active measures to try to maintain air temperatures within the vegetation layer above the

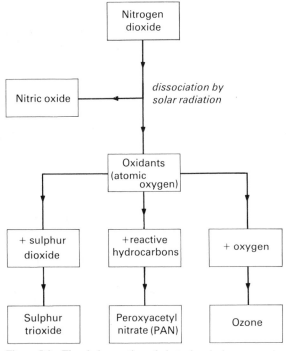

Figure 5.2 The chain reaction of photochemical processes in the atmosphere originating with emissions from motor vehicles and from combustion.

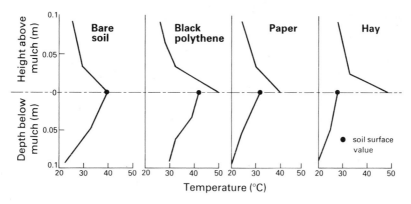

Figure 5.3 The effect of surface mulches of black polythene, paper and a 6-cm-thick layer of hay on soil and air temperatures on a summer day. (Sandy loam soil, Connecticut, USA.) (After Oke 1978.)

critical level for frost damage. The techniques used are effective only in marginal conditions where temperatures need be raised only by a few degrees. Equally they can be used only for sites affected by radiative (*in-situ*) cooling of air. Advective cooling (cold air blowing in) involves continual replacement of artificially warmed air by cold and would require impossibly large inputs of energy.

A common method is to place artificial heaters (particularly in orchards) within the crop zone (Fig. 5.4). The convective currents generated mix and warm the lower 5–15 m of air, breaking the temperature inversion and cold air layer at the ground that characterise radiation frosts. Fans to

agitate the air can also be used to break the inversion and mix in warmer air from above without the addition of artificial heat.

A somewhat riskier method of temperature control involves using the latent heat of fusion released when freezing of water actually occurs. When the temperature has fallen to just below freezing point, a fine spray of water is directed on to the plants. As it freezes the heat given out will help to retard any further cooling.

5.5.2 Shelter belts
Passive methods of local climatic change are much more common than the example above. One of the

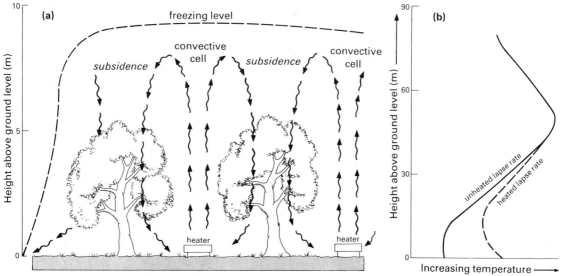

Figure 5.4 Frost prevention in an orchard by the use of artificial heat sources: (a) local convective circulation within the orchard; (b) temperature–height relations (lapse rates) within and without the heated zone. Within the heated zone, ground temperatures are higher and a normal lapse rate prevails in the lowest few metres of the air.

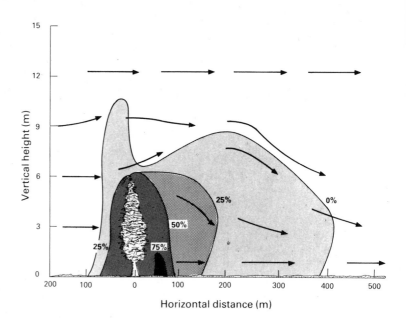

Figure 5.5 Reduction of wind speeds in the vicinity of a 6-m-high permeable shelter belt of trees.

oldest such methods, first noted in Norfolk in the 18th century, is the planting of rows of trees (one or more trees thick) to act as windbreaks and to provide a more desirable local climate in their immediate vicinity. The purpose of the shelter belt may be to screen an exposed dwelling, to lessen wind erosion of soil or to retain soil moisture by decreasing wind speed and consequent evaporation rates. The effects of a shelter belt on wind velocity and direction are illustrated in Figure 5.5, which shows the small upwind and extensive downwind zone of lessened wind flow and hence of modified local climate. The extent of the zone of influence and the degree of change of climate will depend on the height, thickness and nature of the shelter belt. Although shelter belts are used in Britain (often as hedges rather than lines of trees), it is in areas that are marginal for arable agriculture due to the lack of rain and risk of soil erosion that shelter belts are most valuable. Following the 'dust-bowl' of the 1930s in America, 30 000 km of shelter belt were planted in the affected region of the mid-west. Increases in crop yield of 5–25 per cent have been claimed for fields protected by such windbreaks.

5.5.3 Atmospheric moisture modification

An example of some degree of success in manipulating an aspect of climate on a meso-scale is given by man's attempts to alter atmospheric moisture

conditions. Particular efforts have been made to disperse cloud droplets (fog dispersal) and to induce droplet coalescence (rain making). Fog dispersal is possible over limited areas, usually airfields, provided that the fog is not too firmly entrenched – in other words, when a leverage point exists to alter atmospheric conditions to those that will not sustain the suspended water droplets. Freezing fogs may be 'seeded' with tiny particles of dry ice or silver iodide to encourage the water droplets to freeze on to the particles, eventually forming crystals large enough to fall to the ground under gravity. Warm fogs are harder to disperse, although mixing the foggy air with drier air from above using helicopter rotors is sometimes successful. The fog may be seeded with hygroscopic particles (lithium hydroxide or urea) which absorb water vapour, thereby drying the air and causing the fog to evaporate. The commonest method is to artificially heat the fog layer, thereby increasing its water vapour capacity to a level sufficient to evaporate available moisture. The Turboclair system at Orly airport in Paris consists of 12 jet engines in underground chambers, and is capable of fog removal over a 1.2-km length of runway.

The seeding technique described above is also used to attempt to trigger precipitation from clouds in regions with insufficient rainfall. The method is based upon the assumption that clouds at the right temperature that do not produce precipitation lack sufficient tiny particles around which coagulation of the cloud droplets can occur in order to create large enough crystals of ice to fall to the ground. The addition of supercooled particles of dry ice or silver iodide or mists of ammonium nitrate or urea is intended to rectify the deficiency. The particles are added either by aerial spray or as a smoke from ground level. Cloud seeding is only successful when natural conditions are close to those necessary for precipitation to occur. Man's effect is to push the system beyond the threshold into the precipitation state. It is, of course, difficult to be sure whether or not any rain falling from a seeded cloud is due to the seeding or would have fallen in any case. However, projects in Australia and the USA claim increases in annual precipitation of 10–30 per cent over areas of several thousand square kilometres.

Hurricanes have also been seeded in order to cause rapid freezing of water droplets and so the release of latent heat of fusion. This appears to reduce maximum wind speeds in parts of the hurricane circulation, if the area just outside the 'eye' is seeded. In 1969 the American Project Stormfury seeded five Caribbean hurricanes at 2-h intervals with silver iodide at a height of 10 000 m. Wind speeds were decreased by 15–30 per cent.

Equally spectacular have been the efforts to prevent crop-damaging hailstorms by firing shells containing coagulation nuclei into clouds that are likely to produce hail in an attempt to cause precipitation before the hailstones have formed.

5.6 Conclusions

Compared with the man-induced changes discussed in the remainder of this book, human impact on climate is much more difficult to assess. It is certain that on a very local scale, in the vicinity of buildings for example, the climate is altered. On larger scales the problem is that the tiny scale of change that might be caused by man can be swamped by natural change. Our knowledge of the global atmospheric system is still very limited.

Even if man-made climatic change is more a future possibility than a present fact, the consequences of such change are enormous. The atmosphere and the solid Earth are the two most independent aspects of the Earth system. Therefore, changing climate will provoke a cascade of changes in geomorphic, soil and vegetational processes which in turn, by feedback, will further modify climate.

6 Water

6.1 Introduction

It might be argued that fresh water is mankind's single most important resource. On a global scale the expansion of agriculture and settlement into vast areas of land is inhibited by insufficient water. Locally, water resources may determine the location of specific industries such as power stations and, in the past, settlement patterns showed a close relationship to surface water supplies and springs: an extreme example being desert oasis settlements.

From the human viewpoint the constraints imposed by water are that there may be too little water available (deserts, droughts) or too much (marshes, floods). Equally, in a particular area seasonal or occasional excesses or deficits may occur.

It is in part because of the absolute importance of fresh water that modification of its occurrence in time and space was one of man's earliest attempts to alter the natural environment. Indeed, the development of agriculture and of organised society was closely linked with water control, especially for irrigation. The civilisations of ancient Egypt and China, and of India and Mesopotamia have been termed 'hydraulic civilisations'. Their rise and subsequent fall was intimately related to their use and misuse of water.

Tampering with the hydrological cycle has continued to the present day. With the advent of modern technology the degree of interference has increased dramatically, and now there can be few drainage systems in the world that are wholly natural in character. Although regulation of hydrological systems is greatest in the developed countries, inadvertent modifications to the system are universal, commonly due to land-use changes.

Apart from the economic and social benefits, a further reason for the high degree of human interference in the hydrological cycle is that very great modifications are relatively easy to achieve and the benefit quickly realised.

In terms of the leverage points discussed in Chapter 2, the hydrological system offers many such points at which a relatively small modification provokes a large change in the functioning of the system. This is especially true of the terrestrial part of the hydrological cycle, whereas altering the atmospheric and oceanic parts is much more difficult. Ideally, man prefers to intervene in the water system at points where the benefits obtained to cost involved ratio is greatest, using current technology. In fact, the technologies of dam building, river diversion, land drainage and groundwater extraction are highly developed. The prospects of larger dams, grandiose water diversion schemes and of towing icebergs across oceans tend to bring a gleam to the eye of the engineer and the planner alike. As with other aspects of environmental control, so particularly with water, man's ability to create changes has outstripped his wisdom in terms of the likely consequences of change. 'If it can be done, it will be done' has often been the philosophy.

The functioning of the hydrological cycle, particularly on the land, has, in part at least, been understood by man since early times. This is in marked contrast to other aspects of the natural environment – erosion and nutrient cycles, for example. Thus there has been a tendency to perceive and act upon the workings of the hydrological cycle as an integrated and interrelated whole. However, this has led to a neglect of the relationship between water and other aspects of the natural world. It is only recently that the idea of integrating water management with that of, say, land or energy has emerged.

Scales of intervention in the hydrological cycle range from the minute to the mighty: from the 'shadufs' (counterbalanced buckets) used in India and Egypt to transfer water from the river to an irrigation channel to the proposed continental diversion of river systems in the USSR; from rainwater tanks collecting roof runoff to vast manmade lakes – the USA stores approximately 100 days of mean runoff in reservoirs.

6.2 The hydrological cycle – points of intervention

6.2.1 Introduction
The hydrological cycle may be thought of as a series of water stores linked by transfers (Fig. 6.1).

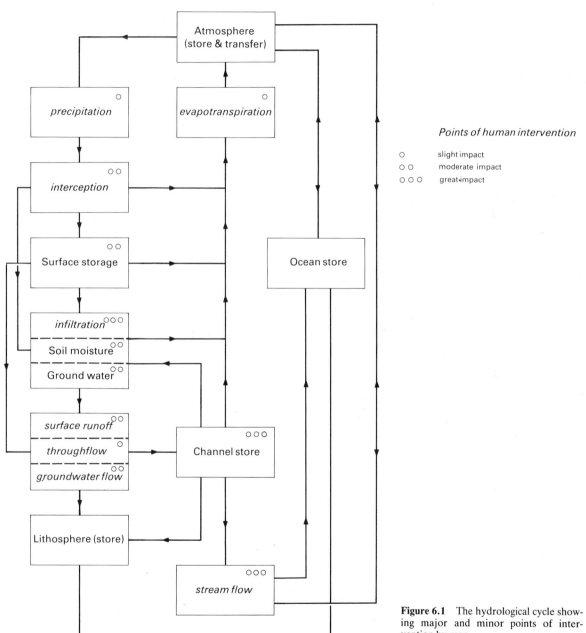

Points of human intervention

○	slight impact
○ ○	moderate impact
○ ○ ○	great impact

Figure 6.1 The hydrological cycle showing major and minor points of intervention by man.

In fact, many of the 'stores' are really slower transfers (e.g. ground water) and some of the faster transfers (e.g. rivers) also have a limited storage function. Figure 6.1 may be seen as a plumbing system through which water drains steadily downwards towards the lowest point of the system, the oceans. Several side vents allow 'steam' (evapotranspiration) to escape directly to the atmosphere.

In practice, each of the storage boxes could be subdivided into smaller interconnected units. High degrees of feedback exist between many of the stores. The routes taken by water through the plumbing system from the entry point (precipitation) will vary from place to place on the earth's surface depending on the nature of the land and the climate. The distribution of water will also change through time at any one location. (For fuller details, see *Landscape processes*, D. and V. Weyman, or *Elements of geographical hydrology*, B. J. Knapp, George Allen & Unwin, 1977 and 1979 respectively.) On the surface of the land, water becomes concentrated into individual drainage basins, each of which operates its own series of stores and transfers of incoming water. The outflow from many basins may unite before the water reaches the sea. Some of the routes available to water within a particular river basin are shown in Figure 6.2. The individual boxes (stores) in the diagram are shaded in accordance with the approximate proportion of total precipitation that is likely to pass through each box. Some idea of the importance of the various transfer mechanisms is indicated by the thickness of the lines linking the stores.

Obviously, no two river basins will deal with incoming precipitation in exactly the same manner. The approximate values in Figure 6.2 correspond to those for a medium-sized basin underlain by permeable rocks in a climate such as that of Britain. All incoming water must pass through the 'surface' store, but thereafter the routes it can follow are various. So, for example, in a semi-desert region almost all the water entering the surface store might promptly leave it via evaporation, the remainder of the plumbing system being unused.

Man can alter the capacity and efficiency of many of the storages and transfers. If the interference is made with surface or soil transfers or storages, it is likely that a chain reaction will cause changes to occur throughout the remainder of the storages and transfers. The lower down the system

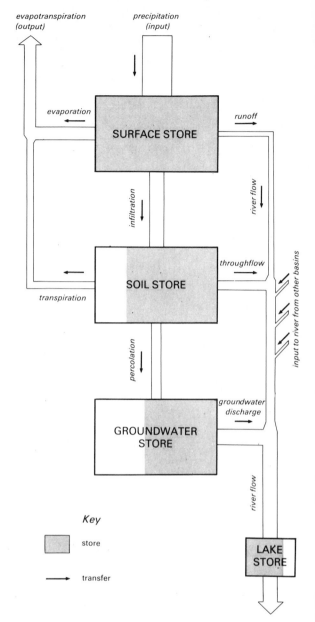

Figure 6.2 Simplified flow-diagram of the land-based section of the hydrological cycle. Stores are shaded according to the proportion of total input water that they process. Transfer line thicknesses are approximately proportional to the importance of the transfer mechanism. The data relate to an 'average' agricultural river basin in Britain.

is the point of intervention, the fewer elements in the hydrological system are likely to be affected, although the existence of feedback mechanisms in the system would, of course, allow chain reactions to work back 'up' through the system. A lessening of the ability of the soil to absorb rainfall, due perhaps to a change in land use, might affect the distribution of water through all the succeeding routes, whereas groundwater abstraction might only affect river flow, lake storage and flow to the ocean. An example of artificial feedback in the system would be the use of abstracted ground water for irrigation of the land surface above.

In the following sections, some of man's impacts on individual water storages and transfers are examined, and then examples of integrated modification of several aspects of the hydrological cycle are considered.

6.2.2 Surface stores and transfers

A number of pathways may be followed by rainfall immediately it reaches the ground surface. The more important stores and transfers are illustrated in Figure 6.3. Vegetation plays an important role in redistributing water at this stage. Interception of rainfall by plant leaves (with probable re-evaporation of some water) will vary according to the density of vegetation and the plant species. For example, a cereal crop with a dominantly vertical structure intercepts less water than plants such as potatoes that have a spreading, horizontal structure and a large leaf area. Similarly, a forest area is likely to intercept more water than either cropland or grassland. Thus a change in vegetation cover is likely to affect the amount of interception water

lost to evaporation. Deforestation or afforestation commonly has a considerable effect on water losses. Loss of tree cover, in the short term, lessens loss of water from the soil by transpiration as deep tree roots are removed, and induces more direct surface runoff from the land as the former buffering layer of dead leaves (litter) is replaced by bare soil. Thus direct runoff to the stream is likely to increase. Figure 6.4a illustrates the effect of forest clearance on river flow from a small (c. 500 ha) basin in the Appalachian mountains of the eastern USA. Streamflows in this basin and an adjacent similar basin have been measured since the mid-1930s, the data from the second basin in which land use remained unaltered being used to check for natural changes in discharge over the years. In the first basin the deciduous forest was cleared in 1940. The response in terms of stream flow was immediate and dramatic, annual discharges increasing sharply – the equivalent of a 20 per cent increase in rainfall. During the succeeding 23 years the forest was allowed to regenerate and water yields from the basin fell accordingly. In 1963 a

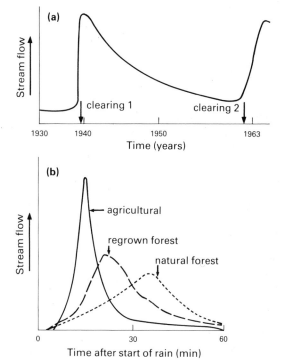

Figure 6.4 The effects of forest clearance on river flow in Appalachia. (a) Water yield from a small basin cleared of forest in 1940 and again in 1963. (After Hibbert 1967.) (b) Storm hydrographs from basins in the same area under differing land uses: natural forest, regenerated forest and agriculture. (After Dib 1957.)

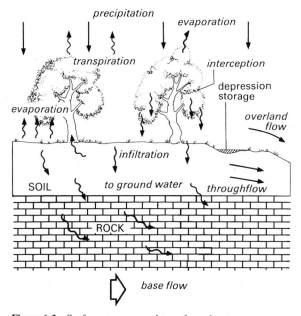

Figure 6.3 Surface storages and transfers of water.

second clearance of the trees provoked a second sharp increase in stream flow. However, in regions where much of the precipitation falls as snow (e.g. the USSR, Sec. 6.3.5), forest may, in fact, give a higher water yield than adjacent farmland as trees trap and retain the winter snows more effectively.

The increase in total water output via the stream is not the only hydrological effect caused by deforestation: the rate of runoff of water into the river as well as the amount of runoff is increased. In Figure 6.4b the stream flows (hydrographs) resulting from individual storms are shown from similar Appalachian basins. The three hydrographs represent runoff from three different land-use types – native forest, partly regenerated forest after clearing and a basin devoted wholly to farming (50 per cent pasture, 50 per cent crops). The agricultural catchment responds quickly to rainfall and produces a much larger flood wave in the river. The natural, forested basin processes the same input of water very differently, stream discharge increasing slowly after the storm and reaching a maximum flow at a much lower level. The partially reforested basin has a form intermediate between the two extremes.

Afforestation decreases the amount of rainfall available to pass through the successive stages of the hydrological cycle. In the Tropics in particular, attempts have been made to reduce transpirative losses of water while still retaining the same vegetation type. Spraying leaf surfaces with substances such as atrozine has reduced water losses by up to 50 per cent for short periods and over small areas.

In vegetated areas of moderate or gentle slopes comparatively little flow of water directly overland to streams is likely except following very heavy rainfall. Man's activities (ploughing, for example) may expose bare earth. This may have the effect of lessening any possible flow of water overland by creating a rough surface with innumerable small hollows, which trap water until it subsequently evaporates or infiltrates into the ground. This is especially true of contour ploughing (Fig. 6.5) and, indeed, it is usually undertaken to minimise soil erosion (due to overland flow) and to increase soil moisture storage. In the USSR and in Canada, autumn ploughing was found to lessen direct runoff by up to 45 per cent. However, if heavy rains compact and flatten the ploughed surface before vegetation regenerates, overland flow may be encouraged on the smoother, less permeable surface.

Figure 6.5 Surface water retention in plough furrows illustrating the lowered infiltration rates and increased depression storages that result from ploughing land.

In areas of semi-aridity or seasonal drought, the effects of land-use change on hydrology are most apparent. These are also the areas most liable to soil erosion (Ch. 3) for the same reasons. Measures may be taken to lessen accelerated and increased runoff from a basin while still allowing agriculture to continue. Figure 6.6 shows river flows due to heavy rainfall (storm hydrographs) from a small basin in Nebraska, USA before and after the adoption of water conservation practices. The conservation methods used included terracing, contour ploughing, pasture re-seeding, stripcropping, irrigation and the construction of storm-water storages. The overall effect of these measures has been to reduce the amount of water reaching the stream by up to 40 per cent, so partly restoring a forest-type hydrological regime to the area.

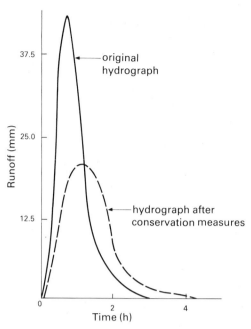

Figure 6.6 The changed form of the runoff hydrograph generated by 60 mm of rainfall with the adoption of land conservation practices. Runoff is presented as the depth of water in millimetres available to runoff per hour over the basin. (Hastings basin, Nebraska, USA.) (After Pereira 1973.)

The most extreme alteration in the character of surface stores and transfers occurs in an urban area where a high proportion of the surface is made wholly impermeable by concrete, tarmac or house roofs. Vegetation is largely absent and surface storage of water is minimised on the graded roads and pavements and sloping roofs. Thus evaporation losses are very low and far more water is available to flow through the remainder of the system. However, as Figure 6.7 illustrates, man has ensured that the options open to the water are severely limited. The great majority must run off via drains and storm sewers, the lower transfers and storages scarcely being used at all. Examples of these effects are given in Chapter 10.

The changes in natural stores and transfers and hence in the functioning of the hydrological cycle are shown diagrammatically in Figures 6.8 (under deciduous forest), 6.2 (agriculture) and 6.7 (urban conditions).

6.2.3 Soil stores and transfers

For thousands of years attempts have been made to alter water conditions in soils. The intention may be to add to stored water (irrigation and methods of cultivation) or to lessen stored water

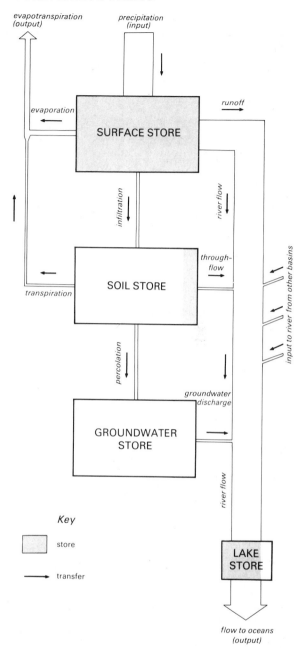

Figure 6.7 Changes in the hydrological cycle following intensive urbanisation. Compare with Figure 6.2.

(land drainage); to increase the rate of movement of water in soil (changing structure and texture), or to decrease movement (adding organic matter, compaction). Modifications to both surface and soil stores, and transfers of water are rarely intended as direct attempts to alter the hydrological cycle. Rather, the subsequent hydrological

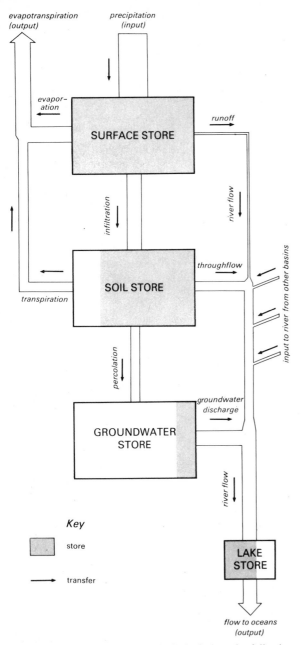

Figure 6.8 Changes in the hydrological cycle following afforestation of a basin. Compare with Figure 6.2, which shows conditions in a comparable unforested basin.

extend 'upwards' towards the atmosphere and 'downwards' to the lower portion of the cycle.

Considerable hydrological effects are brought about by land drainage. In intensively farmed areas with a humid climate such as Britain's, almost all agricultural areas have been drained to some extent.

The purpose of land drainage is twofold: first it serves to lower seasonal or permanent water-table levels and secondly it removes excess water from the land via artificial channels, more rapidly than under natural conditions. Thus both storage and transfer mechanisms are modified. Field drainage (under-drainage) is usually carried out by installing parallel lines of either plastic pipes or earthenware tile drains some 1–2 m below the surface. In heavy soils unlined conduits called mole drains may also be made by dragging a bullet-shaped implement through the earth at shallow depth. Mole drains run at right angles to tile drains, which in turn empty into ditches usually running round the perimeter of the field. The ditches form part of an integrated drainage system ultimately discharging to a natural stream course (Fig. 6.9).

Of the 160 000 km of waterways in Britain, some 96 000 km are artificial ditches and a further 3000 km are canals. It is estimated that in England and Wales there are 1–3 km of natural channels per km^2 (drainage density 1–3). Artificial drainage conduits raise this drainage density to c. 2–6 km/km^2. These figures do not take into account the vast numbers of mole and tile drains, and as field drainage has been practised for several hundred years it is very difficult to estimate their extent. Figure 6.10 indicates the approximate extent of under-drainage in England and Wales in 1973–1974. In practice, the drains, gutters and storm sewers of urban areas serve the same function as do land drains in a rural area, even though they are designed to remove surface water.

The hydrological impact of land drainage is greatly to increase the drainage density of an area. This means that the distance an individual raindrop has to travel between landing on the soil and reaching a stream channel is much reduced. In addition, total soil water storage is reduced (Fig. 6.11), and modified soil water tables will increase the rate of flow of soil water towards the drainage channels. Water now reaches stream channels more rapidly and in greater quantities, lessening the amount available for distribution or storage elsewhere through the hydrological system, and so

changes have been spin-off effects, beneficial or otherwise. The soil system is the pivot of the terrestrial part of the hydrological cycle, acting as the buffer zone between atmospheric and groundwater systems. Changes in soil hydrology can

Figure 6.9 High-density land drainage (the ditches are 2 m apart) in an upland area due to be afforested. Natural drainage of the soil is very inefficient due to the underlying shale bedrock.

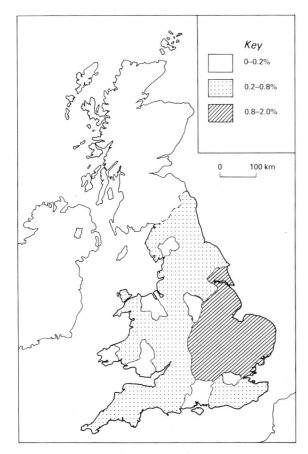

Figure 6.10 Percentage of total land area with under-drainage in England and Wales, 1973–4. (After Green 1979.)

Key

☐ 0–0.2%

▨ 0.2–0.8%

▧ 0.8–2.0%

0   100 km

storm flow in rivers is likely to increase significantly.

An extreme example of man-made additions to the natural drainage system is given in Figure 6.12. Figure 6.12a shows the drainage system of the Clarinbridge river basin, 90 km² in area, in County Galway, western Ireland as it was in the early 19th century before land drainage commenced. In this area of partly cavernous or karstic lowland limestone overlain by hummocky glacial deposits, there were no continuous natural streams. The drainage system was a series of disjointed sinking streams and seasonal lakes called turloughs. The land-drainage programme has involved not simply under-drainage and the excavation of a rectilinear net of drainage ditches, but also the creation by blasting of wholly artificial river channels leading to the sea. In Figure 6.12b only the rivers and major field drains are shown. Figure 6.12c is an enlargement of a small area showing the full drainage network. The original drainage density in this area was $c.$ 0.2 km/km². Present-day drainage density is $c.$ 20 km/km² excluding under-drainage. The effects on groundwater storage and movement, on lake levels and on river flows have been dramatic and often adverse from man's viewpoint. During the summer months there is no surface water in the area as the excess rainfall of the winter is rapidly discharged to the sea by the highly efficient drainage system. Summer rainfall sinks into the underlying limestone. Groundwater levels have fallen by 2–10 m in the summer due to the

65

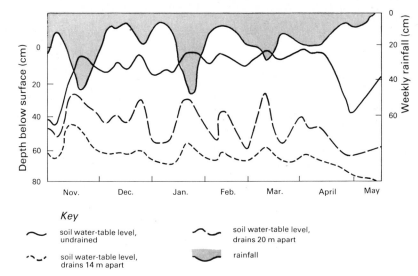

Figure 6.11 Changes in soil water-table levels due to field drainage with mole and tile drains; winter 1974–5, Suffolk. With closer spacing of the drains, the lowering of the water table is greater. (After Green 1979.)

Key

soil water-table level, undrained

soil water-table level, drains 14 m apart

soil water-table level, drains 20 m apart

rainfall

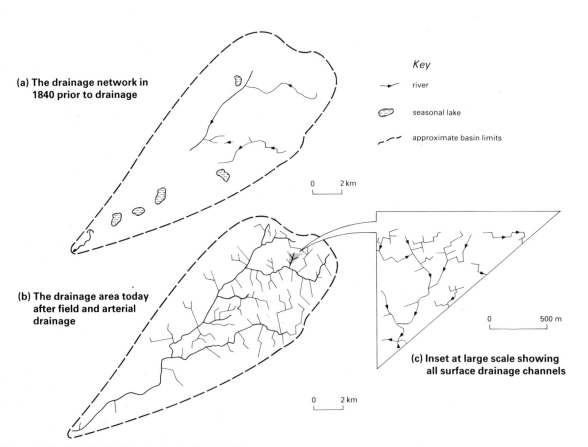

(a) The drainage network in 1840 prior to drainage

Key

river

seasonal lake

approximate basin limits

0   2 km

(b) The drainage area today after field and arterial drainage

0   2 km

0   500 m

(c) Inset at large scale showing all surface drainage channels

Figure 6.12 The Clarinbridge river basin, County Galway.

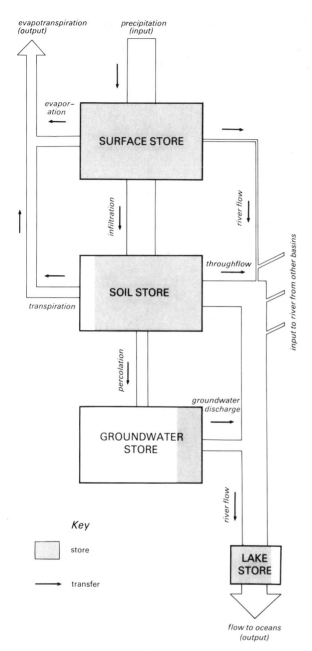

evapotranspiration (output)

precipitation (input)

evapor- ation

SURFACE STORE

infiltration

river flow

transpiration

throughflow

input to river from other basins

SOIL STORE

percolation

groundwater discharge

GROUNDWATER STORE

river flow

Key

store

transfer

LAKE STORE

flow to oceans (output)

Figure 6.13 Changes in the hydrological cycle following land drainage. Compare with Figure 6.2.

amounts of sediment and fertiliser residue in the coastal zone. This in turn appears to have reduced yields in an area of commercial oyster breeding. The intention was simply to improve soil drainage, but the result has affected groundwater supplies, surface water supplies, the local ecology and flooding. The general effects of land drainage on the hydrological cycle, which are rarely as adverse as these, are shown in Figure 6.13.

6.2.4 Ground water

In areas underlain by permeable rocks, some of the rainfall filters down through the soil and rock to become ground water. In the hypothetical basin shown in Figure 6.2, c. 20 per cent of rainfall enters the groundwater store. Underground water is in motion and eventually must reappear at the Earth's surface, commonly discharging into river channels and less often into lakes, seas or from springs (Fig. 6.1). Man may extract water from an aquifer (water-bearing rock) at any point that he chooses by pumping from wells. If the rate of abstraction of water is equal to or less than the natural rate of replenishment (recharge), then the overall effect is simply to short circuit a part of the hydrological cycle. Discharge of water from the groundwater store can be made when and where it suits man via wells and boreholes, but natural outflows from springs and into river channels will be correspondingly reduced. Ground water may be used for many purposes. It may be pumped into a river to increase low flow levels – such usage simply speeds up a natural transfer process. Alternatively, the ground water might be used for irrigation. In this instance the water is returned to its initial surface store via an artificial loop in the hydrological system.

The consequences may be very different when water is taken from an aquifer at a rate greater than the rate of natural recharge. In order to sustain such an abstraction rate, water must be removed from storage in the rocks and so water-table levels drop in the abstraction area. The effect is similar to baling out water from a basin that is simultaneously being filled by a tap. If water is removed from the basin at the same rate as the tap water is filling it, water level will remain constant. However, if water is emptied out faster than the inflow rate, water level in the basin will decline. The lowering of water-table levels may be slight in the case of a single well, but can extend over a large area if, say, an urban area derives its supply from ground water. If the topography of the ground-

deepening of river channels and to the larger proportion of water removed from the land by direct channel flow. Consequently, more shallow wells are now seasonally dry and water has to be delivered by tanker to farms. Winter flooding of the rivers is also encouraged by the efficient runoff system, damaging river banks and depositing large

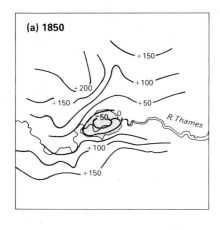

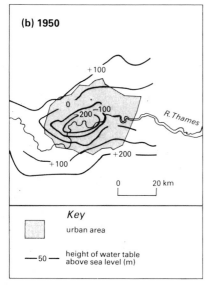

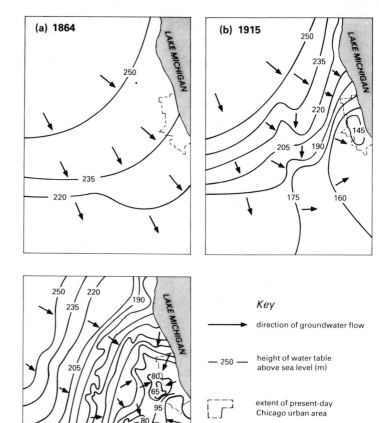

Figure 6.14 Changes in groundwater levels in the London basin aquifer between (a) 1850 and (b) 1950. (After Water Resources Board 1973.)

Figure 6.15 Changes in groundwater levels in the Chicago area between 1864 and 1958. (After Suter 1959.)

water table changes, so will the direction of groundwater flows.

Figure 6.14 shows the changes in the water table in the London area since extensive well pumping began at the beginning of the 19th century. Until the early 1950s water-table levels fell continuously. Flow in rivers with headwaters in the chalk strata diminished, and even minor land subsidence occurred as the de-watered rock compacted. The fall in water levels has now been arrested in west and central London as the pumping rate has lessened.

In coastal regions excessive lowering of the water table may allow sea water to enter the aquifer, contaminating the supply, and this has happened to a limited extent in the rocks underlying the Thames estuary. In southern California, salt-water contamination is such a problem that it has been necessary to pump fresh water into the ground near the coast to artificially raise groundwater levels and thus to lessen saline water encroachment.

An example of large-scale alteration of groundwater conditions is given in Figure 6.15. Progressive changes in groundwater levels in an aquifer of sandstone and dolomites are shown in the Chicago area of Illinois. The first wells were drilled into the aquifer in 1864 and, as may be seen (Fig. 6.15a), the natural form of the water table at this time was a gentle slope to the south-south-east. By 1915 (Fig. 6.15b) Chicago was obtaining much of its water from wells and water-table levels had fallen by as much as 100 m beneath the urban area. Figure 6.15c shows the form of the water-table surface in 1958. Water was then being removed over a much wider area and levels were up to 230 m lower than under natural conditions. Flowlines of ground water in the area have been reversed.

The removal of large quantities of water from groundwater storage has accelerated in this century throughout the world. This has had the effect of transferring this water to other points in the hydrological cycle. It has been suggested that recent rises in sea levels as well as increases in the amount of polar ice might represent the displaced ground water entering new storages via evaporation and precipitation. Were changes in climate responsible, then if ocean levels rose, polar ice would diminish, but it seems that the *overall* amount of surface water is increasing.

6.2.5 River control

Both river and groundwater modifications by man are usually deliberate attempts to improve the water resources of an area: this is in contrast to the often inadvertent modifications to surface and soil storages and transfers. Although groundwater ex-

ploitation is growing rapidly, especially in semi-arid regions, direct manipulation of rivers or even of whole river systems remains man's most profound impact on the hydrological cycle. Rivers are used for many purposes of which water supply is merely one, and the ways in which they have been altered reflects this diversity of function.

The natural function of streams is to transmit runoff derived from varied sources (Fig. 6.1) to the regional base level – commonly the sea. Although rivers are primarily transfer mechanisms, they also have a limited storage capacity, which is much increased if a part of their course consists of natural lakes. The discharge in most rivers is variable through time depending on the level of inputs from ground water, soil water and surface flow. In human terms this variation in flows may mean at one extreme, flooding and at the other extreme, a shortage of water.

Human intervention in river systems is normally concerned with one or more of the following: regulating discharge, storing water, increasing total flow, abstracting water or altering river channels. The direct and side-effects of these activities are summarised in Table 6.1, and the following sections describe each of these categories in turn.

Regulation of discharge. The quantity of water that can always be reliably abstracted from a river is determined by the minimum flow, and if this can be raised, then the guaranteed supply will also be

Table 6.1 River control: methods and effects.

Control type	Techniques	Subsidiary and feedback effects
discharge regulation	headwater reservoirs sluices	new aquatic environment (lake) – ecology increase sedimentation interrupt fish migration increase evaporation, create new local climate
water storage	storage reservoirs estuary storage	as above alter estuarine environment, especially via sedimentation, destroy estuary wetlands Alter coastal deposition/erosion/currents
increasing flow	groundwater inputs inter-basin transfer basin runoff controls	lower groundwater levels mix chemically different waters alter fluvial geomorphology
decreasing flow (abstracting)	artificial recharge inter-basin transfer basin runoff controls	mix chemically different waters raise groundwater levels alter fluvial geomorphology
altering river channels	deepening, widening straightening concreting diverting	alter velocities and therefore erosion and deposition prevent water exchange between banks and river and vice versa alter soil hydrology and therefore local runoff to river

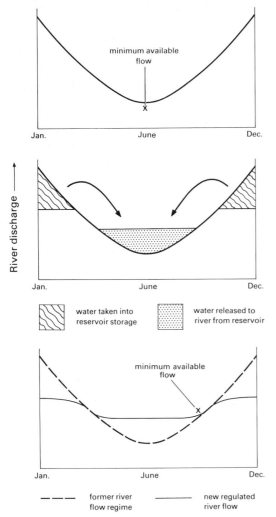

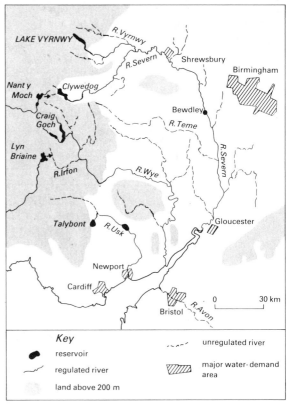

Figure 6.17 Regulation of river flow in the Severn–Wye catchment. (After Water Resources Board 1973.)

Figure 6.16 The effects on the flow regime of a river of regulatory reservoirs.

increased. The most usual technique for flow regulation is the construction of dams in the headwaters of a river. The waters stored in the resulting reservoir may then be released in sufficient quantities to maintain the desired minimum flows further down stream. The greater the seasonal fluctuation in river flow, the more useful will be such regulatory reservoirs (Fig. 6.16). Mediterranean streams with high winter flows and very low summer discharges have long been subject to control by regulating reservoirs (Sec. 6.3.4), and very few rivers around the world still have a totally 'natural' flow regime, unaltered by man.

In Britain the Severn–Wye system is an example of a major drainage unit in which river flows are being determined artificially to an increasing extent (Fig. 6.17). The headwaters of these basins drain much of the central Welsh upland, and are thus liable to violent flooding and large seasonal variations in discharge.

Flow in the Severn is now severely regulated by a series of headwater reservoirs (e.g. Clywedog) that control input variations in discharge. During the summer, reservoir levels are allowed to fall giving sufficient storage volume to retain a part of the winter flood water. For example, the Clywedog reservoir is reduced to that level which gives 8.5 million m³ of available storage by 1 November of each year. The level is then allowed to rise until 1 May, when flow augmentation of the River Severn normally begins. Addition of water to the river from Clywedog storage has raised minimum annual flows in all but the lowest reaches of the Severn – at Bewdley, flow is kept above 27 per cent of mean flow compared with 10 per cent minimum prior to regulation. The same storage capacity is also used to absorb flood waves generated by heavy rainfall in the upper catchment and thus affords a measure of protection to the floodplain sites such as Shrewsbury that are liable to flooding in the middle reaches of the river. Abstractions of water can be made from points on the river closest to demand areas rather than piping water directly from reservoirs to cities. Thus, flow regulation has the effect of evening out variations in discharge and of enabling man to exploit the river's natural transfer function to suit his demand for water.

Increasing natural storage. Although most modern reservoirs are primarily intended to regulate river discharge, they also retain their former function as stores of relatively large quantities of water, thus supplementing existing channel or lake storage. Headwater storage sites are still the commonest reservoirs, but recently attention has been turned towards the possibility of storage at the lowest point on the river system, the estuary. This would be achieved by embanking the estuary and so making available virtually all of the residual flow in the river. In Britain several such projects have been suggested and a River Dee estuary store seems the likeliest to materialise. Estuary storage, as with the original type of headwater reservoir, involves constructing artificial water transmission conduits (aqueducts) to pipe the water to where it is needed. Many of the world's major cities are served by such aqueducts: for example, much of Manchester's water comes from the Lake District (Thirlmere, etc.), 130 km distant, New York is fed by an aqueduct 225 km long and Los Angeles water is piped from more than 400 km away. The effect of such artificial transfer mechanisms from artificial storages is that water may be returned to the hydrological cycle at a point distant from its origin. Although most reservoirs behave more or less as do natural lakes in terms of ecology and geomorphology, estuarine barriers may create serious, widespread environmental changes.

Increasing total flow in rivers. If water is to be added to a river to supplement its flow (usually at low flow periods), it must be obtained from some other store within the hydrological cycle. In suitable locations ground water may be pumped to the surface and discharged into the river. For example, some of the tributary streams of the Thames flow across extensive chalk and Jurassic limestone aquifers. Low flows in the Thames are increased by pumping up to 500 000 m³ of water daily from boreholes. There is no real overall gain

by this means, simply a transfer of water from a long-term store (ground water) to a short-term store/transfer (the river). Secondly, water may be imported from a completely separate river basin by aqueduct. Such inter-basin transfers are becoming common and are considered in Section 6.3.

Lessening of river flow. An estimated 2 per cent of the total discharge of the world's rivers is abstracted for use by man. Most users (domestic, HEP, industrial) return the water, though often in a polluted form. However, the single largest water use by far is for irrigation. Water is led away from the river in order to increase the soil water store. If irrigation is efficient, then all of this water will be used by plants and thus short circuit the remainder of the cycle, depleting stream flows accordingly. This is a consumptive use of river water. As more than 80 per cent of water use on a worldwide basis is for irrigation, this represents a major deflection of the natural hydrological cycle. The Nile (Sec. 6.3.4) now has virtually all of its discharge taken off for irrigation.

Channel alterations. In hydrological terms, one of man's less significant activities involves the alteration of river courses. Channel form may be changed by deepening, widening, constricting or by modifying channel sides and base, in extreme cases by concreting (Fig. 6.18). Usually these changes are intended to prevent flooding by accelerating flow and lessening obstacles to flow. This involves improving the efficiency of the river as a transfer mechanism. Most rivers have had their courses modified in this manner to a greater or lesser extent (Chs 7 & 10). Problems may occur if a long reach of river flows in a concrete channel, as natural exchanges of water between the soil and groundwater stores and the river water are prevented. Flood flows will be increased, but low flows will diminish as flow into the river channel from the banks is no longer possible.

Alterations to the river course may consist of permanent diversions for the whole flow. The course of the Mississippi river below its junction with the Ohio river has been shortened by 150 km by constructing bypasses to natural meander loops. Alternatively, spillway (floodway) channels may be built that only carry overflow water from the main channel in high flood. The changes in fluvial landscapes that may be brought about by such engineering are discussed in Chapter 7.

Figure 6.18 A greatly modified river channel, the course has been straightened, the channel deepened and graded.

6.3 Large-scale modification of surface water

6.3.1 Introduction

Partly because of the many uses for which water is required and partly because of the relative ease with which it can be accomplished, large-scale manipulation of water, involving several aspects of the hydrological cycle on a basin or inter-basin level, is becoming common. The four case studies that follow illustrate various scales of intervention in different environments.

6.3.2 The Kielder scheme

Britain's largest river control and water transfer scheme is to link the major rivers of northeastern England – the Tyne. Derwent, Wear and Tees (Fig. 6.19). A 1000-ha headwater control reservoir, the Kielder Water, is being created behind two dams on the River North Tyne, upstream of Falstone. In this way 200 million m³ of water can be impounded, and will be released to maintain constant low flow discharge in the River Tyne down stream, and also to lessen the severity of flooding by using reservoir capacity to absorb storm runoff in the upper catchment. Just below the junction with the South Tyne, surplus water (over and above that needed for the Tyneside conurbation) is to be pumped southwards for

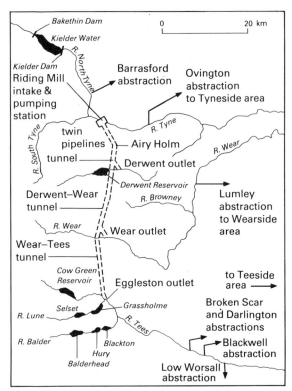

Figure 6.19 The Kielder water scheme in north-east England, showing the regulatory reservoir and the proposed transfer aqueduct. (After Kirby 1979.)

72

40 km via pipes and tunnels, terminating at the headwaters of the River Tees near Eggleston. Minimum flows in the Tees will thus be increased helping to alleviate the water shortages experienced in the Teeside industrial area. Between the Tyne and the Tees the aqueduct will have outlets to the Derwent and Wear rivers, again allowing some degree of regulation of their flow regimes.

6.3.3 The Tennesee Valley Authority

Probably the best known example of large-scale, multi-purpose modification of river basin hydrology is the work of the Tennessee Valley Authority (TVA) in the southeastern USA. The basin of the Tennessee river, an area of 100 000 km², was one of the areas most affected by the 'dust-bowl' conditions of the 1930s. Subsistence farming, overgrazing, deforestation and other forms of mismanagement had exposed vast areas of land to sheetwash, gully and wind erosion, stripping the topsoil, causing sedimentation in rivers and increasing flood intensities. Control measures were undertaken on both the land and the rivers. The main river from upstream of

Knoxville to the confluence with the Ohio river at Paducah is virtually one long lake impounded behind a series of nine major dams constructed between 1935 and 1944. A further series of dams on tributaries (Fig. 6.20a) means that river flow is now wholly regulated, not by a single headwater reservoir but by a whole series of dams along the course of the rivers. The TVA scheme was designed to be multi-purpose, improving navigation, generating HEP and draining swamps. Concurrently, conservation measures were applied to the land in order to minimise surface runoff. For example, the Parker Branch basin (43 ha) was typical of the worst affected areas. One-third of the land was gullied and abandoned after the stream floods caused violent erosion. Restoration work involved reforesting steep slopes with pine trees, planting black locust trees in the erosion gullies to stabilise them and carrying out agricultural conservation techniques (Sec. 6.2.1). Within 10 years agricultural yields from the basin had doubled, flood peaks from summer storms had halved and sediment yields in the stream had declined by 65 per cent (Fig. 6.20b). Although the small Parker

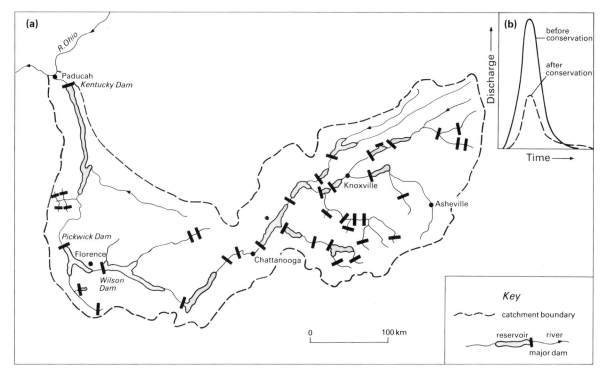

Figure 6.20 Large-scale hydrological control: the Tennessee Valley Authority area, USA. (a) The Tennessee basin showing major dams; (b) storm hydrographs before and after the application of agricultural conservation techniques in the Parker Branch basin. (After Pereira 1973.)

Branch basin was selected for special investigation by the TVA, similar changes in land use and hydrology have been made throughout the Tennessee basin.

6.3.4 The River Nile

Introduction. Of all the world's great rivers none has been subject to such drastic control over such a long period of time as has the Nile. The evolution of early civilisation in Egypt depended completely on the water of the Nile, flowing through what was otherwise an arid, inhospitable land (Fig. 6.21). Throughout history the population levels (and sometimes economic prosperity) have been tied closely to the availability of Nile water for irrigation. In a sense the Nile cultures represent an example of the natural environment exerting a powerful control on man's activities. Yet, within the constraints of a marginal environment, human activity has exploited the vital resource of water to such an extent that the environment of large areas of the Nile valley has been wholly transformed. As increasing supplies of water have been made available, so the Egyptian population has risen – eventually to the extent that further projects have become necessary to obtain yet more water. This demand cycle continues to the present day.

Hydrology of the Nile. The 6700-km-long Nile system drains 10 per cent of the African continent (Fig. 6.22). The catchment extends into parts of Egypt, Sudan, Ethiopia, Zaire, Uganda, Tanzania and Kenya. Over 60 per cent of the river's discharge is provided by the Blue Nile which rises in the Ethiopian Highlands. This region lies in the seasonally wet–dry Tropics, but its climate is modified by the mountains. The White Nile drains a much larger area, but contributes less than 30 per cent of total discharge, the remainder of the flow being derived from the Atbara tributary draining part of the northern Ethiopian Highlands and part of the Sudan. Below the Atbara confluence the Nile flows north to the Mediterranean for 2500 km with virtually no further tributaries.

Figure 6.21 The contrast between the fertile irrigated strip and the adjacent desert in the Nile valley. (Photograph by M. Murphy.)

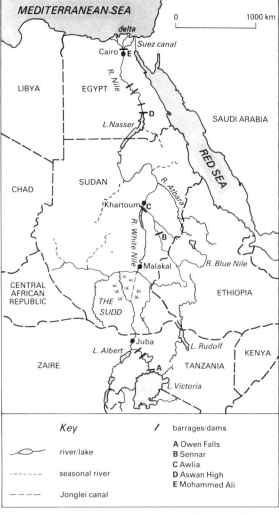

Figure 6.22 The Nile drainage system showing the major river control structures.

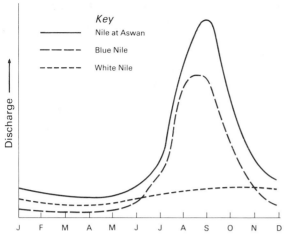

Figure 6.23 The flow regimes of the Nile and its main tributaries.

The White Nile originates in the equatorial zone with no pronounced dry season. Its discharge is therefore relatively constant throughout the year, and this effect is reinforced by the regulating effect of Lakes Victoria and Albert through which the river flows. In contrast, the Blue Nile and Atbara headwaters lie in regions with a marked concentration of rainfall in the summer months. The resulting flow regime for the Nile (Fig. 6.23) as it flows across the Egyptian desert is characterised by a violent flood peak and very low flows for the remainder of the year. The annual flood reaches Aswan in July–August and northern Egypt a month or so later. Up to two-thirds of the annual flow in the Nile occurs between August and October. Because of this uneven flow regime through the year, the primary aim of water resource engineering within the Nile basin has been to spread the flow more evenly over the year and so make available a greater quantity of water in every month of the year.

Taming the Nile. In pre-dynastic Egypt, society adapted to the character of the Nile. The summer flood overtopped the natural levees, filling natural basins, 70–100 km² in area, on the floodplain. The flood wave surged northwards, and so flooding occurred successively down valley. As the waters receded leaving a layer of alluvium, sowing of crops took place, yielding one crop per year over perhaps 65 per cent of the floodplain.

This harmonious relation with natural conditions was breached some 5000 years ago when King Meres caused the first dam to be built on the Nile. A small structure, south of Memphis, it nevertheless marked the beginning of man's battle to conserve the wasted waters of the Nile flood. As Egyptian society became increasingly coherent and disciplined under the pharaohs, so more ambitious river control structures were built. About 1500 BC Lake Qarun, 30 km south-west of Cairo was walled around to detain sufficient water to irrigate 20 000 ha of new land by gravity feed. Later, the invention of the Archimedean screw and shaduf (Fig. 6.24) allowed water to be lifted above its natural level to irrigate the land.

During the colonial period in Egypt, the technology of the Industrial Revolution allowed larger-scale manipulation to be undertaken. In the 19th century the French and Belgians built a barrage north of Cairo, diverting water into three canals to irrigate areas of the Nile delta. The British raised the height of the Cairo barrage and built the first Aswan Dam, 3 km long and designed to let the early, silt-laden flood through, while retaining a part of the clearer receding flood flow. By 1933 the Aswan Dam had been raised to 40 m in height and had a capacity of 500 million m³ – this in response to the rapidly growing Egyptian population. Regulating reservoirs were also constructed higher up the Nile system. The Sennar and Roseires Dams on the Blue Nile allowed a large area between the

Figure 6.24 Primitive irrigation using a shaduf in the Nile valley. (Photograph by M. Murphy.)

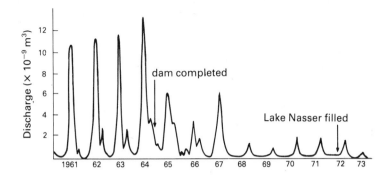

Figure 6.25 The Nile regime at the delta before and after construction of the Aswan High Dam. (River flow measured at Cairo.) (After S. el Din 1977.)

Blue and White Nile south of Khartoum to be irrigated, and a dam at Owen Falls in Uganda, partly controlled flow of the White Nile from Lake Victoria.

The most ambitious project to date has been the construction of the Aswan High Dam on the Egypt–Sudan border. The resulting Lake Nasser has an area of 5700 km^2 and a storage capacity of 15.5×10^9 m^3 of water. This storage goes beyond regulation of seasonal variations in discharge and is intended to compensate for several years of below-average flow in the river. Perennial irrigation rather than seasonal basin flooding is now possible over vast new areas and at least two crops per year can be grown. The extent of control structures on the Nile system is shown in Figure 6.22.

The cumulative effect of these regulating reservoirs and irrigation schemes on the regime of the Nile has been profound. Below the Aswan High Dam one of the world's great rivers is now little more than a canal. The change in the annual flow pattern of the Nile in recent times is shown in Figure 6.25. During the period 1964–74 the Aswan High Dam was completed and filled, and downstream the Nile flood is a thing of the past. Over 80 per cent of the Aswan discharge is abstracted with only a relative trickle of water reaching the Mediterranean. This represents almost total exploitation of the river as a water resource. However, total annual flow in the river is now *less* than before reservoir construction began, due to water losses from evaporation over the lakes – it is the distribution of flow through time that has been altered to man's advantage.

The Jonglei canal. Yet more modifications to the Nile are planned. Between Mongala and Malakal in the Sudan the White Nile flows for 400 km through the extensive swampy area of the Sudd.

The marshes of papyrus and reeds are flooded in the summer months and between a third and a half of the discharge of the river is lost in evapotranspiration. This is roughly equivalent to evaporation losses from Lake Nasser. In 1978 work began on the Jonglei canal, a 320-km-long bypass channel to the swamp. The 50-m-wide channel has been constructed carefully to maintain flow velocities of *c.* 1 m/s – too rapid to allow excessive deposition or waterweed growth, but too slow to cause bank or bed erosion.

Although the Jonglei canal project has been under consideration for many years, its implementation has been delayed, partly for economic reasons, but also because of an awareness of the great environmental changes that are likely to occur over the 33 000 km^2 of the Sudd. In addition to the probable changes in vegetation, wildlife and human patterns, it is expected that shrinkage of clayey soils that are presently seasonally flooded will produce a landscape of hummocks and hollows over a large area. The swamp removes a large proportion of the solutional load carried by the White Nile, so when the canal is completed, dissolved salt concentrations will rise sharply downstream. Unlike many of the earlier Nile projects, a considerable amount of research has been undertaken into the likely environmental effects of the canal. Wherever practicable, attempts have been made to minimise adverse effects. Looking further into the future, even more ambitious schemes have been proposed for the middle and upper reaches of the Nile until, from source to mouth, the drainage system will be exploited to the full.

Other consequences of controlling the Nile. As with virtually every attempt by man to modify natural systems, so with the Nile regulation,

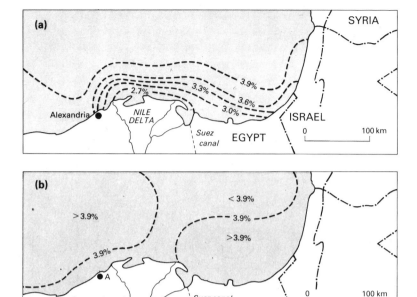

Figure 6.26 Changes in salinity (per cent) in the southeastern Mediterranean sea (a) before and (b) after the construction of the Aswan High Dam. (After S. el Din 1977.)

changes have occurred in other aspects of the environment. Some of the changes were foreseen, others were not.

Lakes and reservoirs act as sediment traps, much of the finer material settling out on the lake floor. Lake Nasser removes virtually all of the suspended load of the Nile. Accordingly, its water storage capacity is steadily reducing, while deposition of valuable silt on the floodplain down stream has ceased. A part of the hydroelectricity generated at Aswan is used to manufacture artificial fertilisers which are needed to replace the lost, soil-enriching silt on the floodplain.

Before construction of the Aswan High Dam, 60–180 million tonnes of sediment per year were laid down at the mouths of the Rosetta and Damietta distributaries on the Nile delta. Deposition has now ceased and marine erosion is beginning to gnaw at the delta. The lack of groundwater recharge from the river in this area is allowing saline water from the sea to pollute the alluvial aquifer of the delta, and soil salinity levels on old farmland are rising.

Down stream of the Aswan High Dam the relatively constant discharge of the river has enabled bankside vegetation and water weeds to form stable colonies, and so narrow channel width and increase the transpiration of water.

The small residual flow of water entering the Mediterranean has caused changes within the southeastern Mediterranean itself. Coastal and especially estuarine zones are normally one of the most productive areas biologically. The lack of nutrients formerly brought in by the Nile water may be responsible for the great decline in sardine and shrimp catches offshore since the Aswan Dam was constructed. Some 18 000 tonnes of sardines were caught annually; now the harvest is negligible and 30 000 fishermen have lost their jobs.

More directly, the lack of freshwater input has affected marine currents and salinity levels in the delta area and perhaps as far distant as the coast of Israel. Prior to dam construction, a 100-m-deep surface layer of less saline water flowed north and east from the Nile estuary during the flood season. Salinity levels were less than 3.9 per cent for 80 km out from the coast. This flow of less saline water has now ceased and as may be seen from Figure 6.26 salinity levels now exceed 3.9 per cent even in coastal areas.

Other effects on the biology of the river and the Levant sea are becoming apparent. The low, steady flows in the lower Nile favour the molluscs that host the flukes of schistosomiasis, a parasitic disease easily contracted by humans. The incidence of this debilitating disease has increased sharply in the delta area in recent years. Finally, the lack of freshwater discharge into the Levant sea has speeded up what is termed the **Lessepsian** migration of organisms from the Red sea to the

Mediterranean, via the man-made Suez canal. This one-way movement has been taking place ever since the construction of the Suez canal in the late 19th century and it is estimated that 200–500 alien species have reached the Mediterranean in this manner. The loss of the freshwater flow into the western outlet of Suez has made the migration easier.

6.3.5 Continental water modification – the USSR

River discharge control and small-scale inter-basin transfers of water are now commonplace. Relatively few such schemes have been executed on a continental scale with the exception of examples in North America and the Snowy river scheme in Australia, though these might be considered as very large-scale regional projects. This lack is not due to an absence of ideas or of technology. Schemes ranging from the eminently practical to outrageously lunatic have been put forward, and man undoubtedly has the engineering ability to transform global drainage patterns as he sees fit. Rather, the restraint has been due to the enormous costs involved and, much more recently, to an awareness of possible undesirable environmental repercussions.

One such scheme which many scientists feel may verge on the unjustifiable due to uncertainty as to its possible side-effects is examined here. For many years the USSR has considered the re-routing of rivers draining to the Arctic ocean so that they drain southwards instead across the semi-arid lands of Kazakhstan to the land-locked Caspian sea. The plan is now in the drafting stage and will be completed by 2010. There are obvious advantages to such a scheme. Much needed irrigation water would be available for the potentially highly fertile grainlands of the south. Secondly, the northward flowing rivers, whose water is largely unused, are subject to severe spring flooding as, at winter's end, their headwaters unfreeze some time before the more northerly lower reaches. The abstraction of large quantities of water from these rivers would reduce this hazard.

The most ambitious of these plans (Fig. 6.27) involves diversion of the waters from the northward draining Ob–Irtysh system with a catchment area of $2\,500\,000\,km^2$. A dam below the confluence of the rivers would create a lake (or sea!) twice the area of England and Wales. Some of the outflow

will be transferred south to Tobolsk by canal, and a part of the water used for a local irrigation scheme. The remainder of the flow is then to be pumped over the watershed of the Irtysh, into a storage reservoir and then south to feed into the Amu Dar'ya river in Uzbekistan and thence to the Caspian. *En route* the water will be piped beneath the course of the Syr Dar'ya river. The total distance from the Ob Dam to the Aral sea is 2500 km. A further link to the Caspian sea from the Aral sea may extend this scheme still further.

An even more grandiose version involves the damming of the other main river draining north over the western Siberian lowland – the Yenisei river and also its tributary, the Angara river. Water from this lake would be transferred to the 'Ob sea'. More than $10\,000\,km^2$ of steppe in western Siberia and Kazakhstan could be irrigated by this means.

Water levels in the Caspian and Aral seas have fallen rapidly in recent decades, and a further aim of the diversion scheme would be to halt or reverse this decline. The Caspian sea derives 75 per cent of its inflow from the Volga river. Deforestation in the Volga catchment has reduced natural storage of water, and upstream of Volgograd a series of dams has reduced the river to a series of man-made lakes from which more than half the river's discharge is removed by abstraction and evaporation. This loss of inflow may explain the fall in Caspian water levels since 1930. Levels fell by 2 m between 1961 and 1971 alone. The shallowness of much of the northern part of the sea has meant that large areas of former sea bed have been exposed, and the Volga delta has extended 32 km seawards over the past 30 years. Fisheries in the Caspian have been adversely affected.

The potential benefits of the Ob–Irtysh–Yenisei diversion, therefore, seem to be great. However, the scale of the project is such that the consequences might be felt at a global scale. At present it is not possible to predict the effects of lessening freshwater flow to the Arctic, creating a great new freshwater body and irrigating large areas of the steppe. It has been argued that the Arctic ocean will remain ice-free all year round over extensive areas. In turn this would allow a new airmass to form above it, warmed by the water. The climate of western Siberia might become less continental, and increased precipitation could result from the high levels of transpiration over the irrigated steppe.

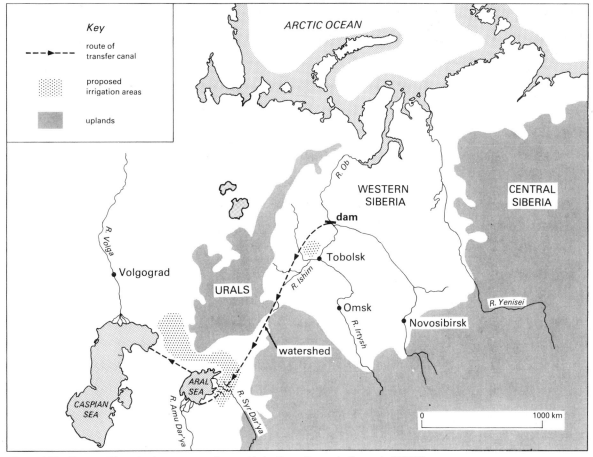

Figure 6.27 Proposed inter-basin water transfers and irrigation schemes in the central USSR.

6.4 New sources of water

An extreme form of human intervention in the hydrological cycle is the introduction of 'new' water into the system. As yet the quantities of water involved are an insignificant fraction of the total, but in the future, and especially in semi-arid regions, 'artificial' fresh water may affect the functioning of the hydrological cycle.

Desalination of brackish water or sea water using flash distillation or membrane methods is becoming increasingly common, particularly in coastal areas of affluent states. World desalination capacity in 1976 was c. 2400 million litres of sea water per day and is increasing by 16 per cent annually. In countries such as Israel, Australia and Kuwait and in the western USA, medium-sized desalination plants have been in operation for

some years. Limitations to the expansion of desalination have mainly been due to the large energy inputs required.

A more bizarre scheme for creating more fresh water involves towing icebergs from Antarctica to coastal areas of water shortage. Ideally, such icebergs would be stable and tabular in form with a volume of c. 1 km³. South Australia, Saudi Arabia and southern California are likely importers.

Finally, proposals have been made for the construction of giant condensers filled with cold sea water to be located on coastlines with prevailing warm, wet, oceanic winds. Some of the atmospheric moisture would then be trapped by condensation. A gain of 4000 m³/day was suggested for such a series of condensers to be located on St Croix in the Virgin Islands.

It is difficult to assess the impact of any of the above-mentioned techniques for generating fresh water. In each case water is being forcibly removed from a store (ocean, ice and atmosphere), but it will require a higher level of technology and investment than that prevailing at present before the quantities of water involved are important on any but a local scale.

6.5 Conclusions

The range of scales of hydrological change and the degrees of intensity of change illustrated in this chapter demonstrate both the relative ease with which man can manipulate fresh water, but also the necessity to his survival and prosperity of doing so. Economic and social factors are often the limitations on water modification. The importance of changes in hydrological conditions are such that they are mentioned in the chapters (3–8) concerned with human impact on other aspects of the environment, in contexts as various as soil water, vegetation, fluvial landforms, mass movement, local climates and arid region settlement.

7 Landforms

7.1 Introduction

Following the construction of the Hoover Dam and the creation of Lake Mead in 1935, mild earthquakes were felt in this hitherto stable area of the USA. In 1937 100 quakes were recorded. Elsewhere, the Koyna earthquake of December 1967 which killed 200 people is also thought to have been a result of reservoir construction. Mercifully, man's effects on the internal workings of the Earth are as yet localised, and in a global context wholly irrelevant. The same may also be said for intervention in geomorphic processes and so in landform shaping (Figs 7.1 & 2). The scales of time and space on which the landscape-forming mechanisms operate make the prospect of significant intervention by man a remote likelihood. Landforms are a product of geological structure, time and geomorphic processes, and it is only the last mentioned factor that can be modified significantly. Geomorphic processes are largely climatically determined (weathering, transportation) or gravity controlled (mass movement), and with the exception of fluvial and similar transport systems (Ch. 6) are commonly characterised by diffuse rather than concentrated energy flows. Thus they are not readily 'controllable'. Leverage points are few and thresholds to change are high; man-made changes are local rather than regional, intensive rather than extensive. There are exceptions to this rule: sensitive environments such as rivers, coastlines, semi-arid regions, the sub-Arctic, these can be destabilised as the examples in the succeeding sections of this chapter show. (A fuller account of the operation of the natural tectonic and geomorphic systems is given in *Tectonic processes*, D. Weyman, and *Landscape processes*, D. and V. Weyman, George Allen & Unwin, 1981 and 1977 respectively.)

Weathering processes can be accentuated by changes in local climate as with enhanced chemical weathering in urban areas (Ch. 10), though much of the increased weathering takes place on man-made structures. Mass movement can be accelerated by destabilising slopes during construction, and local erosion intensified by footpath trampling in recreation areas of the countryside (Ch. 2). Transport mechanisms, particularly fluvial and coastal can be modified. The mechanical excavator is now a geomorphic agent; 'bulldozogenesis' can create new landforms and destroy existing ones.

As with all aspects of the natural environment, man-made changes in landforms can be deliberate or the inadvertent consequence of some other activity. Artificial 'valleys' can be created by road or rail cuttings or can develop by centuries of erosion of a trackway as with the sunken lanes of Devon. Drainage systems may be constructed to control the hydrology of an area or natural intense gullying may occur as a result of land misuse (Figs 7.3 & 4, Ch. 6). New land may be created by infill of lagoons or marshes (Fig. 7.5) or may be generated by estuarine deposition of excess sediment load introduced to rivers by soil erosion – an extra 250 km² of land has accumulated at the head of the Persian Gulf in historical times due to erosion in the basins of the Tigris and Euphrates. Hollows may be excavated for mineral extraction or may result from land subsidence due to mining or land drainage.

Only with respect to changed rates of soil erosion and sedimentation (increases up to several thousand-fold in some highly disturbed areas) does man appear to alter landform development on a regional to continental scale. Otherwise, man is a significant geomorphic agent on a relatively small scale or to a limited degree, as the following examples demonstrate.

Figure 7.2 An ancient man-made excavation, an artificial channel 20 m deep and cut through solid rock in order to drain a coastal swamp. The excavation was made in the Etruscan (pre-Roman) period in Tuscany, Italy.

Figure 7.4 Creating a new landscape: making terraces for agricultural use in the same area.

Figure 7.1 A man-made landform of prehistoric date, the 15-m-high burial mound, 5000 years old, at Newgrange, Ireland.

Figure 7.3 'Destroying the landscape: accelerated gully erosion in Mexico.

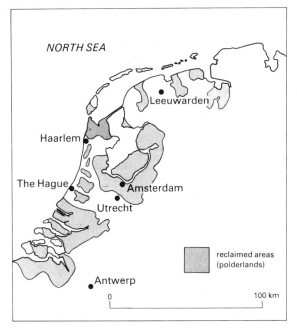

Figure 7.5 The extent of land reclaimed from the sea in the Netherlands over the past eight centuries.

7.2 Permafrost regions

One-fifth of the Earth's land surface is permanently frozen, to depths exceeding 1000 m in places. Half the area of Canada and of the USSR and 80 per cent of Alaska lie in the permafrost zone. Until recently settlement in these areas was minimal, but the exploitation of forestry and mineral resources has led to a great expansion in human colonisation of the sub-Arctic, particularly in the USSR. A failure to appreciate the nature of the environment caused serious local problems initially, and man has been forced to adapt his practices to the constraints of the environment.

The tundra has already been mentioned as a marginal and unstable environment in terms of soils and vegetation, and the same is true in terms of landforms, where the instability arises from the seasonal melting of the surface layer (active layer) of the earth. A thickening or thinning of the active layer can result from a variety of natural or human factors (Fig. 7.6), and although natural processes are still of greater importance by far, man-induced changes are of considerable local significance. If the thickness of the active layer is reduced by compression of the surface or by excavation, melting extends deeper into the permafrost. Tracks or pipeline routes then become lines of highly erodible terrain, and can act as the focus of water erosion during the spring melt period. As the channels are deepened, so thawing will extend deeper down thus allowing still further vertical erosion – a positive feedback mechanism leading to ever more erosion (Ch. 2). Entrenchment of up to 3 m in one season has been recorded along motor trackways in northern Canada. Excavations that create a pit cause similar thawing and, if they become lakes, melting of the permafrost beneath becomes intensified causing the hollows to enlarge by bank slumping and erosion. The melting zone is deepened directly by artificial heat sources such as buildings or pipelines and by removing the vegetation layer from the surface. Vegetation acts as an insulating layer, minimising heat transfer between air and earth, and when it is removed atmospheric heat is conducted to greater depths below the surface. Figure 7.7 shows the effect of progressive removal of scrub vegetation near Fairbanks in Alaska. Tree felling caused the frost table to fall by 28 m within 10 years, and total vegetation clearance caused the active zone to deepen by 38 m over the same period. Although the clearance shown in Figure 7.7 was undertaken for research purposes, more extensive devegetation for agricultural or settlement purposes has led to large-scale and complex land subsidences. Clearance of 2 km² of land for grazing in the Tanara valley near Fairbanks led to uneven thawing and within 3 years the fields were a mass of hummocks 1 m in height, rendering the land unusable.

Man has been forced to adapt to the permafrost environment in order to survive in such areas. The vegetation mat is maintained and insulation reinforced by gravel pads wherever construction is undertaken. Buildings are set upon foundations of poles set deep into the permafrost and are raised above ground level, all pipes are above ground and excavations are avoided wherever practicable. One of the most controversial projects, the construction of the pipeline to carry oil south from the north slope of Alaska, was realised only when all practicable steps had been taken to minimise the likelihood of environmental change. Tampering with the permafrost environment has produced such immediate and from man's point of view, adverse responses, that a more cautious attitude now characterises the approach.

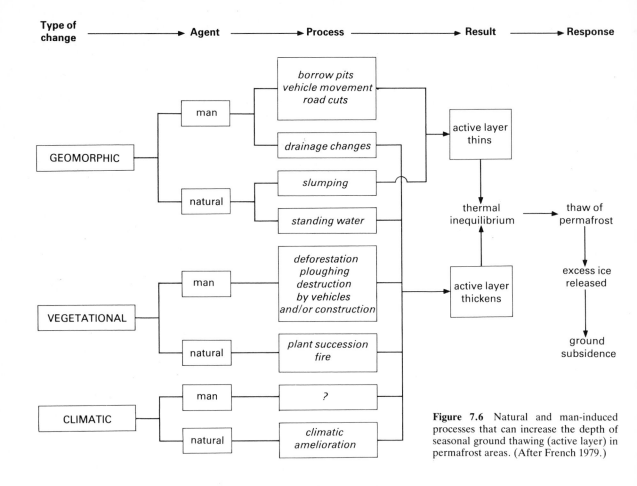

Type of change ——→ Agent ——→ Process ——→ Result ——→ Response

GEOMORPHIC

man

*borrow pits
vehicle movement
road cuts*

drainage changes

natural

slumping

standing water

active layer thins

thermal inequilibrium → thaw of permafrost

VEGETATIONAL

man

*deforestation
ploughing
destruction
by vehicles
and/or construction*

natural

*plant succession
fire*

active layer thickens

excess ice released

CLIMATIC

man

?

natural

climatic amelioration

ground subsidence

Figure 7.6 Natural and man-induced processes that can increase the depth of seasonal ground thawing (active layer) in permafrost areas. (After French 1979.)

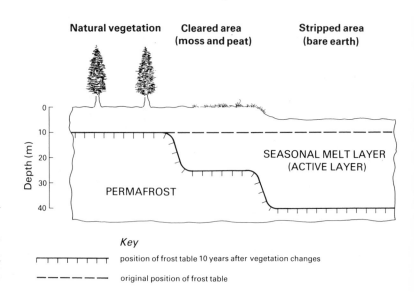

Natural vegetation   Cleared area (moss and peat)   Stripped area (bare earth)

Depth (m)

SEASONAL MELT LAYER (ACTIVE LAYER)

PERMAFROST

Figure 7.7 Deepening of the active layer over a 10-year period in a permafrost area of Alaska due to differing degrees of vegetation removal. (After Linnell 1960.)

Key

⊢⊢⊢⊢⊢⊢⊢ position of frost table 10 years after vegetation changes

– – – – – – – original position of frost table

7.3 Fluvial landforms

Alterations made to river systems in hydrological terms were discussed in Chapter 6. However, whatever the purpose of such alterations, whether to increase or decrease flow, for reservoir building, channel modification or for construction of bridges or jetties, the natural dynamic equilibrium of the river is upset (Fig. 7.8). The balance between erosion and deposition is changed, both in location and intensity, and changes are rarely confined to the immediate zone in which they are carried out – local river channel deepening may affect the behaviour of the river for many kilometres up and down stream. Many of the changes caused by man are accentuations or reproductions of natural processes. Reservoirs may simulate the effects of natural lakes, acting as sediment traps, building deltas and, by removing the existing load of the river, allowing intensified channel erosion down stream. Alternatively, if water is abstracted directly from the reservoir and downstream river flow reduced, this may reduce erosion and allow the channel to partially infill. Increases or decreases in discharge accelerate changes that variations in precipitation would induce. The great increases in sediment load reaching rivers in areas undergoing urbanisation or intensive agriculture simulate natural periods of erosion. In all

instances, man's effect is to compress such changes in time and to intensify them in effect. The case study that follows illustrates some of the consequences that can flow from modifications of a river system.

The Willow river in Iowa, USA, ultimately a tributary of the Missouri, is cut into thick, compact silts in its upper course. Prior to modification at the beginning of the century, the river channels were wide (20–30 m) and meandering, with a mean gradient of 1 m per 1000 m. The main channel of the Willow river was canalised to a uniform 6 m width and straightened, thereby increasing the mean gradient to 1 m per 660 m. The changes in fluvial regime, due mainly to the increased flow

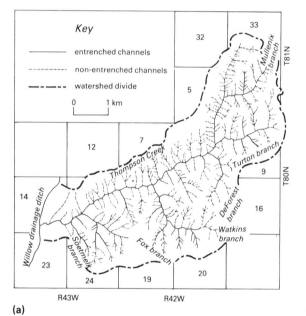

(a)

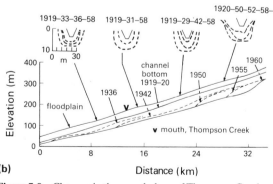

(b)

Figure 7.9 Changes in the morphology of Thompson Creek, a tributary of the Willow river, following channel modifications. (a) Entrenchment of river channels. (b) Changes in the long profile and in channel cross section. (After Ruhe 1971.)

Figure 7.8 Levees on the Mississippi river intended to alleviate flooding.

velocities, were rapid and dramatic. A 3-m knick-point moved upstream through the headwater channels, eventually eliminating the effects of grading and causing subsequent widening as well as deepening of the channels. As Figure 7.9 shows, the effects on the channel network and longitudinal profile were extensive and closely resemble those induced by a natural fall in base level that are termed **rejuvenation** features. A further effect of this man-caused 'rejuvenation' was to increase bank slumping, and therefore sediment load in the river. The sediment was deposited in the lower reaches of the basin and necessitated dredging to keep the channel clear. In the headwaters the same bank erosion initiated gullying and land degradation, while the entrenchment of the river to a lower level caused well water levels to fall by 3–5 m over the area. Such a drastic response of a fluvial system to human interference is exceptional and relates to the low threshold levels prevailing in the particular area. However, few river systems in the world have remained entirely unaltered by man's activities.

7.4 Coastal environments

Two factors are responsible for the fact that coastal environments have been altered more by man than have most other geomorphic environments. First, coasts throughout the world are foci of human settlement. Two-thirds of the world's population live close to the sea; half of the world's cities with populations greater than one million have a coastal location. Thus the pressure on the coastal zone is great and modifications to better suit human purposes are widespread. In the Netherlands (Fig. 7.5) 75 per cent of the coastline has been radically modified by man, as has 40 per cent of the coastline of the coterminous USA. Only in the north of Scotland do large stretches of untouched coastline remain in Britain. In Japan the 100 km stretch of coast between Yokahama and Kisarazn is almost wholly artificial, consisting of man-made islands, peninsulas, embayments and plains.

The second factor is the relative fragility of many coastlines, particularly those in wave-lashed (high energy) marine environments. Natural energy and therefore material flows are often easy to disrupt, deflect, decrease or amplify. Intentional coastal modifications are designed to prevent erosion or to reclaim land, to facilitate coastal economic activity or to promote recreational activities. The natural processes affected are similar to those operating in rivers – currents, tides and waves. Erosion and deposition of material through the intensive use of beach zones for recreation has often created particular problems such as the destabilisation of sparsely vegetated dune systems due to footpath erosion and subsequent blow-outs (Fig. 7.10). One such example of coastal modification leading to a succession of related changes is at Seaford Bay in Sussex.

The dominant southwesterly wave direction on the Sussex coast causes a dominant north-west to south-east longshore drift of beach material. The Newhaven area shown in Figure 7.11 exemplifies what may happen when longshore drift is impeded by a man-made structure. The harbour wall (shown in black) at the mouth of the River Ouse was built to provide protection against storm waves. The breakwater extends for some 800 m into the sea and effectively blocks the eastward movement of beach material. In the 250 years since its construction considerable accumulation of beach material has taken place updrift (west) of the barrier forming a beach 300 m wide in places. To the east of the Ouse estuary, longshore drift has continued but with no replacement for the east-ward moving material. Thus the beaches, the natural protection against cliff erosion, have been depleted allowing wave erosion of the cliff line to increase. In turn, this has necessitated the con-struction of artificial sea walls which themselves alter the direction and erosional capabilities of the waves, so changing scour and deposition patterns offshore.

Although many coastlines may be regarded as 'sensitive' environments, some areas are par-ticularly unstable and liable to considerable change due to a relatively small degree of human interference. The cliffed section of the coastline of East Anglia is characterised by rapid cliff recession (up to 1 m per year) under natural conditions and high rates of longshore drift of material. Attempts to protect the cliffs by building a sea-wall in front of them have been only partially successful. Often the beach to seaward of the wall is rapidly eroded, leaving the wall as the only line of defence but, more importantly, if the cliffs are protected from marine erosion, then the primary source of beach material for that section of coastline is cut off. Some 95 per cent of beach sand is derived from the cliffs, the sluggish rivers of East Anglia con-tributing only the remaining 5 per cent.

The resort of Clacton, south of Harwich, is

Figure 7.10 Dune erosion by wind creating a 'blow-out' hollow due to the loss of vegetation caused by excessive trampling (in this instance, recreational use).

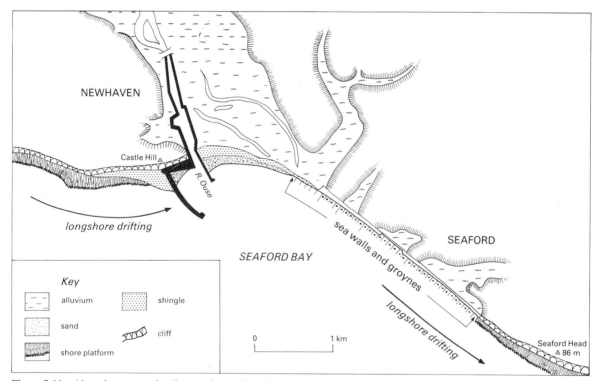

Figure 7.11 Altered patterns of sedimentation and erosion on a part of the Sussex coast due to the construction of the Newhaven harbour breakwater. (After Bird 1979.)

rapidly losing one of its major attractions, its beach, due to man-provoked changes on this part of the East Anglian coast. Longshore drift in this area is to the south at a rate of $c.$ 40 000–70 000 m³ per year. Some of the sediment builds up the spit of Colne Point at the mouth of the Blackwater river, but the remainder maintains the beaches to the north (Fig. 7.12). However, the estuary at Harwich is dredged, some 250 000 m³ of sediment being removed annually and taken away to be sold inland. As a result longshore drift has continued to the south of Harwich, but without replacement of sufficient material, leading to extensive losses from Clacton beach and to the almost total denudation of the coastline at Walton-on-the-Naze to a coastal platform of the underlying London Clay.

Examples of chain reactions stemming from a single alteration in the coastal environment are

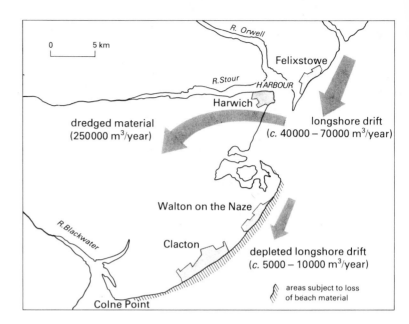

Figure 7.12 Erosion of beach material in the Clacton area due to sediment removal by dredging from Harwich harbour.

widespread. For example, the Santa Barbara breakwater in southern California traps 200 000 m³ of beach material annually and within a few years of construction had led to extensive loss of beach deposits over a distance of 16 km down drift.

7.5 Mass movement

Downslope movement of soil and regolith material (mass movement) under gravity is universal on slopes. The rate and nature of such movement varies with the nature of the material, the topography, the climate and the vegetation, but can be imperceptibly slow (creep) or spectacularly rapid (slides or slumps).

Any changes made by man to slope conditions, whether by building or excavation, drainage or agriculture, may alter rates or types of mass movement. The slumping of material in road cuttings is a common example where slopes have been steepened by man.

Sometimes man's intervention in slope processes can be catastrophic. The Vaiont reservoir was constructed in a narrow valley in northern Italy in a zone naturally liable to landslides. The upper 100–150 m of rock is of interbedded limestones and clays, the limestones having been subject to extensive solution along the fractures in the rock. Even without human interference these

valley slopes would have been inherently unstable with the heavily fractured limestone liable to slip down slope over the underlying clays. However, human intervention in the form of the reservoir construction led directly to sliding on a disastrous scale. Groundwater levels beneath the valley slopes rose as the reservoir filled, weakening the limestone strata still further and lubricating the clay layers. A period of heavy rain in October 1963 raised groundwater levels still further, and increased the weight of the top layers of rock until, finally, a mass of rock slid down slope into the reservoir. The slide took place within one minute, but contained 240 million m³ of rock, an area of valley side 1.8 km by 1.6 km being affected. The reservoir dam was overtopped by displaced water and a 100-m-high flood wave raced down the valley killing 2600 people. In this instance the results of pushing a natural system beyond its threshold were calamitous from the human point of view.

7.6 Artificial tectonics – land subsidence

Land subsidence associated with human activity is the best documented instance of artificial tectonic activity. Subsidence can result from the abstraction or addition of liquids to the ground or from the extraction of solids from below ground in mining. Superficial subsidence is common when organic

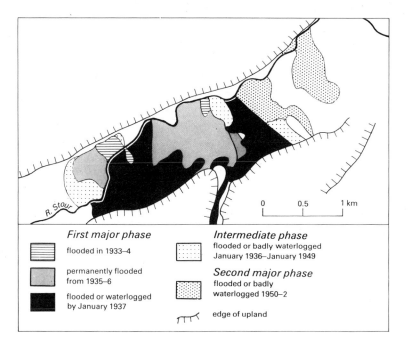

First major phase

▤ flooded in 1933–4

▨ permanently flooded from 1935–6

■ flooded or waterlogged by January 1937

Intermediate phase

⠠ flooded or badly waterlogged January 1936–January 1949

Second major phase

⠶ flooded or badly waterlogged 1950–2

⌒⌒⌒ edge of upland

Figure 7.13 Successive stages in the growth of a subsidence lake due to coal mining in the Stour valley, Kent coalfield. (After Coleman 1955.)

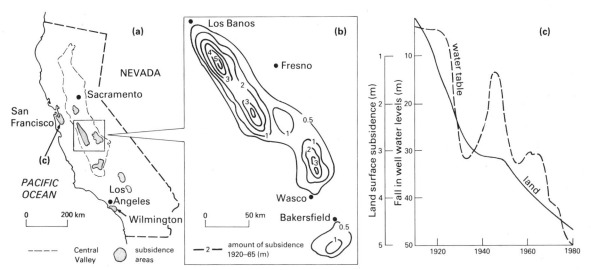

Figure 7.14 Land subsidence due to groundwater extraction in California. (a) Areas of California affected by subsidence. (b) Subsidence in the southern part of the Central valley 1920–65. (c) Changes in well-water levels and in land surface levels in the San Francisco area 1920–80. (After Poland 1973.)

soils with a high water content are drained. The English Fens, the Florida Everglades and the Dutch polders have all experienced land subsidence over large areas following drainage and subsidence may occur when irrigation takes place. Certain low-density, unconsolidated sediments may be stress resistant when dry, but when thoroughly wetted for the first time during irri-

gation their intergranular strength falls leading to rapid compaction and subsidence. Loess and alluvial fan materials are especially liable to this phenomenon – in the southwestern part of the Central valley of California 4.5 m of subsidence occurred on a newly irrigated fan disrupting the canal system and ruining the irrigation network.

Deep seated subsidence of the land is common

to many regions of extractive industry. The 'flashes' of Cheshire are water-filled hollows resulting from salt extraction underground. Coal-mining settlements often show the results of subsidence dramatically with tilted buildings and deformed road surfaces. The surface subsidence can extend horizontally for a distance of up to half the depth of the workings and a vertical extent up to two-thirds of the thickness of the coal seams removed. Figure 7.13 shows a part of the floodplain of the River Stour on the Kent coalfield. Small-scale subsidence (up to 60 cm) took place during the 1930s following the mining of a 1.2 to 1.5 m thick coal seam. Almost 4 km^2 are now affected and are subject to flooding. Subsidence may occur catastrophically rather than gradually. In the gold-mining region near Johannesburg, collapses 50 m in diameter and 30 m in depth have formed at the surface following heavy rain which weakened the overlying strata.

The most extensive subsidence phenomena are those due to extraction of ground water, particularly from a pressurised (artesian) aquifer. Some 9000 km^2 of land in the Central valley of California has subsided by more than 30 cm during this century as the groundwater reserves in the major aquifers have been emptied. Figure 7.14a shows the areas of California most affected, and Figure 7.14b shows the extent of subsidence above the aquifers at the southern end of the valley. Water levels have been lowered by 60–140 m by pumping in these areas. Figure 7.14c illustrates the relationship between declining water levels and the lowering of the land-surface – in this case the San Francisco area. Note the much reduced rate of subsidence between 1936 and 1943 when water abstraction was reduced and groundwater levels were allowed to recover.

Oil extraction can produce intense but highly localised subsidence. The Wilmington oilfield near Los Angeles (Fig. 7.14a) is perhaps the most spectacular example. An ellipse of subsidence occurred between 1928 and 1971 with a maximum fall in land level of 9.3 m. As much of the area was only 2–3 m above sea level, elaborate sea walls have had to be built. The horizontal and vertical displacements of the overlying strata ruptured pipelines and destroyed buildings.

7.7 Conclusions

Although the examples given in this chapter have tended to emphasise the spectacular impact of man upon landforms, it is probably the less obvious, less intense but more widespread man-induced changes such as soil erosion that are important on a global scale. Many of these alterations in geomorphic processes are an indirect result of some of the human actions described in the other chapters in this part of the book – on water, soil, vegetation and climate, for example. Ultimately, man would have the greatest impact on geomorphic processes and therefore on landforms were he to succeed, deliberately or otherwise, in changing global climate.

8 The oceans

8.1 Introduction

Seven-tenths of the Earth's surface are ocean, and yet this chapter is the shortest of those concerned with aspects of the environment. An optimistic view would be that the reason for the brevity is the lack of human impact on the oceans. The pessimistic opinion would be that so little is known of the workings of the oceans that it is not possible to say with any confidence what effects in degree or kind man's activities are having.

What is certain is the importance of the oceans in controlling global energy flows and hence the large-scale environment of the whole Earth. Although all the oceans are interconnected and the only barriers to water exchanges are temperature and salinity differences, the ocean waters are not as mobile as the atmosphere. Nevertheless, they act as very efficient dispersal and dilution agents. The oceans may be considered as the Earth's giant flywheel, giving stability to the Earth system as a whole. This is particularly the case with regard to the heat budget, the oceans storing vast quantities of solar radiation, but gaining and releasing heat only slowly. A consequence of the flywheel function is that any deviation in its workings, man induced or otherwise, will greatly transform the entire planetary environment. Unfortunately, it is not yet clear just how delicately balanced is the oceanic flywheel; what degree of stress is required to alter its function.

Although they are at the lowest level of the food-chains in the oceans, the phytoplankton (microscopic sea plants, mainly algae) are central to the functioning of the global carbon and oxygen cycles. Their role in photosynthetically fixing atmospheric carbon dioxide releases 75 per cent of the Earth's free oxygen and also provides a global carbon sink (Ch. 2). Thus the oceans also occupy a central position in the maintenance of the chemical cycles. Figure 8.1 shows in simplified form the exchange and sink functions of the oceans.

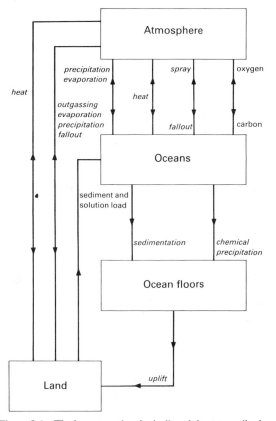

Figure 8.1 The long-term (geological) and short-term (hydrological) functions of the oceans in the general workings of the global energy system.

8.2 Man and the oceans

8.2.1 The nature of the relationship

It is almost true to say that more is known about the Moon than about the depths of the oceans. The marine environment is wholly alien to man, and its life-forms have evolved quite separately to those on land; comparatively little is known about the basic ecology or food-chain system operating in

91

the oceans. This ignorance means that man is insensitive to the effects of changes he makes in the underwater environment, the consequences need not be the same as those on land and organisms may not possess the necessary negative feedback mechanisms to resist changes.

Man still has a mesolithic, hunting and gathering, relationship with the oceans, with the exception of embryonic experiments in mariculture, yet the technology he possesses has allowed him to impinge upon the oceans to a measurable extent. It is believed that the temperate waters of the north Atlantic and north Pacific are now being fished to their full potential and that particular species are overfished – the sardine off California; the salmon in the north-west Pacific; the herring in the Atlantic. The blue whale, a mammal, though now protected, has been depleted to the point of extinction. Degrees of human influence vary, being at a maximum in estuarine and continental shelf areas (8 per cent of the ocean area), and least in the deep oceanic zones and in unpopulated coastal areas. However, it cannot now be assumed that the oceans are still a natural environment.

8.2.2 Oceanic pollution

A major difficulty in assessing human impact on the oceans is presented by the huge scale and slow response rate of the great water bodies. The length of time involved and the possible transmutations of the chain of cause and effect make it very difficult to understand how man's actions affect the workings of the oceanic environment, and this is particularly true of the effects of pollution. The oceans are the global dustbin where 'out of sight; out of mind' is still the prevalent attitude. The oceans are not a bottomless sink, however, any more than they are an endless source of food. Although they are a vast energy store, the energy is thinly distributed throughout the oceans, and this may mean that they are a fragile ecosystem.

The frequent oil spillages at sea are spectacular and receive considerable publicity when they are sufficiently large and damaging. An estimated 6 million tonnes of petroleum hydrocarbons reach the oceans annually (90 per cent of them due to man). It is thought that thin oil layers may concentrate trace pollutants such as heavy metals, DDT and amino acids. It is these chronic, low concentration pollutants rather than oil itself that may eventually have the most marked effects on the workings of the oceans. The persistence of such substances in sea water varies greatly: sodium, a

naturally abundant element, remains in solution for more than 100 million years, but aluminium compounds precipitate out on to the ocean floor within 100 years. The residence periods for man-made compounds in the ocean are largely unknown. Mixing times for the oceans are similarly great, probably 1000–3000 years. There is a distinction in terms of intensity of effect and perhaps in response, between the continental shelf areas and the ocean basins proper (Fig. 8.2). Shelf areas are more comparable to inland waters in that they receive concentrated inputs of pollutants including organic and fertiliser residues. The equivalent of algal blooms occur in coastal waters when excessive nutrient enrichment occurs: for example, the 'red tides' of dinoflagellates that took place in sewage-polluted waters off north-east England in 1968 and Nova Scotia in 1972. The ocean deeps tend to receive only the more persistent chemicals, but the long residence time means that marine organisms are exposed to them for extended periods.

Radioactive substances are now present throughout the oceans: there are caesium 137 and strontium 90 from nuclear weapon tests, but now much more significantly a wide variety of radioactive isotopes from nuclear power station effluent. Figure 8.3 shows the levels of radioactivity in bottom-dwelling organisms of the Irish sea derived from the nuclear processing plant at Windscale in Cumbria.

Halogenated hydrocarbons of high molecular

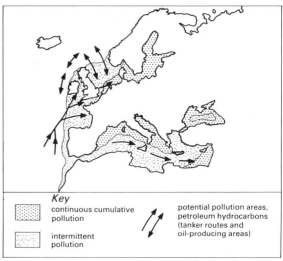

Figure 8.2 Degrees of human impact on the European offshore environment.

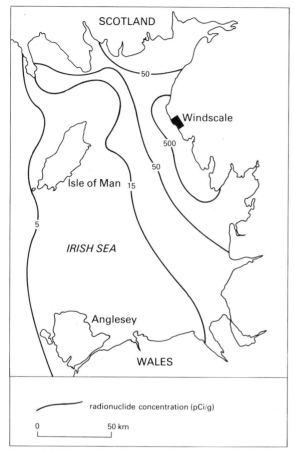

Figure 8.3 Concentrations of man-made radioactive effluent in the Irish sea in 1970.

weight, such as DDT, reach the oceans largely as fallout from the atmosphere and, although of very low solubility, they are very stable compounds (Ch. 9) and are concentrated biologically. Phytoplankton are thought to be damaged by moderate concentrations and so, therefore, are zooplankton (planktonic animals) and species higher up the food chain. Low molecular weight hydrocarbons such as trichloromethane (Ch. 5) are distributed in the environment as aerosols, but again the oceans are ultimately their sink. Six thousand tonnes per annum reach the oceans, and although concentration levels in organisms are well below the toxic level, their long-term effects are unknown.

The increasing mobilisation rates for metals mentioned in Chapter 2 eventually affect the oceans, the final destination for metal wastes or leachates. Although the ability of heavy metals to combine with organic substances to form highly

poisonous organometallic compounds may be important in the long term, thus far only lead levels (from petrol fumes) have measurably increased in the oceans.

The story of man and the oceans is an inconclusive one; we do not know whether even the present levels of pollution or fishing are sufficient to cause significant changes in the oceans. Similarly, the thresholds and leverage points are uncertain. However, the smaller, enclosed seas in the developed world unmistakably show the effects of man's actions.

8.2.3 *The Baltic sea*
The Baltic sea has geographical features similar to the Mediterranean and Black seas in that it is almost cut off from the main oceanic circulation and is surrounded by highly populated areas. However, it is being affected by human activity to a greater degree than the other two seas due to its peculiar morphology and water circulation. The Baltic receives large inputs of fresh water from rivers, and is an enclosed basin with the only outlet to the North sea being through the narrow, shallow (18 m maximum depth) straits between Denmark and Sweden. This combination of factors means that the waters are permanently stratified. A layer of fresher water 50–70 m deep with a salinity of only 0.6–0.7 per cent overlies a saltier and therefore denser (1–1.2 per cent) body of deep water; this salinity gradient is termed a **halocline**. The halocline prevents exchange of water between the levels, and thus the deep water body remains isolated, and is a trap and concentrating zone for pollutants that reach it.

The effects of man on the sea are illustrated in Figure 8.4 using oxygen and phosphorus levels to represent water quality. The data are from the Landsort Deep (*c.* 250 m). Dissolved oxygen levels have declined from 30 per cent saturation in 1900 to virtually zero today. The sea floor is now a reducing (oxygen-lacking) environment, the existence of hydrogen sulphide indicating that sulphate-reducing bacteria are present and that the zone is otherwise virtually lifeless. The deoxygenation has resulted from a reduction in oxygen levels in the inflowing rivers, the difficulty of vertical water exchange and the direct deposition of organic matter which takes up large quantities of oxygen to attain chemical stability into the deeps from human pollutant sources. The enrichment of the surface waters with nutrients (fertiliser

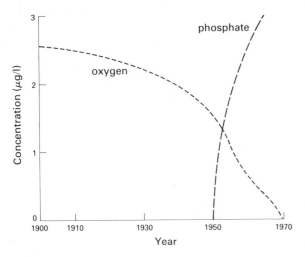

Figure 8.4 Changes in water quality, Landsort Deep, Baltic sea. (This figure first appeared in *New Scientist*, London, the weekly review of science and technology.)

residues, sewage) has increased primary production which in turn causes more organic matter to fall into the depths. The increase in chemical pollutants is shown by the threefold increase in phosphate concentration between 1955 and 1970, a result of increased use of artificial fertilisers and synthetic detergents.

The surface layers of the sea also act as a concentrating zone for alien chemicals. For example, the grey seal population of the Baltic has fallen by 80 per cent in recent years due, it is thought, to their eating fish contaminated with high levels of polychlorinated biphenyl (PCB) chemicals. The Baltic is a marine environment in which irreversible changes induced by man's activities may already have occurred.

8.3 Conclusions

In the past man was overwhelmed by the vastness of the oceans, their apparent limitlessness justifying their role as a global dustbin for wastes from the land. Awareness has now dawned that the oceans are finite and that pollution due to man is becoming significant.

Offshore mining is still a limited industry: oil wells are the best known example, though sulphur, sand and gravel, magnetite, diamonds, gold, chromite, phosphate and tungsten amongst other substances are currently being mined from shallow waters. Manganese nodules are dredged from the deep ocean. As more is learned about sea-bed resources, so mining will increase in scope and in greater depths of water, creating further pollution problems.

Although the open oceans are 'international', nations have had great difficulty in obtaining agreement on how oceans should be managed, particularly with respect to pollution. Economics are responsible for the lack of accord: thus the Moon, with no obvious immediate economic value, now legally belongs to no one and human activities thereon are governed by international law.

Part C THE OVERALL HUMAN IMPACT

9 The rural–agricultural environment

9.1 Introduction to agriculture

Part C of this book examines the total impact of man on his environment caused by his two main social–economic activities: agriculture (rural life) discussed in this chapter and industry (urban life) in Chapter 10. Sections 9.1–3 provide an introduction to agriculture, and the remainder of the chapter is concerned with case studies. Agricultural activity represents man's most widespread attempt to control his surroundings. Unlike urban–industrial complexes, changes due to agriculture are, or were until recently, extensive rather than intensive, partial rather than total. Agriculture has been defined as: 'the art of disturbing the balance of nature most safely to our own advantage' (Wigglesworth). Although this may define good agricultural practice, the primary function of agriculture is to manipulate natural ecosystems in order to maximise their output of foodstuffs (energy) for human use. The more sophisticated the form of agriculture, the more distorted become natural ecosystems and the greater the proportion of the energy flow within the system that is bled off for human use.

On a global scale the ideas of determinism discussed in Chapter 1 might be thought to operate to some extent. Throughout history, agriculture has been at the mercy of natural elements, particularly weather, and as famines, crop and animal disease epidemics show, the dependence on nature is still great. Of the four major vegetational units of the world (grasslands, woodlands, tundra and desert), only the first two are used intensively for agriculture to any extent, and it has been estimated that only 12 per cent of the Earth's surface is available for productive agricultural use.

9.2 Scales of agriculture

The effects of agriculture on the environment relate directly to the scale on which it is undertaken. There are two aspects to consider: first the intensity and degree of change imposed on the pre-existing soil and vegetation, and secondly the area over which the change has taken place. Pre-agricultural (hunting and gathering) economies divert energy from natural storages (fruit, leaves, animals) to man, but as only very low population densities can be supported in this way the overall impact on the environment is negligible. The earliest forms of agriculture (originating some 8000–9000 years ago) were the **swidden (landnam)** types involving clearing a small space in the woodland for crop growing over a period of a few years. When the land shows signs of exhaustion, the plot is abandoned and vegetation is allowed to regenerate naturally. Semi-domesticated plants and animals are used in this activity. The areas involved are small, the artificial inputs of energy (other than human labour) are also small and hence this is an example of low intensity, restricted area agriculture with correspondingly little environmental change.

Early pastoralism, particularly in wooded areas, probably led to more extensive environmental change, as woodlands were thinned or cleared to provide grazing.

At the other extreme are the wheatlands of the North American prairies with a single plant type being given total dominance over millions of hectares, with soil properties determined by the use of fertilisers, insect and microbiological life-forms restricted by pesticide applications and so massive inputs of external energy introduced to the system.

Between these two extremes are examples of high-intensity, limited area systems – gardens or horticultural areas – and low-intensity, large area systems – cattle ranches or areas of sheep grazing. The former type of system causes dramatic changes in the environment over restricted areas and the latter leads to more subtle changes over large areas.

9.3 Effects of agriculture

9.3.1 Direct effects

The biosphere and, therefore, all living things are a product of the interaction of solar energy with the Earth's surface. Under natural conditions, dynamic balances evolve attaining maximum bio-mass production compatible with the particular environment. The natural cycles of energy and mass (Ch. 2) function largely as closed systems as plant nutrients are retained within the soil–vegetation system. Agriculture deliberately upsets this balance with the intention of manipulating certain aspects in order to produce the maximum yield of selected foodstuffs suited to man.

The consequences are that the maturity of the ecosystem is reduced, and in effect it is reduced to a lower developmental (seral) level. The diversity of animal and plant species is greatly reduced as is the variety of soil types. Hence the complex inter-locking cycles of life-support systems are simplified and short circuited. The most extreme example of this effect is the conversion of the vastly complex ecosystem of the tropical forests into monocultural plantations or ranches.

Secondly, the productivity of the land (in terms of primary production of biomass per unit area) is normally reduced. This follows from the simpli-fication of the ecosystem. The most productive terrestrial environment in the world is the tropical rainforest. If the production of this system is

arbitrarily set at 100 units of biomass per unit area, then approximate relative productivities for other systems are as follows:

Natural systems	
tropical rainforest	100
temperate forest	30–40
prairie grassland	5
desert	0.5
Man-imposed agricultural systems	
wheat	3.5
rice	5
maize	4
potatoes	4
wheat and fertiliser	15
vegetables – irrigated desert	4

The last two examples illustrate the third con-sequence of agriculture. Agriculture, other than at the most primitive level, requires the input of external energy into its ecosystem partly to replace losses from nutrient leaching and harvesting, and partly to increase productivity as in the case of irrigated areas. Thus agricultural areas are zones of higher energy throughput than their natural counterparts. They are also much more open systems than natural ecosystems. A feature of modern, intensive agriculture is the high degree to which natural energy flows are distorted and to which external energy is funnelled into the land. Fertilisers, irrigation and machinery are examples of what are termed **energy subsidies**, over and above the natural solar energy falling upon the area.

Figure 9.1 illustrates diagrammatically how energy subsidies vary with differing agricultural systems, and also how energy subsidies have in-creased with improving technology through time. A subsidy ratio greater than 1.0 means that more energy is being obtained from the land than is being put into it – stored energy (effectively stored sunlight as biomass) is being used. A subsidy·ratio less than 1.0 means that more energy is being applied than is being obtained. Energy subsidies are at their highest in areas such as Britain and the USA where agriculture is most 'efficient' – for example grass-fed beef in Britain is subsidised to the extent of 3000–5000 kcal (1 kcal = *c*. 4200 J) per kg of protein produced. Less intensive systems have lower subsidies, 400 kcal/kg for rice in India, for instance.

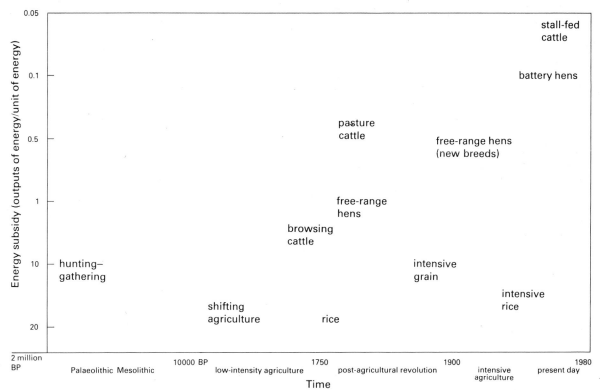

Figure 9.1   Energy subsidies associated with various agricultural practices.

9.3.2   Indirect effects

The results of the alterations, amplifications, reductions and distortions of natural cycles of energy and mass described above are far reaching. In Chapters 3–8 man's impact on particular aspects of the environment was considered, especially with regard to processes. Agriculture is concerned with the skin of the Earth, and it is within that region that the greatest changes can be made in most of the characteristics of the natural environment. Table 9.1 summarises some of the effects of agriculture on the various facets of the environment. The right-hand side of the table could be extended indefinitely as chain reactions are set off. Notice also the degree of interconnection whereby a change, say, from pastoral to arable agriculture may alter soil character, microclimate, local hydrology, rates of soil erosion and hence river sediment load. In turn, feedback effects may then alter the properties of the various environmental factors once more – increased erosion will alter soil texture and soil moisture, which will change soil fertility, crop yield and hence microclimate.

Many of the changes shown in Table 9.1 have

already been discussed in early chapters, so only some examples of changes imposed by agricultural activity will be looked at in more detail.

Fertilisers.   The direct effects of fertilisers upon soils were mentioned in Chapter 3. However, in recent years rates of application of artificial fertilisers have increased greatly, particularly in the developed countries. Usage rates of 90 kg/ha of nitrogen–phosphorus–potassium (NPK) fertilisers are the norm for cropland in Europe, and the USA uses some 30.5 thousand million kg per year. In these regions nitrogen and phosphorus have ceased to be limiting factors on plant growth, and there is evidence to suggest that *excess* fertiliser, nitrogen in particular, is being used. Supplying nitrogen to the soil is difficult because in its available form as nitrate it cannot be stored in the soil and is easily washed through into ground water or streams. Thus more needs to be applied to the ground than can actually be used by plants. It is estimated that less than half of the nitrogenous fertiliser applied is actually taken up by the plants. The final destination of the remaining nitrate is not

Table 9.1 Some effects of agriculture on aspects of the environment.

Sphere of change	Change imposed	Intended effects	Unintended effects	Possible effects
biological	crop growing	maximise food output	restricted flora, fauna changed microclimate	encourage specific diseases, predators
	harvesting	transfer of energy to man	reduce soil fertility, biology	alter soil structure
	grazing land	animal protein, etc.	alter flora, fauna	?
	selective breeding/genetics	improve productivity	?	
	use of pesticides	destroy harmful fauna }	chemicals may reside in } soil and enter food chains	water pollution } soil chemistry changes animal/plant mutations
	use of herbicides	remove unwanted flora		
pedological	addition of fertilisers	energy input – more production	change soil chemistry	water pollution, change soil structure
	tillage	facilitate sowing/change land	alter soil structure, infiltration rate, albedo	soil erosion, climatic change
	liming	change pH/minor nutrient	alter availability of other chemicals	alter chemistry of ground water/runoff
climatic	greenhouses	control temperature and moisture	almost total control	
	mulching/frost spraying	prevent frosts	change microclimate	
	shelter belts	lessen erosion	alter microclimate	alter soil conditions
hydrologic	irrigation	increase soil moisture }	alter leaching rates and soil chemistry,	oasis microclimates salinisation
	drainage	decrease soil moisture	vegetation, soil flora and fauna, runoff, evaporation	river flooding increased solutional load
topographic	terracing	prevent erosion on slopes	change mass movement processes	
	flooding	growing specific crops (rice)	new ecosystem	?
	levelling	economic use of machinery	altered geomorphic processes	
	reclamation	new land	new habitat	

known with certainty, but nitrate concentrations are known to have tripled in some rivers in southern England in the past 30 years. In East Anglia groundwater nitrate levels have approached the maximum levels considered safe for human drinking water (10 mg/l). It has also been suggested that eutrophication (overenrichment with nutrients) in lakes and rivers is associated with excessive use of fertilisers. Increased use of fertilisers is associated with more intensive farming, including land improvement, and it may be that land drainage (Ch. 6), accelerating runoff with a high nitrate concentration, is at least as important in contributing to higher nitrate levels in ground and surface waters as is over-application. Levels of solute load of non-fertiliser chemicals have increased by up to 30 per cent over the past 30 years in England.

Herbicides and pesticides. The ambiguous results of land drainage also seem to be apparent in respect of herbicides. As with fertilisers, runoff is the primary means by which herbicides and pesti-cides move beyond the area in which they are applied. Unlike fertilisers, however, they are intended to be toxic and their persistence in the environment has already led to undesirable side-effects elsewhere in the ecosystem.

The substances that have most effect on their surroundings are those that are slow to break down under natural conditions. Pesticides based on organochlorines (DDT, aldrin) take many years to decompose. Organophosphate or carbonate pesticides (e.g. Malathion) are relatively non-persistent. The herbicides Simazine and Linuron persist for more than a year but Chloroprophon is broken down within 4–5 weeks. It is the long-life substances that are potentially the source of significant damage.

The best documented example of the effects of pesticide residue is that relating to DDT. Although DDT is now banned in many developed countries, its relative cheapness makes it attractive to less developed states, and here its use is increasing by 10 per cent per year. DDT can be moved from the site of application by wind, as particles or vapour, or in water. It is insoluble in water (1×10^{-3} p.p.m. saturation) compared with other pesticides, but much more soluble in lipids or fatty tissues – living bodies. This leads to an instance of biological concentration, whereby although concentrates of DDT in the inorganic environment may be very low, because living organisms concentrate and retain the substance, they may build up concentrations thousands or millions of times greater. For example, at an estuary, water may have a very low DDT concentration. Zooplankton concentrate the chemical 1000-fold. Further up the food chain the concentration in small fish is 10 000 times original levels, and in the gulls which eat the fish 1 million times estuary water levels. The long-term effects of such concentrations are unknown, but the short-term effects can be dramatic. Birds eating seed dressed with DDT may be killed and, in the USA, forest spraying to eliminate spruce budworm, contaminated streams and killed fish in the 1950s. Pesticides, including DDT, are usually more harmful to predators on the particular pest than to the pest itself, as the predators may be poisoned via the pest and the predator population is less numerous and therefore develops less immunity to the pesticide. Also, as the pest population declines so, from lack of food, does the predator, but a recovery in pest numbers is followed only after a considerable time lag by an increase in predators, by which time larger concentrations of pesticide have been used, and so the cycle continues (Ch. 4).

A further, inadvertent effect of the use of specific pesticides is the development by mutation of genetically based immunity to the substance by many insects. In California, 16 of the 25 major pests formerly controlled by DDT have developed immunity. Cotton, which receives half of all the pesticides applied in the USA, is now attacked by pests which have immunity to all the commonly used chemicals.

Pesticides enter the food chain at a high level and therefore have affected man directly. This is almost certainly the reason for the degree of concern that has been shown regarding their use.

The use of herbicides has lagged behind that of pesticides. They are used most intensively in association with 'no-till' planting which involves leaving crop residues in the fields, so dispensing with ploughing and harrowing. No-till techniques are used on a quarter of US farmland today, a threefold increase since 1970.

Pesticide and herbicide application is a result of the rapid strides in agricultural technology in recent years. Equally, it is an example of a man-imposed change on the environment leading to an unforeseen chain of linked changes, many of which, from the human point of view, are wholly undesirable. Yet the social and economic pressures that drive modern agriculture (high productivity) make it difficult to survive as an intensive and 'efficient' farmer without the use of such chemical warfare.

9.4 The British landscape

9.4.1 Introduction

Three-quarters of the British people live and work in the highly unnatural environment of the town or the city. Perhaps because of this there is a widespread love for the 'countryside' as the bank holiday exodus to rural areas demonstrates. Conservation of the countryside also receives much support – for example, there has been opposition to reclamation of upland areas such as Exmoor, to re-afforestation of large areas with conifers and to the recent loss of hedgerows. One of the charms of the British countryside is its variety. The manicured landscapes of the south with rich pastures and tilled fields dotted with mature oaks, beech and until recently elm; the bleak, featureless uplands of Scotland and Wales; the grey and green limestone hills and the dark peaty plateaux – all this diversity within a very limited area (Fig. 9.2).

And yet . . . the imprint of man has been planted more firmly on the countryside of Britain than anywhere else in the world with the exception of Holland, the Nile valley and parts of China. Almost all the landscapes we regard as 'natural' in terms of soil, vegetation and sometimes even the contours of the land are largely the work of man. Two centuries ago, before land enclosure was widespread, the rural landscape looked very different, but was still far from being nature's handiwork. Twenty centuries ago, Britain was covered by a quilt of forest broken only by the higher mountains, the boggy patches and the first clearings of man. The British countryside is not the result of the interaction of natural forces, still less does the 'balance of nature' hold sway. Such balance as there is in the environment exists by courtesy of man; it is an imposed and sometimes precarious balance.

It is curious that the most recent trends in agriculture in southern and eastern England have been

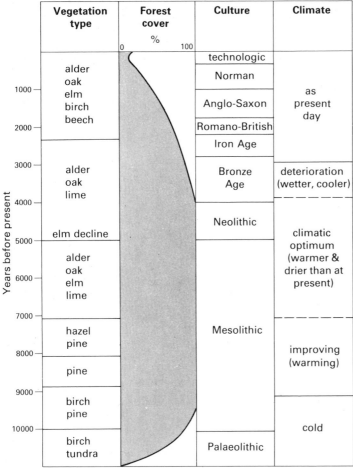

Years before present	Vegetation type	Forest cover % 0 — 100	Culture	Climate
	alder oak elm birch beech		technologic	as present day
1000			Norman	
			Anglo-Saxon	
2000			Romano-British	
			Iron Age	
3000	alder oak lime		Bronze Age	deterioration (wetter, cooler)
4000			Neolithic	climatic optimum (warmer & drier than at present)
5000	elm decline			
	alder oak elm lime			
6000			Mesolithic	
7000				
	hazel pine			improving (warming)
8000	pine			
9000	birch pine			
10000				cold
	birch tundra		Palaeolithic	

Figure 9.2 The typical English landscape of upland rough pasture and enclosed, partly wooded lowland, South Shropshire.

Figure 9.3 The Postglacial chronology of Britain.

directed toward the development of a landscape of vast fields, a treeless prairie of grass or cropland. Seen from a distance, such a landscape might resemble that of 14 000 years ago when tundra conditions prevailed following the retreat of the ice sheets.

The intervening centuries have seen the colonisation of Britain, first by shrubs and then by a succession of forest types which reached their greatest extent during the period of the climatic optimum some 6000 years ago. Since that time man has become the single most important agent in determining the soil, vegetation, drainage pattern and increasingly the geomorphology of the country. Look again at Figures 3.1 and 4.3 which show world patterns of soils and natural vegetation. Southern Britain is included within the forest soil group and northern Britain within the weakly podsolised group. Natural vegetation is forest, largely deciduous. In reality only 7 per cent of Britain is forested – more evergreen than deciduous – and the actual pattern of soils is a complex mosaic of man-induced deviations from the original soils.

9.4.2 *Influence of man in rural Britain*
The earliest human habitation in Britain probably occurred during the penultimate (Hoxnian) interglacial period up to 200 000 years ago. For much of the Palaeolithic (Fig. 9.3), habitation was sporadic with numerous invasions and withdrawals. The Upper Palaeolithic ended some 10 000 years ago, the landscape virtually untouched by human activity. The succeeding Mesolithic was based upon the economy of the hunter and gatherer. The population was small and scattered. As in areas of the world where mesolithic cultures still exist today, so in Britain, humans had to adapt to natural systems. The technology and organisation that man needed to alter conditions to his own advantage were lacking. The exact degree of influence of Mesolithic man on the British scene is still not fully understood, but it would have been limited in extent and degree.

It was from the Neolithic period (5000–4000 years ago; Fig. 9.3) that human activity first began to affect the environment materially. The Neolithic or New Stone Age marked the beginning of agriculture, and thus the first distancing of man from an absolute dependence on his immediate surroundings.

At the beginning of the Neolithic most of Britain was forested. Oak, beech and elm pre-

Figure 9.4 Natural deciduous forest in England, the Mark Ash Wood in the New Forest. (Photograph courtesy of the Nature Conservancy Council.)

dominated with ash being locally important and pine in Highland Scotland (Fig. 9.4). The forest was dotted with marshes and bogs in ill drained areas. The upper limit of tree growth was 700–900 m OD (the present limit for oak on Dartmoor and in the Lake District is *c.* 450 m above sea level and *c.* 640 m above sea level for pine in the Cairngorms). Only on the highest summits was the forest absent, replaced by scrub or grassland with arctic–alpine plant communities (Fig. 9.5). Brown-earth soils were widely developed as a response to the climate and forest cover. On the lowlands the forests were dense and the soils often heavy. On acidic, coarse grained or overdrained soils especially in uplands, the forest cover was thinner. It was these more lightly wooded areas that were the weakest link in the soil–vegetation–climate system, and therefore the point of man's first effective intervention. The Neolithic lies within the period of time known as the **climatic optimum** when temperatures were a few degrees warmer than those of today and rainfall probably slightly less.

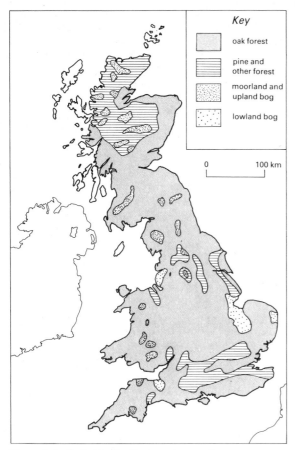

Figure 9.5 Probable distribution of vegetation c. 6000 years ago, before human interference. (After Eyre 1968.)

The Neolithic invasions of Britain brought with them the near-Eastern culture of polished stone axes, animal domestication and crop cultivation. The basic agricultural practice was that of the landnam – a small, temporary clearance in the forest that was used for agriculture or grazing for a few years, then abandoned and allowed to regenerate. On heavy soils this technique would scarcely alter natural conditions, but Neolithic man showed a strong preference for the lighter soils of the chalk and of sands and gravels. Dry soils of this type are slower to regain their fertility and their original vegetation following exploitation. It may be that some of the heaths and open chalk uplands in southern England were deforested at this time and have remained treeless ever since. The coastal area around Gwithian in Cornwall was forested in pre-Neolithic times, but after it had been converted to pasture in

the Neolithic, blowing sand was able to blanket the area preventing forest regeneration. Thus, the first permanent changes had been made in isolated areas. Towards the end of the Neolithic and during the subsequent Bronze Age, the balance between man and nature began to tilt in favour of man. Soil, vegetation, water and topography still exerted a strong influence on human settlement patterns, but gradually the influences were becoming less deterministic as humans were able to decide the character of their surroundings to some extent. Studies of fossil pollen grains preserved in boggy areas show that during the Neolithic the number of elm trees declined sharply. Elm is one of the more demanding trees in terms of soil fertility and its decline is regarded as a likely result of human influence. The tradition, still practised in parts of Europe, of using elm branches as fodder may have originated at this time. Birch, hazel, grasses and weeds began to replace elm indicating more open land with less fertile soil.

During the Bronze Age and early Iron Age the climate deteriorated somewhat, becoming cooler and wetter until by c. 500 BC it was very much the same as that prevailing today.

The Iron Age (500 BC onwards) saw irreversible changes in the landscape. A new technology based on iron tools, new agricultural methods and an increased population allowed man a greater control over his immediate surroundings. The distinctive landscape of the uplands was created at this time. Uplands that were deforested degenerated rapidly in the cooler, wetter climatic conditions. Brown-earth soils were leached to become more acid and podsolic, and soil erosion was severe on steeper slopes. Natural vegetation declined accordingly and the use of the land for grazing would have made tree regeneration impossible. Blanket peat spread over upland areas that had been recently cultivated or forested, as is shown in Figure 9.6. (Blanket or hill peat covers upland slopes and plateaux unlike the lowland fen and raised-bog peats which develop at low points in the landscape.) It may be that such environmental changes would have happened without man's presence as a direct result of the change in climate. However, the brown earth–deciduous forest system is very stable except in the wettest areas of Britain, and it is highly likely that deforestation was the action that destabilised the whole soil–vegetation system in the uplands. The cultural and physical contrast between highland and lowland Britain that we now take for granted was established more than 2000 years ago and has persisted ever since.

A graphic illustration of environmental change in Bronze–Iron Age times is given in Figure 9.7. This is a section through a prehistoric burial mound (barrow) on the North York Moors in what is now an inhospitable acid moorland area. The soil around and above the barrow is acidic, podsolised and relatively infertile. Beneath the barrow is the now fossilised, buried soil that must have existed in the area when the structure was built. This soil is a forest brown earth and contains tree and cereal pollen grains. Similar barrows built at a slightly later period have much inferior, podsolised soils preserved beneath them. Thus a drastic change in soil and vegetation conditions seems to have occurred within a very short time span. Forest clearance to allow cereal cultivation and grazing may have tilted the balance of a marginal environment, allowing the soil to become leached of nutrients and eventually to become acidic and infertile. There is also evidence that, at the same time, sediment accumulated rapidly in lakes and on river floodplains. This helped to constrain lowland rivers into a single channel rather than the braided courses they may have followed before. Soil erosion on the slopes is the likely reason for this increase in sedimentation. At Llancarfan in Glamorgan a 3-m depth of material of Iron Age–Roman date overlies the prehistoric valley floor, and the modern river has cut into these deposits to form terraces. The material that accumulated was probably derived from the valley slopes that were deforested in this period. The enclosure of fields by banks or walls also began in pre-Christian times. Where enclosures were on a slope, the first human modification of mass movement processes began as soil accumulated on the upslope of the barrier and thinned out on the downslope side.

Serious exploitation of the lowland forests dates from Iron Age–Romano–British times. Road systems gave easy access to formerly remote areas and the use of the mouldboard plough allowed heavier soils to be worked: for example, those of the Cotswold Hills. The brown-earth soils of the lowlands were well drained in the topsoil zone. As

Figure 9.6 A wall of Neolithic age excavated from beneath a peat bog at Belderg Beg, County Mayo, Ireland.

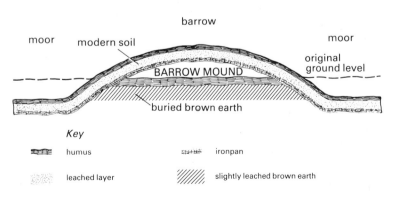

Figure 9.7 A fossil brown-earth soil preserved beneath a Bronze Age burial mound in an area of podsolic soils on the North York Moors. (After Evans 1976.)

cereal growing expanded, so nutrients were lost to the soil by harvesting and by lack of liming or manuring together with more direct exposure to rainfall. Soil structure deteriorated and with the loss of the deep rooted trees, drainage worsened. The present-day organic content of these soils is about 3 per cent compared with about 8 per cent in Roman times. However, colonisation of the lowlands and especially of the Midlands was a slow and patchy affair: for example, the Saxon diffusion up the river valleys of southeastern England and Nordic clearance in parts of northern England. Much of southern Britain retained its forest cover until the late mediaeval period.

After the Norman conquest the creation of a man-made landscape accelerated, in part due to the more centralised economic and social systems. Mediaeval forest clearances (**assarts**) encroached on the heavier soils and gradually the cultivated lowland soils developed an 'agric' horizon or topsoil, lacking the original horizons and the result of ploughing. This period also saw man make deliberate changes in the fauna of Britain. There were deliberate exterminations, of the wolf and bear for example, but also introductions such as the rabbit which would eventually significantly affect the ecology of the countryside (Chs 2 & 4).

Minor changes in landforms were being made by this time. For example, the practice of ridge and furrow cultivation (see Fig. 9.8) has left its mark in many areas, particularly in the Midlands, though large areas have subsequently been destroyed by later ploughing techniques. The ridges, up to 5 m wide, may have been units of land division or simply methods of improving yield by growing crops on only the better drained ridges.

In sloping areas the equivalent landforms are the **strip lynchets**, created over a period of 1000 years or more (Fig. 9.9). They are the equivalent of un-irrigated mediterranean terraces. Some are deliberate constructions, others are the product of contour ploughing over a long period of time. As is shown in Figure 9.10, their effect has been to modify the processes of mass movement naturally occurring on slopes. Thick accumulations of soil exist on the positive lynchets and much thinner deposits on the negative lynchets. Soil moisture and vegetation are altered accordingly. Lynchets now appear as distinctive terrace-like features in many upland areas.

The mediaeval period also saw the use of organised labour to begin landform modification on a large scale. The drainage of the Somerset Levels

Figure 9.8 Evidence for former ridge and furrow cultivation, once common on the lowland soils of Britain.

between the 10th and 14th centuries by local abbeys (e.g. Glastonbury), and the construction of reclamation dykes in Lincolnshire are examples. Hand-cutting of fen peat in Norfolk and subsequent flooding of the excavation in the wetter 15th century formed the Norfolk Broads – until comparatively recently thought to be natural lakes. These large water bodies were kept open only by artificial means – reed cutting and marginal cultivation. When these activities lessened, vegetation began to invade the Broads and the area of open water grew less. Without further human interference the Broads would soon disappear.

In later mediaeval times the forest areas diminished rapidly with increased demand for timber for fuel, housing, and ship building. The landscape was one of scattered settlements surrounded by large cleared areas of pasture and arable land with still extensive clumps of virgin forest remaining. The 16th, 17th and 18th centuries saw many of the changes that created the landscape we know today. The great enclosure movement replaced the vast open field system with a patchwork of field boundaries that characterise Britain. At the same time pastoral activities increased greatly. In ecological terms, the tens of thousands of kilometres of hedge that were mainly deliberately planted created entirely new habitats and microclimates (Chs 4 & 5). They offered refuges to animals and insects displaced from the forests, and allowed woodland bird numbers to be maintained. Ash and elm were replanted in the hedges, especially in the Midlands, to give the graceful isolated trees that were regarded as so essentially 'English' before the spread of Dutch

Figure 9.9 Strip lynchets forming terraces on a hillside near Austwick, Yorkshire. Although the lynchets were originally used for crop cultivation, the area is now devoted almost entirely to livestock rearing.

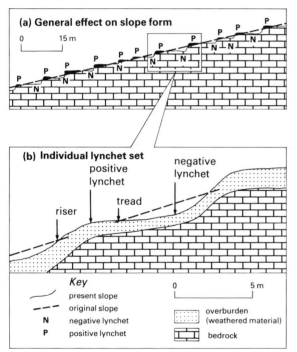

Figure 9.10 Section through a flight of strip lynchets. (After Evans 1976.)

elm disease, which killed off a large proportion of elms during the 1970s.

Land reclamation created artificial polder landscapes in eastern England, the scale of the projects increasing as the Industrial Revolution provided new sources of power and technology. Changes in land use had provoked changes in soil character-

istics since agriculture began, but with the coming of the Agricultural Revolution deliberate attempts were made to alter soil properties on a large scale. The sandy heaths of Norfolk were sheep lands until the 18th century. By 1800 the same areas grew cereals as deep ploughing had mixed the sandy topsoil with the heavier subsoil to form a fertile loam.

During the long period of change from pre-Christian to post-Agricultural Revolution, the uplands remained almost unaltered, the degraded soil and vegetation systems being maintained by grazing. As with all of man's impact on the natural environment, so the alteration of rural Britain has proceeded slowly until recent times. New agricultural ideas, improved technologies, changing social and economic structures all played their part in determining rates of change and the nature of the change. However, until the Agricultural Revolution, perceptible changes in the landscape occurred on a time scale of centuries. Scales of change were also slow to increase. The early farmers could hope only to tame very small plots around their settlement and, even by mediaeval times, intakes of land were commonly only a few hectares in extent at a time. This leisurely pace of modification of the countryside is now a thing of the past. The technological, social and economic upheavals of the 20th century have been reflected in agriculture. Nowhere more than in Britain is agriculture now agribusiness. The changes are not simply due to improved technology but to factors such as British agriculture becoming a part of a wider European (EEC) system, the increased role of government in determining agricultural policy and the increasing trend for land to be owned by, and managed for, large companies.

9.4.3   The countryside today

A second, less obvious agricultural revolution has been taking place in the past few decades. A new look has been taken at the land through the eyes of the scientific agriculturalist, forester and soils expert – and, equally important, through the eyes of the agricultural economist – as farming becomes more capital intensive.

In arable areas, soil structure and chemistry are being greatly modified by harrowing techniques and the heavy use of artificial fertilisers. Intensive cropping is replacing rotational systems, with pesticides and fertilisers replacing natural recovery methods for the soil. More intensive grazing is made possible by ploughing, fertilising and re-seeding grassland with short-term pastures. The practice of keeping animals enclosed and bringing fodder products to them from the fields means that natural manuring, grazing and trampling has lessened. Inputs of energy foreign to the local agricultural system (e.g. animal feeds, artificial fertilisers, fuels) mean that in many areas of rural Britain the soil–vegetation–animal system is operating at a productivity level that is considerably higher than natural environmental factors alone would permit (Sec. 9.3.1).

Soil-moisture regimes are being altered over wide areas – the area drained increased sixfold between 1930 and 1970 (Ch. 6). Field sizes and shapes are changing and tending to what is thought to be the optimum size economically of 20 ha. Hedges and other forms of field boundary are being removed accordingly, particularly in eastern England.

Even the upland areas and other regions rendered marginal by man's earlier activities are being reclaimed in part. For example, the heaths of Dorset (Fig. 9.11) are vanishing as they are used for forestry, building and for sources of sand and gravel. Thus the heaths, themselves created and artificially maintained by man, are now destined to change again. Increasingly the land, vegetation and climate of Britain are becoming 'raw materials' that man can shape to his ends via technology.

Figure 9.12 summarises the present pattern of land use in the UK compared with that which probably prevailed just prior to the beginnings

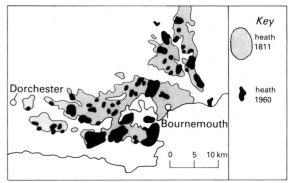

Figure 9.11   The reduction in the extent of Dorset heathland between 1811 and 1960. (After Moore 1962.)

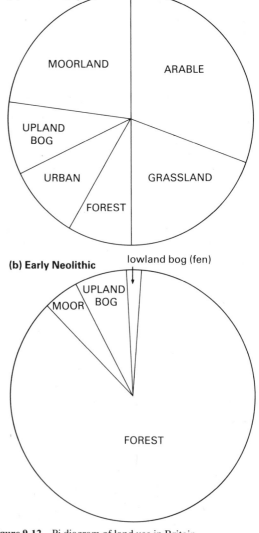

Figure 9.12   Pi diagram of land use in Britain.

of serious agriculture. The great increase in the amount of 'bare' (arable) land is noticeable. The decline and change in forest and the creation of new grass and moorland environments is also noticeable.

In the succeeding section a more detailed examination is made of man's impact on particular and distinctive environments in the British Isles.

9.4.4 The Burren, County Clare

One of the strangest landscapes in the British Isles is the limestone plateau of the Burren on the coast of County Clare in western Ireland. Although less than 300 m in altitude, a large part of the 400 km^2 upland consists of bare limestone seamed with open joints containing pockets of vegetation. It is a stone desert in an area of abundant rainfall (1300 mm p.a.) and mild temperatures (frosts are rare). It used to be thought that glaciers had stripped the surface clean and that soil and vegetation had been unable to recolonise the limestone since the ice retreated. Yet there are indications that the barrenness may be the work of man rather than of nature. Soil erosion on a catastrophic scale is not thought of as occurring in the climatic regime of north-west Europe. The environment is regarded as being relatively resistant to erosional processes (a stable ecosystem) compared with semi-arid areas with high-intensity rainfall (Chs 2 & 3). Yet the Burren is an example of a potentially very fragile soil–vegetation system with little ability to absorb environmental stress. Even the very limited technology of the earliest farmers in the area was sufficient to initiate an irreversible degradation of the soils and hence the vegetation. For the period of historical records the Burren is always described as having its present-day appearance. 'No water to drown a man; no tree to hang him from', one of Cromwell's lieutenants is supposed to have remarked. At present the region supports a farming population of a few hundred people using the patches of upland pasture for winter grazing of cattle.

In prehistoric times population densities were much greater and economic activity more widespread even in what are now the most barren areas. Numerous tombs made of large slabs of rock, burial cairns and settlements of the Neolithic period onwards are widespread, and field systems perhaps thousands of years old enclose what are now bare rock surfaces (Figs 9.13 & 14). Studies of fossil pollen from the area show that in Postglacial times a light forest covered the Burren and the

stumps of a pine forest are still visible beneath a thick peat cover on nearby non-limestone rocks. This forest grew in a brown-earth soil derived from glacial drift. The remnants of this soil are now found washed into fissures in the limestone and in caves. That this erosion coincided with the expansion of agriculture on the plateau is shown by the traces of the original soil preserved under man-made structures such as tombs and walls. Figure 9.15 shows a section through a box-shaped stone tomb erected in the Bronze Age. The land surface around the tomb is bare rock covered by a layer of rendzina (thin, organic soil on limestone) in patches. Within the tomb the soil is a brown earth that has been preserved from rain erosion. Monuments and walls built since early Christian times do not have this layer of mineral soil beneath

Figure 9.13 An ancient field boundary wall on limestone pavement that has been denuded of soil in the Burren, western Ireland.

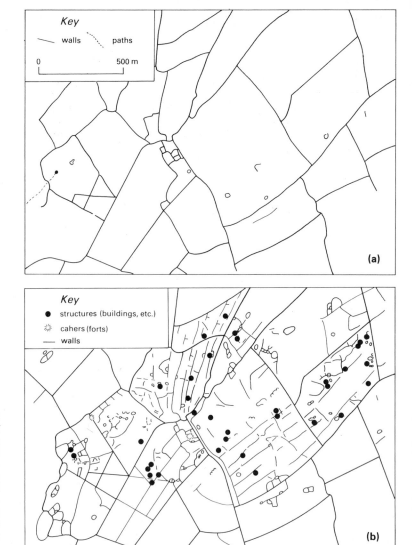

Figure 9.14 Features of the cultural landscape preserved in a 4-km² area of patchy soil and bare rock in the Burren karst of western Ireland. (a) Cultural features (mainly field boundaries) related to the present-day (cattle) economy of the area. (b) All the features of the cultural landscape in the same area including ancient fields, dwellings and cahers (forts). A much more intensive use for land that is now barren seems likely in the past. (After Plunkett Dillon 1979.)

them. Commonly they are built on bare rock. Thus the mineral soil was completely removed by erosion between 2000 and 3000 years ago. Charcoal fragments in the old soil suggest that man, attracted by the light soils and thin woodland of the Burren, cleared the land by burning with disastrous consequences. It has been shown elsewhere in the world that removal of the primary vegetation cover of an upland karstic area of high rainfall may be catastrophic. The thin soil is very subject to erosion without the shelter of vegetation and the binding effect of roots. The highly fissured, freely draining nature of the limestone means that soil particles only need be transported for a few metres at most before being washed underground and lost. Once it has been removed, soil will regenerate only slowly, as would vegetation. Browsing by goats, which were formerly numerous in the Burren, prevented tree or shrub growth as has been the case in mediterranean areas. The present landscape of patches of vegetation alternating with bare rock is artificial, in that only human activity maintains the landscape in that form. During the Irish Famine (c. 1850) much land was abandoned and has lain unused since. In the succeeding 130 years these areas have become

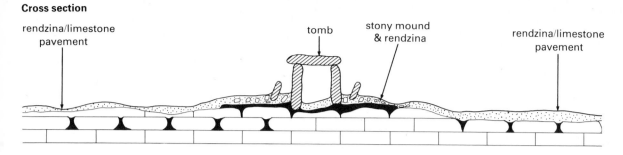

Cross section

rendzina/limestone pavement

tomb

stony mound & rendzina

rendzina/limestone pavement

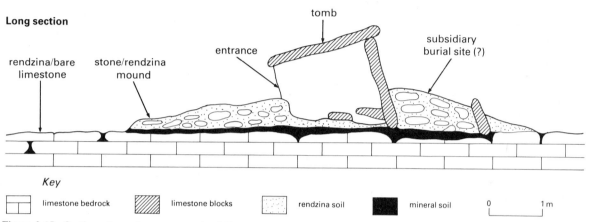

Long section

tomb

entrance

subsidiary burial site (?)

rendzina/bare limestone

stone/rendzina mound

Key

| | limestone bedrock | | limestone blocks | | rendzina soil | | mineral soil | 0 | 1 m |

Figure 9.15 Sections through a stone tomb of Bronze Age on the Burren, western Ireland, showing mineral soil preserved beneath the burial site in an otherwise barren area of patchy rendzina soils.

dense thickets of hazel and brush with a thin organic soil blanketing the bare rock. Old field boundaries are now lost in the sea of new greenery.

The Burren is an example of an area in which the natural equilibrium was sufficiently delicate for a small input from human activity to set in motion fundamental environmental changes. Other upland karsts throughout the world have undergone similar degradation.

9.4.5 The English prairies

The heartlands of British agriculture in southern and eastern England, and particularly East Anglia, Fenland and eastern Yorkshire, are the most efficient in the world in economic terms. The extreme orderliness of the landscape is testimony to the high degree of control exerted by man. These are the areas of large fields (field sizes doubled between 1945 and 1975), and hence the regions in which hedgerows are being removed to the greatest extent. For every kilometre of hedge removed, 1 ha of cultivable land is gained. Over the past 20 years 6500–11 000 km of hedgerow have

been removed annually. At their peak in the 1960s annual loss rates exceeded 1 per cent of the remaining total. When a hedge is grubbed out, the ecosystem that had developed within its zone of influence is also destroyed and the local climate it created is changed. Not all the changes associated with hedge removal have been beneficial to farmers. In the areas of light soils of fen peat or sand in eastern England, the larger fields have increased the local 'fetch' of the wind and so increased its average velocity (Ch. 5). The windbreak effect of hedges has been decreased, and evaporation and hence drying have increased. Autumn ploughing followed by springtime disc harrowing reduces the soil to a very fine tilth. The combination of high wind speeds and fine soil particles has led to increased wind erosion in Lincolnshire and east Yorkshire, particularly. During long, dry windy spells characteristic of early spring, finer particles are moved by saltation or deflation, and in parts of Lincolnshire (Fig. 9.16) much of the topsoil has already been removed (see also Fig. 9.17).

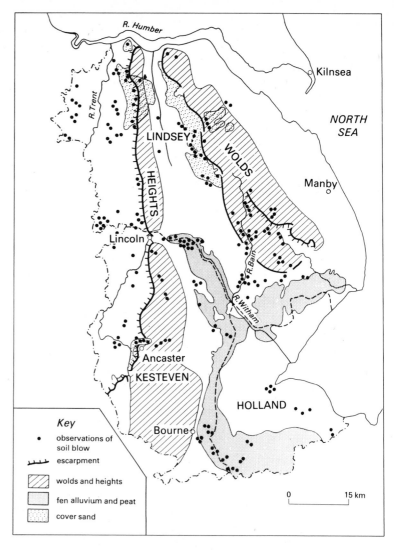

Figure 9.16 Sites at which wind erosion of soil occurred in Lincolnshire in 1968. Soil type is also shown. (After Robinson 1969.)

In east Yorkshire, wind erosion is localised on patches of sandy soil in the east of the Vale of York. The spring of 1967 was mild and dry with persistent west and south-west gales. The soil dried rapidly and wind erosion began. Dust storms up to 15 m high were generated and sand dunes up to 1 m high were deposited in the lee of obstacles. The York to Helmsley road was blocked for a week by sand drifts. Most of the material was redeposited in the vast fields rather than being lost to the area altogether, but the cost of the lost heavily fertilised topsoil was great. Hedgerow removal has declined as the adverse effects have become apparent and conservation measures are being taken. These include the spraying of synthetic organic polymers on to the soil to help to stabilise it and to encourage aggregation of the particles.

In some areas of arable land, overdrainage of land and excessive use of artificial fertilisers may be responsible for the increased level of dissolved salts in the drainage water. Nitrate levels in ground water have also risen appreciably in recent years, though their association with fertiliser use is not a simple one.

The pasturelands of southern England are also being altered. The meadow flowers and associated insects of these fields and meadows were always unnatural in the sense that they could only be maintained by continued grazing and fallow periods. Without such controls grasses and scrub would rapidly invade the areas. Now, such grasslands are ploughed and re-seeded, thus changing

Figure 9.17 Wind eroded soil deposited on a road near Swaffham, 1968. (Photograph courtesy of *Farmer's Weekly*.)

the flora. Pesticides are modifying insect populations. Roadside verges are now becoming the reservoirs of plant and animal life. Motorway verges are a completely new, partially controlled environment to which a full ecological response has not yet developed, though already they are a protected habitat, sheltering species that are becoming rare elsewhere.

9.4.6 The moorlands

The margin of the British uplands in the Lake District, the Pennines and Wales, for example, has a distinctive appearance. Horizontal bands of differently coloured vegetation lead from the valley floors to the high plateaux. In the valley floor and extending some little way upslope are bright green pastures, the product of careful management and fertilisers. Above are the slopes of brown-green bracken and higher still the whitish, coarse grasses dominated by *Nardus*. The summit areas are empurpled with heather or dark with peat bogs. Trees are rare. These vegetation zones with corresponding differences in soil, occur within a remarkably small height range, sometimes less than 500 m. Yet climate changes comparatively little within the same zone. These hill lands (Fig. 9.18) were almost completely forested in prehistoric times, and it is because of the removal

Figure 9.18 The transition from fertile valley meadowland to barren, heathery moorland with accompanying changes in soil type, near Llangollen, North Wales.

of this woodland and the subsequent agricultural use of the land that the complicated present-day pattern of soil and vegetation has developed (Fig. 9.19). The complex of soils typical of such hill slopes is shown in Figure 9.20, and it is reflected in the vegetational zonation of the slopes. Lacking the protective tree canopy, the soils have become severely leached (podsolised), but land use itself can affect vegetation and ultimately soil development. For example, the pattern of land use is generally one of cattle on the lower pastures and extensive sheep grazing on the higher slopes. Sheep, which were introduced by the Cistercian monks in the mediaeval period, are selective grazers, leaving the coarser plants such as bracken to increase. Cattle are much less selective in their grazing, and thus the vegetation cover will differ between sheep and cattle areas (upper slopes and lower slopes) on this basis alone. Abandonment of hill land or less intensive use has also affected soil and vegetational development particularly on the high plateaux. Once deforested, the highest land could only be maintained in pasture by continued manuring and ploughing. When this ceased with land abandonment, leaching, waterlogging and possible ironpan or peat formation followed.

The condition of the uplands has remained largely unchanged over the past 700 years, but now technological man is making his influence felt. For example, 50 per cent of the sheep pastures on the

Figure 9.19 Evidence for a former forest cover on the uplands of the British Isles. The 5000-year-old stump of a pine tree was preserved at the base of a peat bog on what is now a bleak moor.

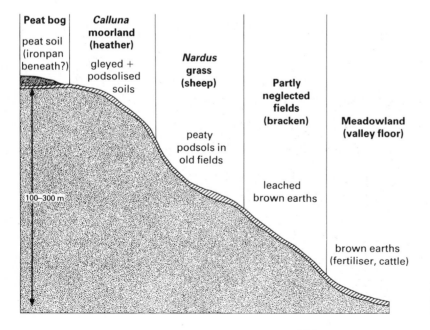

Figure 9.20 Soil and vegetational sequences typical of hill slopes in upland Britain.

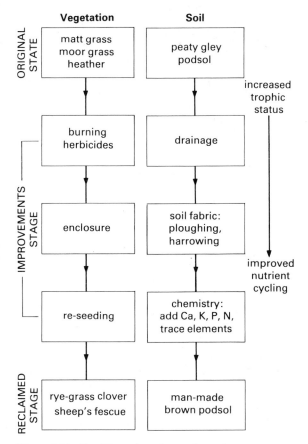

Figure 9.21 Possible reclamation techniques for upland pasture in Britain.

North York Moors have been taken into cultivation or afforested in recent years. Similar reclamation and bog drainage has taken place in other moorland areas. Changing the appearance of these areas is now largely a matter of economic justification as the means to do so are reasonably well understood. Figure 9.21 shows some of these reclamation techniques. The dominance of the less palatable *Nardus* grass rather than *Festuca* and *Agrostis* is due to selective grazing by sheep. Revegetation involves improving soil drainage conditions, altering soil chemistry by adding calcium and phosphorus and then either cutting or burning the vegetation. Re-seeding with rye-grass and clover then follows. The future of the moorlands will be decided by the outcome of the struggle between the farming community and those who wish to preserve this part of the 'natural' heritage.

9.4.7   The Scottish Highlands

Britain's only 'wilderness' area is the Scottish Highlands. Scenically magnificent with its windswept heather moors and bare mountains, it is now beginning to revert to the character it possessed before human interference began.

Four thousand years ago the Highlands were thickly forested with Scots pine. Despite the deteriorating climate, the forest cover maintained

Figure 9.22 Remnants of the original Caledonian forest of the Scottish Highlands at Glen Tanar, Aberdeenshire. (Photograph courtesy of the Nature Conservancy Council.)

itself as the tree litter returned nutrients to the soil, and deep roots helped to prevent waterlogging. Even before Roman times forest clearance had started, fire being the main method. Deforestation continued under the Vikings and later, to allow the cattle-based economy to develop and in order to smoke out enemies from their retreats. Wildlife changed as large open areas were created: the last wolf was killed in 1680. In recent times the demands of the two world wars saw the virtual completion of removal of the original forest (Fig. 9.22). Tree felling produced more extreme results in the Highlands than anywhere else in Britain due to the wetter and colder climate.

As soils degenerated from brown earths to podsolics to peaty podsols, so the forest flora disappeared to be replaced by the monotonous, limited flora of very acid soils. The grouse and the red deer adapted well to the new habitat and new bird species colonised the moors. Following the mass evictions of crofters came the armies of sheep whose grazing ensured the maintenance of moorland conditions. Today only small patches of original Caledonian forest remain, mainly in uneconomic, small clumps on isolated islands. Their persistence and the higher fertility of the soil in which they grow because of nutrient recycling demonstrates that forest can still prosper under the climatic conditions of the Highlands.

Recently tree plantations have begun to be made in the Highlands. Pine and birch have been planted in the drier east, and lodgepole pine and spruce in the damper areas. The soil has become too impoverished over the treeless centuries to support the original forest type. Even with the soil improvements mentioned earlier, the man-imposed forest has to be at a lower seral level than the climatic climax vegetation (Ch. 4). Originally, vast plantations of single tree species were made, giving a dark, dreary landscape. Now a policy of more diverse plantings is being adopted. The new forests have encouraged wildlife immigration including many insect species, birds such as whinchats and in the undergrowth several small mammals. Predators such as the fox, wildcat and owl have followed. Deer damage in the forest encourages the formation of natural clearings which support a more complex ecology. Thinning of the trees after 25 years allows more sunlight to reach the ground and a thicker under-layer of shrubs, brambles and herbs to generate. Slowly, the soil will respond to these changes in vegetation and microclimate and begin its laborious climb

towards greater fertility. Thus a man-made cycle is beginning to close upon itself in the Highlands.

9.5 Amazonia

In the British Isles the assault on nature by man has extended over several thousand years, though with an increasing intensity. There is one area of the world where the natural landscape is being changed out of all recognition, and at a breathtaking pace. Until a few decades ago, the dense rainforests of the Amazon basin were almost wholly undisturbed. The inhabitants were small groups of people living at a mesolithic or neolithic level of culture. As was the case in Britain 5000 years ago, the tribes of the Amazon today are highly adapted to their environment, bending with it rather than seeking to dominate. An example of this harmonious relationship with nature is the practice of swidden agriculture. Swiddens are forest clearings, usually made by burning, that are cultivated for a few years and then abandoned. Minimal disturbance to the environment occurs and seedlings are often 'dibbed' – pushed into the ground without disturbing the layer of ash and residual vegetation in the clearings. Swidden agriculture cannot support population densities in the rainforests of greater than $c.$ 10 people per km². The forest clearings will revert to rainforest provided that they are not too large and provided that the soil has not been exposed to direct sunlight for too long a period. It may take 100 years for a clearing to fully revegetate.

This pattern of land use began to change when colonists first penetrated Amazonia in the 19th century. The major impact, however, has come much more recently with systematic economic exploitation of the region for timber and agricultural land. The culture of the people is being changed from neolithic to modern in an instant. Environmentally, one of the world's most fragile and important zones is being subjected to apparently irresistible technological pressure in what is probably the greatest single landscape transformation that man has yet carried out.

The tropical rainforests have been described as 'forested deserts'. The regions have the greatest input of solar energy of any climatic zone; they have abundant year-round rainfall. They are the most productive terrestrial ecosystem on Earth (a productivity two to three times greater than for temperate forest) with an immensely complicated system of balances between the large number of

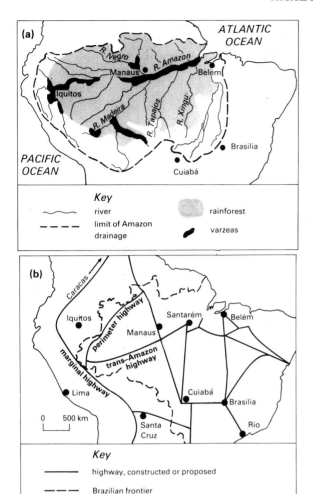

Figure 9.23 The development of Amazonia.

Therefore, the soils are almost barren, though the operation of the rainforest ecosystem disguises this fact very successfully. The luxuriant vegetation creates an illusion of fertility in the soil, but nowhere else on Earth is the relationship between vegetation and soil so weak. The microclimate created by the forest is also very important. Annual rainfall of 1800–3500 mm and temperatures consistently in excess of 30°C would rapidly convert the soil into a sterile laterite if the vegetation cover did not exist. Deforestation in these areas exposes the soil to direct sun over large areas and also removes the greater part of the area's nutrient store. Predictably, the results are dramatic.

The Amazon basin (Fig. 9.23) contains by far the largest remaining undisturbed area of tropical rainforest. The true rainforest occurs on the better drained areas (terra firme), and on the wetter floodplain environments (varzea) a lesser vegetation such as mangrove prevails. In terms of agriculture the varzea are potentially more productive areas as they are periodically flooded and alluvium is deposited.

Extensive forest clearance in Amazonia began at the turn of the century in the Bragantina zone in eastern Brazil. Clearance along the Belem to Braganca railway provided 12 000 ha of land for new settlers to farm. Within a few years much of the land had been abandoned, the soils exhausted. Today it is an area of poverty and economic and social stagnation, covered in a scanty secondary scrub vegetation. Table 9.2 explains why the land was abandoned so quickly – the loss of nutrients by

plant and animal species. Yet the rainforests' system for cycling and storing the great quantities of energy differs from that prevailing elsewhere in the world. A very high proportion of nutrients are stored in the vegetation rather than in the soil and the recycling system is almost closed (Fig. 2.3). Indeed, some of the nutrient cycling is quite independent of the soil. There are epiphytes, plants that live attached to trees, deriving their nutrients from fallen leaves and rain caught in their network of aerial roots. On the ground, nutrients are derived from the shallow litter layer by fungi which then pass nutrients directly to plant roots. The effect of these short circuits is that little leaching of chemicals occurs through the soil and hence to the rivers.

Table 9.2 Decline in soil nutrient status (fertility) following clearance of tropical rainforest and the use of the land for agriculture. Phosphorus and organic levels increase initially due to burning, but subsequent decline in fertility is rapid. Loss of cation exchange capacity (ability to store nutrients) is immediate due to leaching.

| Land use | Soil characteristics (%) | | | |
	Organic content	Cation exchange capacity	Nitrogen	Phosphorus
virgin forest	100	100	100	100
1 year after clearance (unused)	104	82	66	120
after 2 years of cultivation	46	51	36	75

intense leaching is very rapid. Soil fertility may decline by as much as 80 per cent within a few years of forest clearance. Soil erosion may also remove the topsoil particles, adding to river sediment and thereby affecting the fluvial system and the river ecosystem. Rates of erosion even on gentle slopes have increased thirtyfold. Increased rates of runoff from cleared areas may cause Amazon floods to increase in both magnitude and frequency, and although clear data is not yet available, flooding at Manaus is thought to have increased considerably since 1976.

A simplified illustration of the chain effects induced by deforestation is given in Figure 9.24. The degradation sequence may take only a few years; regeneration may take thousands of years.

Although the Amazon basin is shared between eight nations, by far the largest area lies within Brazil. Only 4 per cent of Brazil's population lives within the 40 per cent of the country occupied by Amazonia. In an attempt to exploit what they regard as a 'resource frontier', the government agency SUDAM has co-ordinated a vast scheme designed to open up Amazonia to settlement, industry and agriculture. Central to the policy is the construction, begun in 1970, of a network of highways criss-crossing the Amazon basin. The extent of the proposed road system is shown in Figure 9.23b. The trans-Amazon highway, 5400 km long, is to link Joao Pessoa in the north-east with the Peruvian frontier in the west and a north–south highway (1670 km long) will lead from the port of Santorem on the Amazon to Cuiaba in the Mato Grosso. In total some 14 000 km of roads are planned. Swathes, 70 m wide, are cut through the forest for the highways, and a 100-km-deep strip on either side of the route is designated for agricultural development. Timber is the first target of the developers, but when the trees are gone much of the land is used for ranching, especially in the south-east, closest to the markets. Although the varzea environment is better suited to agriculture, it is on the potentially barren soils of the terra firme that virtually all the ranching and plantation has taken place. A sequence of cut–burn–grass is extending over larger and larger areas. Unless great care is taken during this sequence (for example, by sowing European grass species that protect the land effectively), leaching and erosion follows and the productivity of the pasture falls. Within the first 3–4 years that ranching has been practised, cattle

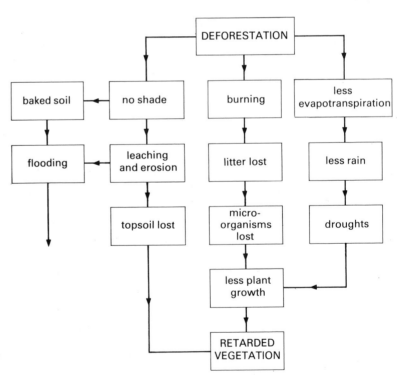

Figure 9.24 The consequences of removal of tropical rainforest.

stocking rates have declined from 2 to 0.5 head/ha. Thereafter, stocking capacities fall at approximately 5 per cent per year. The original area of rainforest was approximately 280 million ha. During the 1960s clearance took place at over 1 million ha per year, but by the mid-1970s the rate was greater than 5 million ha per year.

Amazonia represents man's first, and perhaps last, real chance to develop a vast land area using an ecologically as well as an economically based developmental model. The Brazilian government has shown an apparent concern that the Amazon basin should not be pillaged. In theory there are strict rules governing exploitation: for example, at least a 50 per cent forest cover should be maintained within developed zones. Ideas abound as to how the land should be managed. The methods suggested include the use of organic manures (artificial fertilisers are not retained by the soil); maintenance of a cover of perennial crops; plantation forestry; indigenous crops; natural pesticides; and mixed cropping using small land units. Unfortunately, such is the complexity of the tropical rainforest in terms of natural cycles and interactions, and such is the lack of base-line data concerning the environment, that the best approach to the problem of the development is far from clear.

The prophets of doom have been very active in Amazonia, with various predictions of what might happen if most of the forests are destroyed. Some of the theories are described below. The great number of plant species in Amazonia means that the numbers of any one type of plant in an area are limited. This means that plant-specific diseases or pests are kept severely in check. A change to plantation-type agriculture might allow a population explosion of particular insects or viruses. Similarly, many of the native plants produce repellant or toxic chemicals to ward off predators or disease. These natural defence mechanisms, suited to the environment, would be lost were the species to be eliminated. Amazonia is the world's greatest genetic pool and once species are eliminated they are totally non-renewable.

The most profound consequences of deforestation, though also the most speculative, concern possible changes in the atmosphere. Complete loss of forest and its replacement by scrub would probably increase CO_2 levels by up to 10 per cent and oxygen output to the atmosphere would lessen. It does not seem likely that either effect would be very significant on a global scale. More important would be the change in albedo (reflectivity) that would result from such a change in vegetation cover. The forests reflect back c. 7 per cent of solar energy, whereas a barren scrubland would reflect c. 25 per cent. A computer study suggests that the surface cooling that would occur, together with decreased evaporation, would lessen the upward rise of air in equatorial regions and so cause cooling in the mid and upper troposphere and with steeper lapse rates prevailing. The model predicts 1.5–2.5 per cent more precipitation between latitudes 5–28° north and south, and less precipitation (due to the weakened convection) between latitudes 45°–85° north and 40°–60° south.

These ideas are speculative and may be wildly inaccurate. However, large-scale modifications to the rainforests, part of the engine room of global climate, are likely to provoke changes for better or worse that will be beyond man's power to control once they are set in motion.

10 The urban–industrial environment

10.1 Introduction

Urban–industrial areas represent man's most profound modification of the Earth's surface, of the atmosphere above it and of the ecosystem within it. Unlike the effects of agricultural activity, urban effects are highly intensive and localised. Urban areas are zones of concentrated energy and mass flows, the energy largely being imported from elsewhere. As the energy and mass is used, it reverts to an unconcentrated, diffuse state expressed as heat and wastes. Some 12 per cent of England and Wales is built upon and thereby experiences a degree of direct environmental modification, but much larger areas beyond the concrete landscape are also affected. For example, hydrological changes initiated in the urbanised portion of a river basin may extend up stream and to a much greater extent down stream, possibly altering the functioning of the whole basin. Climatic changes are most obvious in the shallow dome of air immediately above a city, but prevailing winds carry a plume of altered air many kilometres down wind of the source region. Ecological changes induced by polluted or otherwise disturbed environments extend well beyond urban limits.

Virtually all aspects of the environment are changed by urbanisation and industrialisation including landforms, land use, vegetation, fauna, hydrology and climate. In general, the degree of change is associated with the building density (surface area per unit planar area) and with the extent of industrialisation, particularly extractive or heavy manufacturing activity. A gradient of severity of change runs from the rural hinterland through suburbia to the central business district or

Figure 10.1 The urban environment – downtown Chicago.

to the industrial core of the city (Fig. 10.1). Low profile, sprawling urban areas with many green spaces normally modify the environment less than compact, high-rise or highly industrialised centres.

Many of the deflections, accentuations or diminutions of natural processes that are associated with the urban–industrial environment have been described in the earlier chapters of this book, and the remainder of this chapter is concerned with summarising such changes with reference to particular case studies.

10.2   Urban hydrology

10.2.1   Introduction

Although urban areas rarely occupy more than a small percentage of a major river catchment, the changes in hydrological regime may be sufficiently great to extend over a far wider area. This is especially the case if the city is located in the middle or upper part of the basin thus allowing urban-induced flooding and water pollution to affect the downstream zone. The behaviour of small streams lying wholly within the built-up area may be profoundly distorted, whereas large rivers flowing through a city will be less affected. The main differences between the hydrology of rural and urban areas is outlined in Chapter 6 (Fig. 6.5). The intensity of change is dependent on two factors: first, the proportion of the basin that is rendered impermeable by construction, and secondly, the nature of the artificial (drain and sewer) drainage system installed. Doubling the impermeable area within a basin in a British environment increases direct (rapid) runoff by 25–50 per cent. A direct consequence of this increased runoff is the need to provide extensive artificial drainage channels to concentrate and dispose of the excess water. Such conduits range from the guttering on individual houses to large trunk storm sewers beneath the streets. Urban drainage densities are three to 10 times greater than those for the rural surroundings. Milwaukee in the USA, with a city area of $246\,km^2$, contains $60\,km$ of natural river channel but $2200\,km$ of artificial channel. Thus individual water droplets have less distance to travel before reaching a channel than would be the case in rural areas, and this combined with the greater quantity of rapid runoff causes more severe flooding and lower dry weather flows in an urbanised catchment. Hydrological processes contributing to slow flows of water to a river such as soil infiltration, through-flow and groundwater recharge are minimised.

Alterations in water quality are almost inevitable in urban areas. Constructional activity increases sediment and dissolved load 50- to 100-fold; industrial and sewage effluents raise both chemical and organic concentrations in rivers (Fig. 10.2). The headwaters of the River Trent are almost wholly located within the West Midlands conurbation and their flow regime and water quality is determined by man. The River Tame summer flow is 95 per cent effluent where it leaves the urban area, and it renders the Trent lifeless

Figure 10.2 A small river in an urban area showing canalisation and the bed and bank forms created by great variations in river flow.

Table 10.1 Effects of urbanisation on the functioning of various aspects of hydrology. (+ denotes increased effects; − denotes decreased effects.)

	Hydrological processes affected					
Urban processes	Infiltration	Water-table level	Floods	Low flows	Suspended solids	Diss. solids
land clearance; dereliction	− −	−	+ +	− −	+ + +	+ +
buildings; roads	− − −	− − −	+ + +	− − −	+	+
sewage effluent; waste disposal					+ + +	+ + +
storm sewers; channel modification; flood protection	−	−	+ +	− −	+	+

until diluted with the cleaner waters of the Derbyshire Dove and Derwent between Burton and Derby. Further down stream the Trent again deteriorates in quality and is completely deoxygenated in the Humber estuary.

Extractive industry has similar effects on water quality if it is located close to the stream course. Strip mining may cause both sedimentological and chemical contamination, and underground extraction of coal often leads to acid mine drainage entering the rivers, for example as in South Wales. The overall effects of urbanisation and industry on the hydrology of an area are summarised in Table 10.1.

10.2.2 Harlow New Town
The construction of a completely new town at Harlow in a previously rural area of Essex has imposed considerable changes on the small (21 km²) basin of the Canon's Brook. The catchment is underlain by almost impermeable London Clay and lies at an altitude of 36–110 m OD. The Canon's Brook catchment and the stages of urbanisation are shown in Figure 10.3a. Although some road and sewer construction took place in 1951 and 1952, urbanisation proper dates from 1953 as do measurable hydrological changes. By 1960, 10 per cent of the area was covered in concrete or tarmac and by 1968, 16.6 per cent, though 80 per cent of the catchment was considered to be 'urbanised'.

The fact that Harlow is a 'green' city and that it is underlain by impermeable rock has minimised the hydrological effects of construction, but the alterations, particularly in flow characteristics, are still apparent. Figure 10.3b shows the monthly maximum floods during the period of construction. Flow peaks become progressively higher and more abrupt and the moving mean (shaded) indicates the overall trend of increasing flood flow – a two-fold increase since 1951. The unit hydrographs

(Fig. 10.3c) summarise the changes in river flow in response to a single storm event (5 mm of effective rainfall falling in 1 h) at various stages in the urbanisation process. Peak discharges have increased by 460 per cent, time taken to reach peak flow has halved, as has the duration of the individual flood events. All these changes reflect the increase in, and more rapid transmission of, runoff. The effects on flow in the Canon's Brook are much greater in summer than winter. In summer much of the rain falling in a rural basin is stored by the soil and subsequently used by vegetation, whereas in winter the ground may already be saturated, allowing a higher proportion of rain to run off to the river. In the urban environment, conditions vary much less between the seasons because of the high proportion of impermeable area.

10.3 Urban climate

10.3.1 Introduction
The impact of man upon the atmosphere as described in Chapter 5 was seen to be difficult to demonstrate and often speculative except on a very small scale. The exception to this is the urban environment where man-induced changes are measurable and distinctive. Cities are overlain by their own 'climatic dome' within which properties of atmospheric content, temperature, moisture and wind are all deviations to some extent from the prevailing regional climate. Over a major city of a million inhabitants or more the altered climate extends upwards for 50–300 m and for tens of kilometres down wind.

Changes in albedo and modifications of wind flow were described in Chapter 5 in respect of a single building. Cities amplify and complicate these effects on a large scale, but they are significant sources of heat in themselves as a result of the

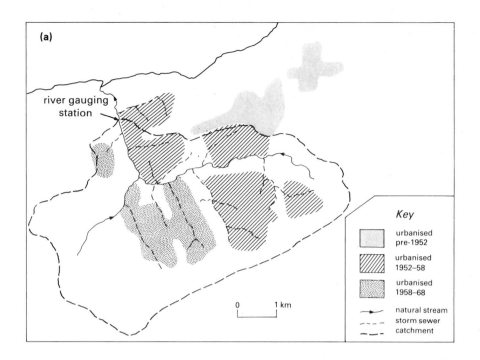

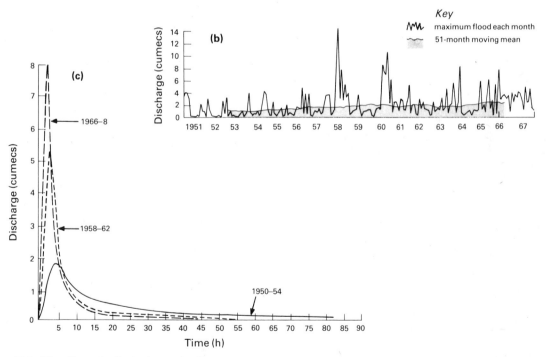

Figure 10.3 The effects of urbanisation on the Canon's Brook catchment, Harlow New Town. (a) The Canon's Brook catchment and the growth of Harlow New Town. (b) The maximum monthly floods in the Canon's Brook 1951–68 and the 51-month moving mean for the maximum monthly flood. (c) Mean unit hydrographs for the Canon's Brook catchment at various stages of urbanisation. (After Hollis 1974.)

Table 10.2 Modification of the regional climate of a large, industrialised urban area.

Aspect of climate		Degree of change
atmospheric composition	nuclei of condensation	+ 1000%
	emission gases	+ 1500%
temperature	solar radiation	− 10%
	annual mean temperature	+ 1°C
	winter minimum temperature	+ 1.5°C
precipitation	annual precipitation	+ 5%
	trace rain days	+ 10%
wind	mean wind speed	− 20%
	calm days	+ 10%
others	ultraviolet radiation (winter)	− 30%
	relative humidity (summer)	− 10%
	fog (winter)	+ 100%

import and combustion of fossil fuels in large quantities. Although the overall production of artificial heat by man is very slight, on a local scale the heat output is significant. The Ruhr–Antwerp–Namur industrial belt emits 17 langleys/day over an area of 500 000 km². Manhattan, the extreme example of urbanisation, produces 250 langleys/day. In these instances heat production is sufficiently great to generate atmospheric processes such as convective plumes, and climatic responses such as warmer temperatures and less precipitation in the form of snow.

Atmospheric changes in both gaseous and aerosol terms are greater above urban areas than elsewhere, though this has less effect on the climate of the actual city than does the altered nature of the ground surface. Atmospheric changes are thought to be responsible for changes in the pattern of solar radiation reaching the ground in cities and perhaps for increased rainfall in urban regions. A summary of the types and order of magnitude of changes associated with the urban–industrial environment are given in Table 10.2, and examples of alterations in climate in the succeeding sections.

10.3.2 The London heat island

In common with other large cities London's pall of combustion products causes haze and screens out sunshine. Compared with the rural surroundings, the outer London suburbs receive 16 minutes less sunshine per day, the inner suburbs 25 minutes less, and the central area 44 minutes less. This loss is, however, more than compensated for by artificially produced heat. The mean annual

temperature is 11°C in central London, 10°C in suburbia and 9.6°C in the countryside. The effect is most marked at night when temperatures are on average 2°C warmer in the centre. The large number of days in the year with temperatures close to freezing in southeastern England means that one effect of London's warmer climate is greatly to reduce the number of frost and snow occurrences – it has a 2-month longer frost-free season than the surrounding country and a 50-day longer growing season.

London's heat island is thus a marked feature of its urban climate, although it alters in size and intensity with season and meteorological conditions. The central area is distinctly warmer than its surroundings all year round, but the suburban heat island is greatest in winter when domestic fuel consumption is greatest. The heat island is thought to extend for approximately 150 m vertically. Figure 10.4 shows the form of the heat island on 14 May 1959 when it was particularly well developed under the clear skies and gentle breezes associated with an anticyclone. The temperature difference between the rural surroundings and central London is 8°C, and the shape of the heat island faithfully reflects the degree of urbanisation. The steep temperature gradient between the densely populated suburbs of East Ham and West

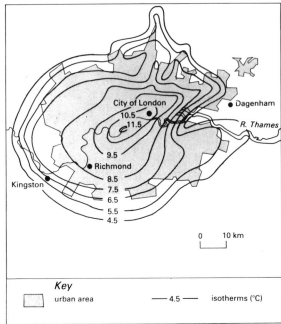

Figure 10.4 The London heat island on the night of 14 May 1959. Isotherms at 1°C intervals. (After Chandler 1965.)

Ham and the Thames marshes on the eastern side of the map is very obvious – the gradient is much greater than is usual in a natural warm or cold front. Thermal gradients are more gentle to the west and south where the urban–rural transition is less abrupt. To the north a tongue of warm air extends up the Lea valley through Poplar, Tottenham and Enfield.

10.3.3 Rainfall in the Houston area
The tendency of large industrial urban areas to trigger precipitation in their vicinity is well demonstrated by the example of Houston in Texas. Located on the flat, uniform plains of the Gulf of Mexico, Houston has experienced great expansion of population and industry in recent decades and a corresponding increase in rainfall. In eastern Texas rainfall decreases from east to west and so isohyets run roughly north–south as is shown in Figure 10.5 for the year 1908. This rainfall pattern has locally been progressively modified to a cellular pattern centred to the north and west of Houston as is shown in the subsequent rainfall maps. Rainfall amounts in the urban area have

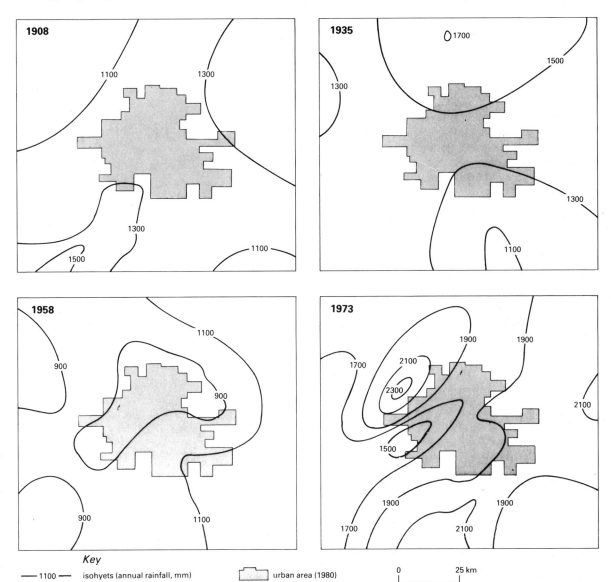

Figure 10.5 Changes in the annual pattern and amount of rainfall in the Houston, Texas area, 1908–73. (After Goldman 1976.)

123

increased by over 1000 mm in some instances. Although there is an area of heavy industry to the east (upwind) of the city emitting aerosol pollutants, it seems likely that the deflection of air by the numerous high-rise buildings in central Houston have been at least as important in provoking this change in rainfall pattern.

10.3.4 Photochemical smog, California

The nature of the changes in atmospheric composition above a city vary. In British cities emissions from the combustion of coal predominate, sometimes creating the impenetrable urban fogs (smogs) of winter. California with its great number of cars and its brilliant sunshine experiences the photochemical smogs containing PAN (Ch. 5) derived from emissions of oxides of nitrogen. Such emissions quadrupled in quantity between 1940 and 1970 necessitating the stringent emission controls now enforced in California.

Figure 10.6 shows the extent and severity of photochemical smog in the early 1960s. The two major population centres, San Francisco and Los Angeles, were most severely affected, but some 60 per cent of the state was affected to some extent.

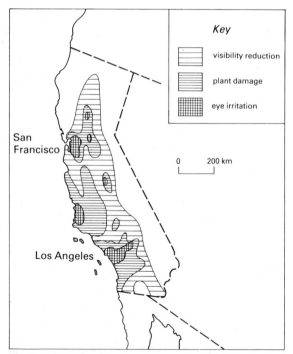

Figure 10.6 The extent and severity of photochemical pollution of the atmosphere, California, 1961–3. (After Leighton 1966. Reprinted from the *Geographical Review*, vol. 56, 1966, with the permission of the American Geographical Society.)

Plant damage due to the chemicals in the air was experienced over some 30 000 km². Los Angeles is particularly liable to severe photochemical smogs as it is located in a broad natural basin subject to temperature inversions and with low wind speeds. These factors allow the smog to intensify and concentrate. From an aircraft the city is often invisible by day beneath its pall, while from below the sky may be uniformly grey despite cloudless weather.

10.3.5 Acid rain

The spread of photochemical smog beyond its source area documented above is paralleled and surpassed by the extent of sulphur dioxide contamination derived from industrial emissions. Sulphur dioxide has a short residence time in the atmosphere as it is readily dissolved in water to rain out as dilute sulphuric acid. Such acidification of rain occurs naturally, due primarily to carbon dioxide being dissolved. This would theoretically give rainfall a pH of 5.6, but in practice various basic substances in the atmosphere largely neutralise this effect. Human-generated emissions of sulphur dioxide now exceed natural, volcanic emissions by a factor of 100. Indeed, one 400-m-high stack at Sudbury in Canada emits as much sulphur dioxide annually as all natural sources combined. However, natural emission of sulphur as hydrogen sulphide is probably comparable with artificial sulphur emissions. Sulphur dioxide output doubled between 1960 and 1980, but equally important has been the use of very high chimney stacks (180 m or more high) which, while lessening atmospheric pollution in the immediate vicinity, allow the gas to reach the middle levels of the troposphere and so to be transported over long distances.

The effect has been an increase in the acidity of rainfall in recent years. Prior to the Industrial Revolution rain was neutral in reaction over much of the Earth, but now global rain is five to 30 times more acidic and locally 100–1000 times more acidic (1–3 pH units). The most extreme recorded example of acid rain was a storm at Pitlochry in Scotland on 10 April 1974, when the rain at the start of the storm had a pH of 2.4, the equivalent of vinegar. Areas down wind of industrial concentrations experience the maximum effect, but areas affected, as well as degrees of acidity, have increased in recent years. Figure 10.7a shows the patterns of acid rain over northwestern Europe in 1956 and in 1974. The extension of the affected zone from Benelux and Germany to include

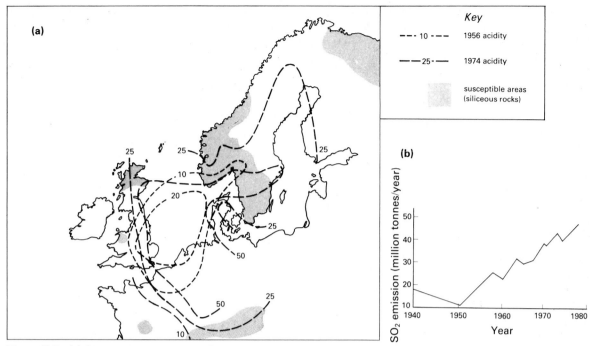

Figure 10.7 (a) Concentration of acid rain over western Europe in 1956 and 1974 compared with (b) emissions of sulphur dioxide. Acidity isolines are expressed in terms of microequivalents of hydrogen ions per litre of precipitation. (From *Acid rain* (G. E. Likens *et al.*), copyright © 1979 by Scientific American, Inc. All rights reserved.)

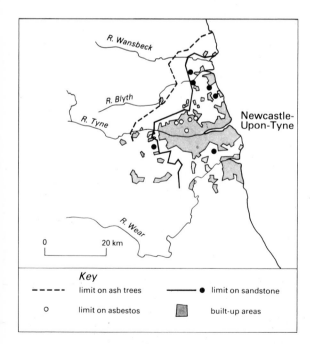

Figure 10.8 The limits of the lichen desert due to sulphur dioxide pollution around Newcastle upon Tyne. (After Gilbert 1970. This figure first appeared in *New Scientist*, London, the weekly review of science and technology.)

Scandinavia and northern France is apparent, as is the rise in acidity. Even higher acidities occur in the north-east of the USA. The increasing rate of SO_2 emission in Europe is shown in Figure 10.7b.

In urban and suburban areas acid rain accelerates chemical weathering – mainly of buildings and particularly if they are made of limestone. The weathering may be by direct solution or by formation and precipitation of calcium sulphate which can accelerate salt-crystal weathering of building materials. Surrounding the immediate urban area is a zone in which the effects of acid rain are also acute, impinging on a rural rather than an urban environment. In Britain such 'fallout' zones extend for tens or hundreds of kilometres beyond the primary emission sources of London, the Midlands, Lancashire, South Yorkshire, the north-east of England and central Scotland. Concentration of sulphur in the soils is greatly in excess of the natural supply from atmospheric and chemical weathering sources, and much exceeds the capacity of plants and decomposing bacteria to process it. Large sulphur concentrations acidify the soil and stunt the growth of many species of plant. Lichens and bryophytes (mosses and liverworts) are particularly sensitive to atmospheric

125

sulphur dioxide and, indeed, they may be used as indicators of the concentration of the gas. Figure 10.8 shows the inner limits of the grey lichen *Parmelia saxatilis* on different surfaces (ash trees, sandstone and asbestos) around the Newcastle-upon-Tyne conurbation. The lichen desert extends furthest beyond the source area to the downwind (southeastern) side and in all some 1000 km² are lichen-free.

Tyneside is one likely source for the acid rain that falls on Scandinavia. The effect of the precipitation upon soils, rivers and lakes is greatest in areas of acid (siliceous) rocks and thin soils where buffering ability is minimal. Such a situation applies over large areas of Scandinavia and has led to a marked increase in the acidity of runoff water in mountainous regions, pH values of under 5.0 being recorded in rivers and lakes over an area of 33 000 km² in southern Norway. The effect has been to cause regression of aquatic ecosystems, inhibiting organic decomposition and in extreme cases killing fish, and affecting the whole food chain. It is estimated that rain with a pH of 4.3 will bring lake pH values to 5.0 in the long term where natural carbonate levels are low (under 2 mg/l) Acid rain also stunts the growth of conifers, the

dominant forest trees of the region. As sulphur dioxide emissions will probably increase by 10–20 per cent by the end of the century, the effects of acid rain are likely to become greater in the foreseeable future. Remedial measures such as the addition of lime to affected rivers are already being undertaken in some areas.

10.4 Urban–industrial landscapes

10.4.1 Introduction

Both urbanisation and extractive industry involve the alteration of landforms, but industry in particular is responsible for the creation of derelict land (no longer used) as a result of quarrying, open-cast mining (Fig. 10.9), spoil heaps (Fig. 10.10), abandonment of buildings or indirectly via land subsidence. In mainland Britain 50 000 ha are classified as derelict and an equal area as 'disturbed' (greatly modified but still used), and the total is increasing by 1500 ha per year.

Dereliction is an extreme change in land use and landform. The landscape may be one of artificial pits, levelled ground and tip heaps surfaced with broken rock, cinder or waste (Fig. 10.11). The

Figure 10.9 One of the world's largest man-made excavations, almost 1 km in diameter – a copper mine in Arizona, USA.

Figure 10.10 Spoil heaps at Bethesda slate quarries in North Wales. The tips form the terraces in the centre of the picture and beyond are the mountains of Snowdonia.

Figure 10.11 Derelict land resulting from coal mining and steel making in Ebbwr Vale, South Wales. The small plantation of trees at centre-right of the photograph is evidence of some degree of reclamation of the spoil heaps.

ecology is similarly transformed to an urban eco-system of the type described in Section 10.5 or, if the wastes are toxic to plants, to a desert. The geomorphic processes operating in such areas are often similar to those in arid regions, as the absence of vegetation leads to extensive gully and

wind erosion as any tip heap will demonstrate. Microclimates in this environment are extreme and again desert-like.

Areas of extreme dereliction may be beyond the threshold of recovery at least for the immediate future and a second round of human intervention often follows, largely for aesthetic purposes, in order to allow and accelerate recovery. In fact, what is created usually bears only a fleeting re-semblance to the original environment as the ground is landscaped, topsoil laid down and vegetation that can survive in the restricted en-vironment planted.

In zones of concentrations of heavy industry, ecological dereliction often extends well beyond the immediate area. Acid rain is an example and, in the case of the Sudbury area mentioned in the previous section, smelter fumes have inhibited growth of vegetation for tens of kilometres around the source region, killing more sensitive plant species. Trunk roads are linear extensions of the urban–industrial complex in this sense. Vehicle-exhaust emissions and spillages on road verges cause build-ups of toxic materials, particularly heavy metals such as cadmium, zinc and nickel, in the soil to five to fifteen times natural levels.

10.4.2 Dereliction and reclamation in the Potteries

The Stoke-on-Trent area has suffered more than most urban centres from dereliction: by 1970, 7 per cent of the city area was in this category, the heritage of the clay and coal industries. The most severely disfigured areas include tips, pits, waste-dumps and subsidence hollows.

Land reclamation has been underway since the late 1960s and is attempting to turn the man-made deserts into man-determined 'parks' in which soils, vegetation, landforms and hydrology are all artificially induced. For example, the Central Forest Park near Hanley was one of the most totally derelict areas. Within its 52 ha were 100-m-high spoil heaps, the waste material from coal mining, and deep flooded marl pits. Tip slopes have been graded, a thin topsoil layer spread and grass species tolerant of the acid, metal-rich substrate planted. Shrubs and birch trees are the successional vegetation planted as the soil 'normalises', and in the future a full deciduous tree cover may be possible perhaps allowing a reversion to the oak forest that covered the area two centuries ago. The marl pits are now lakes and a limited aquatic ecosystem is building up.

10.5 Urban–industrial ecology

10.5.1 Introduction

The prime characteristic of urban areas – high intensity of change – is also apparent with respect to ecosystems. The city is, of course, a complex human ecosystem, but far from being a biological desert for other life-forms it creates, deliberately or accidentally, a variety of environments that are colonised by living creatures. Some of these environments are variants of natural conditions (gardens and parks), but others are completely unnatural. Adaptable species can survive in the city and in some instances may proliferate as do rats, mice and houseflies. Plants such as willow-herb rapidly invade disturbed ground, a ubiquitous feature of urban areas undergoing construction. In rural areas such a niche is comparatively rare. Some 40 ha of central London was turned into rubble by bombing in the Second World War. Within a few years the number of flowering plant species in the area was four times greater than the pre-war level, as wild plants as well as garden escapees such as wallflowers and buddleia prospered on the uncolonised 'soil'.

In Europe, urban fox populations may be higher than rural populations as the fox finds scavenging sufficient to survive. In North America, urban skunks are equally common.

A further distortion of natural ecosystems is the advantage conferred on life-forms that can survive under particularly severe environmental stress. Thus rivers in urban–industrial areas are usually low in dissolved oxygen, heavily polluted with sediment and dissolved load and often eutrophic. Only a restricted spectrum of aquatic life can tolerate this environment. Prior to the Industrial Revolution, the River Thames in London contained a wide variety of fish species: 3.5 tonnes of salmon were caught annually until 1825. As water quality declined, so fish stocks declined in number and variety until eels which are more tolerant of pollution, became the dominant species. Since attempts have been made to improve water quality in the lower Thames, the aquatic ecosystem has gradually become richer once more. The corollary of the above is that intolerant species (for example, the lichens described in Sec. 10.3.5) cannot live in the city environment. Evergreen trees fare badly in the dusty air as the particles accumulate on the leaf surfaces. As London expanded, so the pine trees at the Royal Botanical Gardens at Kew, 15 km from the centre of London, had to be moved further out of the city in order to survive.

10.5.2 The peppered moth

The peppered moth (*Biston betularia*) has adapted rapidly to the deposits of sooty grime in and around the industrial cities of Britain. The moth's main protection against predators is camouflage, a patchy grey-brown colouration that blends well with the lichen-covered tree trunks that are its commonest resting place. As urban and suburban tree trunks became blackened with aerosols from industrial sources, the original camouflage became ineffective and lighter coloured moths became easy prey for birds. Between 1850 and 1900 a dark version of the moth, invisible on black surfaces, came to predominate in industrial areas, while in rural areas they remained a rarity.

This may be an instance of accelerated natural selection in response to the great environmental change brought about by man. With the establishment of smokeless zones and the enacting of anti-air pollution measures in recent years, the number of dark moths has fallen; apparently a direct response to the diminution in sooty environments.

11 Conclusions

11.1 Man's impact on the Earth

It is apparent that man has now modified almost all of the aspects of his habitat. The degree of modification is in part determined by the perceived need for change and in part by the sensitivity or degree of resiliance of the particular facet of the environment. Until the upsurge of industry and technology during the 19th century, habitat change was largely the product or by-product of agricultural activities and so water, soil and vegetation were most affected. Nowadays, the workings of the atmospheric and oceanic systems are also being affected by man, and the extent and intensity of imposed change on the hydrological and biological environments has greatly increased. The high degree of linkage between components of the natural world, emphasised throughout this book, makes possible for the first time, global and uncontrollable environmental change triggered by human action. Only the lithosphere and lithospheric processes such as plate tectonics remain beyond man's capacity to alter significantly, though not beyond his imagination: ideas have been put forward for 'lubricating' the San Andreas fault in California, for example, to lessen earthquake impact.

Man is now an 'unpredictable' species in the sense that his behaviour is not necessarily a response or adaptation to his surroundings in the manner of other organisms. Increasing use of energy transferred by man, particularly nuclear fuels, and developments such as genetic engineering hold out as a real possibility the almost total divorce of at least a part of the human race from its natural environment. The **econosphere** (economic world) will be wholly separate from the ecosphere.

11.2 The future

A great deal of the interest in man–environment relations, reflected in this book, has been generated by the obvious adverse effects of some human activity on the Earth. 'Adverse' in this context relates to human well-being. Only a proportion of man's actions have led to undesirable consequences, nearly always as secondary results of some other action. However, as the doomsday prophets point out, the scale of man's intervention in natural processes may now be sufficient to provoke catastrophic environmental change on a near-global scale and so a degree of interest in the topic is justified! Such a change is likely to be the result of the misuse or thoughtless use of technology, but environmental change is also linked to the ever-increasing demand for resources from an ever-increasing population. The term 'resource' has no fixed meaning except as support systems for humans, and therefore it alters with time, technology and culture, but demand for aspects such as energy, land and materials is currently increasing some three times faster than is population. Inevitably, supply will be less than demand at some point in the future, and the awareness is growing that in a finite world, infinite growth is not possible.

Responses to this future vary. A continuation of the exploitation or 'cowboy economy' is still widely regarded as practicable, using the 'technological fix' as a device for overcoming resource depletion or for rectifying environmental damage. The opposite attitude is represented by the advocates of regressive conservation who would wish man to revert to a lesser degree of environmental control and interference. A more balanced conservationist view is that of conservation as the 'wise' use or management of resources, a reconciliation of human requirements with the constraints of the natural environment. This implies an understanding of the workings of the Earth, and eventually the achievement of an equilibrium or steady state global management.

11.3 Investigation of man–environment relationships

The ancient idea of the Earth as a unitary whole with man as an inseparable part of a system in which everything affects everything else has been revived under a scientific rather than a theological or philosophical guise. The concept of man as a custodian of the Earth is again to the fore, due more to self-interest than to a general benevolence towards the natural world. Such a scientific approach requires a knowledge of global distributions of natural phenomena and an awareness of the workings of natural systems, cause and effect chains, and interactions between systems. The political equivalent of the holistic environmental view is the United Nations and similar global or regional politico-economic organisations. Since the Second World War, equivalent organisations, often UN based, have operated environmental data collection and analysis schemes. For example, the United Nations Environmental Programme (UNEP) is responsible for the study of desertification on a world scale, the International Hydrological Programme collects hydrometric information, the International Biological Programme (1964–74) and the Man and Biosphere Programme (Unesco) drew together information on the living world. The idea of the biosphere as the 'ecological buffer' cushioning the atmosphere–lithosphere interface has emphasised its importance and led to extensive international research into its functioning.

Linkages between the human and physical systems have been modelled on the grand scale and used to predict future scenarios, as for example in the UN World Model which divides the globe into 15 regional models, each with 229 variables including measures of economic demand, available resources and pollution generated.

On a humbler scale are studies of the likely effect of particular human activities on aspects of the natural environment, the (optimistic) assumption behind them being that the proposed action

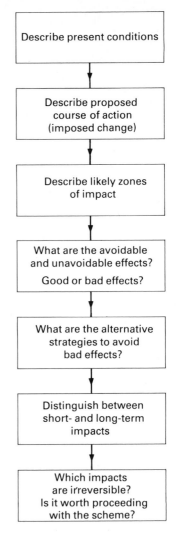

Figure 11.1 Flowchart for the compilation and evaluation of an environmental impact analysis study.

would be modified in the light of any undesirable environmental consequences. The best known method is that of environmental impact analysis (EIA), developed in the United States. It can be applied on a variety of scales – the overall effect of a River Severn estuary barrage or the uprooting of a single hedge on a farm; the building of a chain of nuclear power stations or the draining of a meadow.

The processes involved in environmental impact analysis are shown in Figure 11.1, although the response to the findings are still subject to political and economic considerations as much as scientific logic. Figure 11.2 shows a part of the Leopold

ENVIRONMENTAL IMPACT ANALYSIS

INSTRUCTIONS

1– Identify all actions (located across the top of the matrix) that are part of the proposed project.

2– Under each of the proposed actions, place a slash at the intersection with each item on the side of the matrix if an impact is possible.

3– Having completed the matrix, in the upper left-hand corner of each box with a slash, place a number from 1 to 10 which indicates the MAGNITUDE of the possible impact; 10 represents the greatest magnitude of impact and 1, the least, (no zeroes). Before each number place + if the impact would be beneficial. In the lower right-hand corner of the box place a number from 1 to 10 which indicates the IMPORTANCE of the possible impact (e. g. regional vs. local); 10 represents the greatest importance and 1, the least (no zeroes).

4– The text which accompanies the matrix should be a discussion of the significant impacts, those columns and rows with large numbers of boxes marked and individual boxes with the larger numbers.

SAMPLE MATRIX

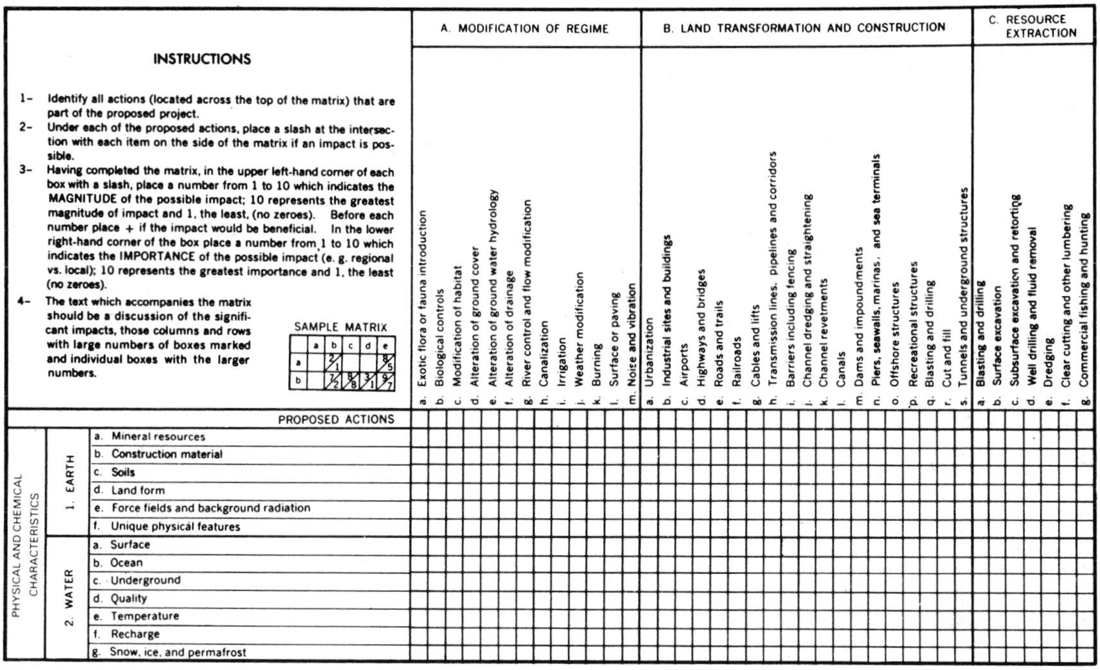

Figure 11.2 A small section of a Leopold environmental impact analysis matrix in which the likely effect of human activities on various aspects of the environment are quantified. (After Leopold *et al.* 1971.)

matrix, one method of impact analysis. The proposed actions are listed on the horizontal axis under general headings such as Resource Extraction, Land Transportation, Resource Renewal, Chemical Treatment, and so forth. In turn, these groupings are subdivided, so under Chemical Treatment, fertiliser, pesticide and herbicide usage would be considered amongst others.

The vertical axis lists factors of the natural and cultural environment such as biological, physical, chemical and aesthetic. Again, these headings are subdivided so that the 'biological' unit includes trees, birds, endangered species and many other categories. The 'cells of interaction' formed by the horizontal and vertical axes are bisected diagonally. In one compartment the magnitude of

the impact is assessed and in the other, significance of the impact, using 1–10 scales in each instance. A positive sign is used if the effect is 'beneficial'. This method gives an overview of the general repercussions on the environment of a single human activity, but it cannot show the series of secondary effects and feedbacks that are equally likely. To model the full effects of even the most uncomplicated of human interventions in the natural environment on anything but the smallest scale would require an analogue of unimaginable complexity.

Perhaps the major limiting factor in the use of such impact analysis studies is the factor that also makes the environmental future so uncertain – man's ignorance of the workings of his world.

Further reading

Because of the wide range of topics covered in this book, most of the books and articles listed below are concerned with particular aspects of the environment (e.g. soils) that have been affected by man. In each case a book that provides a good summary of the principles underlying the topic has been included, together with more advanced texts concerned with man–environment relationships.

General Reading
Arvill, R. 1967. *Man and environment*. London: Penguin.
Detwyler, T. R. 1971. *Man's impact on environment*. New York: McGraw-Hill.
Goudie, A. 1981. *The human impact*. Oxford: Blackwell.
Many relevant articles appear in *Geographical Magazine* and in *Scientific American*.

Chapters 1 and 2
Chorley, R. J. and B. A. Kennedy 1971. *Physical geography: a systems approach*. Englewood Cliffs, NJ: Prentice-Hall.
Haggett, P. 1972. *Geography: a modern synthesis*. New York: Harper & Row.
Odum, E. P. 1976. *Ecology*. New York: Holt, Rinehart & Winston.

Chapter 3
Curtis, F. L. *et al*. 1976. *Soils of the British Isles*. London: Longman.
Knapp, B. 1979. *Soil processes*. London: George Allen & Unwin.
Limbrey, S. 1975. *Soil science and archaeology*. London: Academic Press.

Chapter 4
Bennett, C. F. 1975. *Man and Earth's ecosystems*. New York: Wiley.
Hawksworth, D. L. (ed.). 1974. *The changing flora and fauna of Britain*. London: Academic Press.
Simmons, I. G. 1979. *Biogeography: natural and cultural*. London: Edward Arnold.
Simmons, I. G. 1981. *Biogeographical processes*. London: George Allen & Unwin.

Chapter 5
Breuer, G. 1980. *Weather modification: prospects and problems*. Cambridge: Cambridge University Press.
Hanwell, J. 1980. *Atmospheric processes*. London: George Allen & Unwin.
Matthews, W. H. *et al*. 1971. *Man's impact on climate*. Cambridge, Mass.: MIT Press.

Chapter 6
Chorley, R. J. 1969. *Water, earth and man*. London: Methuen.
Hollis, G. E. (ed.) 1979. *Man's impact on the hydrological cycle in the UK*. Norwich: Geo Abstracts.
Knapp, B. 1978. *Elements of geographical hydrology*. London: George Allen & Unwin.

Porter, E. 1978. *Water management in England and Wales*. Cambridge: Cambridge University Press.

Chapter 7
Coates, D. R. (ed.) 1971. *Environmental geomorphology*. Binghamton: State University of New York.
Cooke, R. U. and J. C. Doornkamp 1974. *Geomorphology in environmental management*. Oxford: Oxford University Press.
Tank, R. (ed.) 1973. *Focus on environmental geology*. Oxford: Oxford University Press.
Weyman, D. 1977. *Landscape processes*. London: George Allen & Unwin.

Chapter 8
Drake, C. L. *et al*. 1978. *Oceanography*. New York: Holt, Rinehart & Winston.
Wooster, W. S. 1969. The oceans and man. *Scient. Am.* **221**, 218–23.

Chapter 9
Bourne, R. 1978. *Assault on the Amazon*. London: Gollancz.
Davidson, J. and R. Lloyd 1977. *Conservation and agriculture*. New York: Wiley.
Lenihan, J. and W. W. Fletcher 1975. *Food, agriculture and the environment*. London: L. Blackie.
Odum, H. T. and E. P. Odum 1976. *Energy basis for man and nature*. New York: McGraw-Hill.
Simmons, I. G. and M. Tooley (eds) 1981. *The environment in British prehistory*. London: Duckworth.

Chapter 10
Coates, D. R. (ed.) 1976. *Urban geomorphology*. Geol. Soc. Am. Sp. Pap., no. 174. Denver.
Manners, I. R. and M. W. Mikesell (eds) 1974. *Perspectives on environment*. Washington, DC: Am. Assoc. Geogs.
Wallwork, K. L. 1974. *Derelict land*. Newton Abbot: David & Charles.

Chapter 11
Leopold, L. B. *et al*. 1971. *A procedure for evaluating environmental impact*. US Geol. Surv. Circular 645. Washington, DC.
National Academy of Science 1972. *The Earth and human affairs*. San Francisco: Camfield Press.
Scientific Committee on Problems of the Environment 1973. *Global environmental monitoring system: action plan for phase 1*. Paris, Unesco.

Index

Italic numbers refer to text figures, and bold numbers refer to text sections.

acid rain **10.3.5**, *10.7*
aerosols 53, 93, 122, 124, 128
afforestation 61–2, 73, 99, 114
agric horizon (soil) 33, 104
Agricultural Revolution 105–6
albedo alteration 18, 27, 29, 50–4, 117, 120
Amazonia 53, **9.5**, *9.23*
Antarctica 6, 9, 47, 79
Arctic 9
assarts 104
Aswan dam 76–7
Australia 44, 78–9

Baltic sea 16, **8.2.3**, *8.4*
Bering Strait 50
biological concentration 16, 99
Britain
    Breckland 27
    Clywedog reservoir 70
    Dee, River 71
    Dorset 106, *9.11*
    East Anglia 86–7, *7.12*, 98, 109
    Exmoor 36–7, *3.5*, 99
    Fens 7–8, 48, 89, 109
    Kielder Water 72–3, *6.19*
    Lake District 6–7
    London 8, 10, 122–3, *10.4*, 128
    Norfolk 105
    Norfolk Broads 104
    North York Moors 103, *9.7*
    Potteries 127–8
    Scottish Highlands 99, 101, **9.4.7**
    Severn, River 70–1, *6.17*, 130
    Somerset Levels 104
    Sussex 86, *7.11*
    Tees, River 72–3
    Thames, River 71, 128
    Trent, River 119–20
    Tyne, River 72–3
    Yorkshire 3, *1.2*, 109–10, 125
Bronze Age 102–3, 107
Buddhism 2
Bushmen (Kalahari) 5

Canada 8–10, *1.6*, 52, 62, 83, 124, 127
carbon cycle 14, 50, 53, 91
carbon dioxide 18, 50–1, 53–4, 117
carbon monoxide 54
Caspian sea 78
chain reactions 12, *2.11*, 39, 50, *5.2*, 60, 97, 99, 130
chemical weathering 32, 81, 125
Chile 45
China 1–2, 58, 99
Christianity 1–2
climatic dome 120
climax vegetation 40, 114
cloud seeding 51, 56–7
Congo, River 50
conservation 129
Corsica 45–6, *4.8*

dams 70, 72–4, 78, 81, 88
Darwinism 2–3, 39
deforestation 15, 18, 24, 34, 41, 45, *4.4*, 50–1, 53, 61–2, 73, 96, 102, 112, 114–17
desalination 79
desertification **2.2.3**, Table 2.1, 51–3, 130
deserts 4–5, 23–5, 96
determinism **1.2.1**, 95, 102
domestication 39
drainage – *see* land drainage
dust, atmospheric 18, 50, 52–3
Dust Bowl (USA) 56, 73
dynamic equilibrium 17, **2.9**, 21, 31, 96

econosphere 129
ecosystem 2, 13, 18, 23–5, 27, 39, **4.3.2**, 92, 95–6, 107, 109, 115, 127, *10.5*
ecumene 9, *1.6*
Egypt 29, 58, **6.3.4**
elm decline 102
enclosure movement 25, 99, 104
energy
    flows 12–13, *2.1*, 20, 39, 51, 81, 91, 95–6, 118
    stores 12–13, 92, 95–6
    subsidies 96, *9.1*
environmental impact analysis 130–1, *11.1*, *11.2*

estuary storage 71, 130
EEC 7, 106
eutrophication 98

feedback mechanisms 20–1, *2.11*, *2.12*, 60, 92
fertilisers, artificial 13–14, 24, 31, **3.4.1**, *3.4*, 37, 77, 93–4, 96–8, 106, 110, 131
fog dispersal 51, 56
freons 54

Galapagos Islands 46
Germany 3, 124
Greenland 10
groundwater
    aquifers 18, 67–8, 77, 90
    extraction, storage 6, 61, 65, 67–9, *6.14*, *6.15*, 71, **6.2.4**, 88, 90
    pollution 68, 77, 99
Gulf Stream 50

Haber process 14
halocline 93
heat island 52, 122–3, *10.4*
heavy metals 16, 92–3, 127
hedgerows 3, 25, 41, 56, 99, 104, 106, 109, 130
herbicides 44, 98–9, 131
horticulture 8, 96
hydrocarbons 54, 92–3
hydrological cycle 58, **6.2.1**, *6.1*, *6.2*, 63, 69, 79

India 35–6, 52–3, 58, 96
Industrial Revolution 75–6, 105, 124, 128
insecticides – *see* pesticides
inter-basin transfers 71, **6.3.5**, *6.27*
International Hydrological Programme 130
intrazonal soils 32, Table 3.1, 34–5
introductions
    animals 18, **2.2.2**, 39, *4.1*, *4.2b*, 47–8, 104
    plants 18, 39, *4.1*, *4.2a*, 41, 44
Ireland
    Aran Islands 31
    Burren **9.4.4**, *9.14*, *9.15*
    Galway Co. 65, 67, *6.12*
    Kerry Co. 37, *3.6*
    Mullet of Mayo 4, *1.3*
Irish sea 92. *8.3*
Iron Age 102–3
irrigation 6, 25, 30, 32, 34–6, 50, 53, 58, 61, 67, 71, 75–6, 78, 96
Islam 2
Israel 29, 77, 79

Japan 86
Jonglei canal 76
Judaism 1–2

Kuro Shivo current 50
Kuwait 79

land
    drainage 15, 17, 30, **6.2.3**, *6.10–13*, 81, 98, 104, 106, 113, 119, 130
    reclamation 105, 113
landnam (swidden) agriculture 95, 102, 114
Lessepsian migration 77–8
leverage points 18, 21, 24, **5.2**, 56, 58, 81, 93
lichen desert 126, *10.8*, 128
local climate – *see* microclimate
lynchets 104, *9.10*

Malaysia 48
Man and the Biosphere Programme 130
marine erosion 86–8, *7.11*, *7.12*
Marxism 2
mass movement 81, **7.5**
Mediterranean
    environment 40, **4.2.4**, *4.6*, *4.8*, 70, 104, 108
    sea 34, 74, 77, 93
mercury cycle 16, *2.6*
Mesolithic 39, 92, 101, 114
Mesopotamia 36, 58
microclimate (local climate) 12, 18, 27, 30–1, **5.3.1**, 52, 56, 97, 104, 114–15, 120, 122–3
mineral nutrient cycle **2.2.1**, *2.13–17*, 114–15
mining 13, 15–16, 81, 88–90, 94, 120, 126
Murray, River 36

Negev desert 29
Neolithic 39, 101–2, 107, 114
Netherlands *7.5*, 86, 89, 99
New Zealand 41, *4.4*, 47
niche v, 39, 41, 44, 128
Nile, River 71, **6.3.4**, *6.22–5*, 99
nitrogen
    cycle 14–15, *2.4*, 22
    oxides 54, 124
    nitrates 14–15, 34, 97–8, 110
no-till agriculture 38, 99

Ob–Irtysh river system 78
oxygen
    atmospheric 117
    cycle 91
    dissolved 93, 120, 128

Palaeolithic 101
PAN 54, 124
peat 34, 102, 104, 111–12
Peru 3
pesticides (insecticides)
 DDT 9, 48, 92–3, 98–9
 general 46, 96, 98–9, 106, 111, 117, 131
phosphorus
 cycle 15–16, *2.5*, 22
 phosphates 33–4, 93–4, 97
photochemical fog *5.2*, 124, *10.6*
plaggen soil **3.5.2**, *3.6*
plagioclimax vegetation 41
plough pan 31, *3.2*, 33
population 9–10, *1.8*, *1.9*, 129
possibilism **1.2.1**

rabbits **2.2.2**, *2.18*, *2.19*, 44, 46–8, 104
radioactivity 18, 54, 92, *8.3*
red tides 92
reservoirs 6, 50, 59, 70–3, *6.16*, *6.19*, 75, 78, 85, 88
resources 3, 6, 10, 129–30
ridge and furrow 104
rivers
 channel alteration 64–5, 67, Table 6.1, 71, 85–6,
  103, 119
 flooding 27, 69–73, 75, 116, 119–20, *10.3*
 flow alteration 13, 61–3, *6.4*, 64–5, 68–71,
  Table 6.1, *6.16*, *6.17*, 73, **6.3.4**, *6.23*, 119–20
 sediment 16, 73, 77, 81, 85–6, 97, 103, 116, 119–
  20, *10.3*, 128
Romania 35

Sahel 3, 27
Saudi Arabia 79
Scandinavia 125–6
semi-arid areas 4–5, **2.2.3**, 40–1, 51, 53, 60, 62, 81
shaduf 58, 75
shelterbelts **5.5.2**, *5.5*
soil erosion
 general *3.3.2*, 62
 water *2.7*, 18, 20, *3.3*, 27, 34, 44–5, 73, 81, 83,
  97, 102–3, 107–8, 116, 127
 wind 4, 27, *2.18*, 52–3, 73, 86, 109–10, *9.16*, 127
soil salinity **3.4.2**, 77
soil reclamation 34–5, *3.5*, 113–14, *9.21*, 127–8
Suez canal 78

sulphur dioxide 53, 124–6
swidden – *see* ladnam
systems **2.1.2**, **2.2**, 50, 96, 130

taiga 9, 25, 52
technological fix 129
Tennessee Valley Authority **6.3.3**, *6.20*
thresholds 18, *2.9*, 20–1, 24, 27, 41, 45, 51, 57, 86,
 93, 127
trace elements 8, 22, 34, 37–8
Trans-Amazon Highway 116
transpiration control 62
trigger factors 18, 27, 123, 129
tropical rainforest 23, 31, 40–1, 44, 96, **9.5**, *9.22*
tundra 23, 25, 83

United Nations 27, 130
United Nations Environmental Programme 130
urban areas
 climate 51, 118, Table 10.2, *10.4–6*, **10.3**
 dereliction 126–8
 hydrology 56–7, *6.7*, 64, 85–6, 118, **10.2**, *10.3*,
  Table 10.1
 reclamation 127–8
USA
 Alaska 83
 Appalachia 61–2
 California 44–5, 68, 79, 88–90, *7.14*, 92, 99, 124,
  10.6, 129
 Chicago 69, *6.15*
 Colorado, River 6
 Florida 18, *2.8*, 89
 Great Lakes 48–9, *4.9*
 Houston 123–4, *10.5*
 Iowa 85–6, *7.9*
 Mississippi, River 71
 Phoenix 5–6, *1.4*
 prairies 96
USSR 9, 35, 53, 59, 62, **6.3.5**, *6.27*, 83

Vaiont reservoir 88
Vietnam 44
Virgin Islands 79
Volga, River 78

water pollution (surface) 98, 119–20, 126, 128

zonal soils 30–1, *3.1*, Table 3.1